Relationship Security

A Personal Journey

ALSO BY THE AUTHOR

Dance When the Brain Says No

Relationship Security

A Personal Journey

Kathleen Price

4505 Dulcinea Drive, Las Cruces, New Mexico 88005

Copyright 2020 by Kathleen Price

All rights reserved, including the right of reproduction in whole or in part in any form.

Manufactured in the United States of American

Published in 2020 by Forest Dale Publishing Company

LIbrary of Congress Control Number: 2020912675

ISBN: 978-0-9841636-2-5

Dedicated to my grandchildren
and the other cherished young people
in my life.

"We learn to move outside static, rigid states of mind and become fluid, changing beings who are not disturbed by inconsistencies in ourselves or in others, who do not demand final conclusions or end states, but recognize that existence means a constant process of becoming."
                                                        Soren Kierkegaard

TABLE OF CONTENTS

Preface

1   My Parents - 5
How Our First Relationships Shape Our Capacity to Love

2   My Childhood - 37
The Effects of Maternal Depression on a Developing Child

3   My Adolescence - 69
Identity Formation in Adolescence

4   Dating, Sexuality, and College - 91
Compassionate Attitudes about Sex

5   Courtship and Marriage - 120
Attachment Security and Adult Romantic Relationships

6   Children - 143
What Do Children Need?

7   Two Years of Psychotherapy - 166
What Motivates Learning, Growth, and Change?

8   Life Transitions - 187
Deceiving Ourselves to Avoid Growth

9   Death and Divorce - 206
What Can Be Gained from Human Suffering?

10   New Love - 236
Why We Simultaneously Desire and Avoid Intimacy

11   An African Adventure - 255
How Unconscious Bias Perpetuates Prejudice

12   Entrepreneurs - 297
Acknowledging our Defenses

13   Family Matters - 313
The Relationship Between Insecurity and Anxiety

14   Retirement - 332
Restructuring Vows and Goals

15   A Sojourn in Salt Lake City - 354
New Insights on Aging and Death

Epilogue

PREFACE

I began working on an autobiography six years ago when I turned seventy-two, an incentive some people have as they grow old and contemplate their death. It was comforting to think that something about me would remain after I'm gone. As I thought about what I would include in my story, I realized there were issues surrounding my most important relationships that I still didn't fully understand. I needed to reach a greater level of self-acceptance if I was to write honestly. Maybe through the process of writing, I could find the congruence I craved, especially if I could identify some progression from one stage of my life to another.

I decided to structure my story by dividing each chapter into two parts. First is a personal narrative section presented in chronological order, focusing on my relationships with the people in my life who have had the most influence—my parents, siblings, two husbands, children, close friends, and teachers. Second is an insight section describing a concept or theory that helps to explain my relationship struggles during that earlier time in my history. I am deeply grateful to the scholars who have developed their ideas, tested their theories, and then cared enough about them to record them in books so others like me might benefit. Often they have had childhood experiences similar to my own.

What I hadn't anticipated was that in the process of preparing for the insight portion of the chapter, I discovered new mentors and new ideas that have expanded my understanding beyond what I had at the time I began this project. In some cases, my research has encouraged me to pursue a new and different direction. Consequently, the process of writing this book has been infinitely more important than the book itself, which is only a representative symbol of the living, growing, changing, synthesizing, and creating that has taken place. The insight section ends with a list of references so that my reader can explore the sources I've used and arrive at their own conclusions.

I subscribe to Jonathan Gottschall's idea, expressed in his book *The Storytelling Animal*, that we create stories in our minds in order to make sense of our experience, a result of our being hard-wired to see cause and effect, and therefore, meaning. He cites research to show that our memories are unreliable, containing omissions and inventions that enhance the best things about ourselves and blur our weaknesses—self-serving perhaps, but also maybe "*faulty by design.*" He suggests that a pliable memory may be useful in maintaining a positive self-image, so that one explanation as to why we are the way we are may work for a time until a new experience comes along to reveal its fallibility. When one story no longer provides the clarity we seek, we are free to create a new and more realistic perspective. "*Like a novel in process, our life stories are always changing and evolving, being edited, rewritten, and embellished by an unreliable narrator.*"

I hope that I am a more reliable narrator now than I was when I was in my forties or fifties, or even at seventy-two when

I began this effort. As my perspectives change throughout the book, it is because I've found something that was more logical, liberating, compassionate, and most of all, helpful to me in my relationships. I've done away with the notion that I can always be certain my important decisions are correct, or that there are absolute truths outside of myself that I can trust to be foolproof. I find the most meaning by accepting responsibility for my judgments, while knowing they are limited and imperfect, mustering the courage to act on them, and then trusting the consequences to lead to the next turning point that will further enrich my life. I am still in good health, so I have yet to come imminently face to face with my death, but I hope this process of writing will prepare me to use the end of my life as another opportunity for growth and change. Then it too will have meaning.

1

MY PARENTS

From the lives of my mother and father, the two most influential people in my life, I discover the origins of my own strengths and weaknesses. Their stories help me understand the emotional undercurrents that were at work within my family growing up. I'm fortunate to have the writings of my mother and my brother, which go back and beyond my own experience, to describe the hopes that inspire my parents, the fears that limit them, and the challenges they face raising a family.

Born on June 26, 1911, my mother, Hope Virginia Grubbs, is the second of four children born in four years, the first of whom died from whooping cough when the baby girl was four months old. From the time she is eleven, Hope keeps a journal, a practice she will continue for the rest of her life. Her first attempt is a notebook with two headings, "A Good Day" and "A Bad Day," in which she records each night why that particular day has been pleasant or unpleasant. *"I write when I can't talk to anyone. It's a way I keep in touch with myself."* Later she will use her journal-writing as a means of sorting things out in her mind and to clarify that which is most important and meaningful.

Hope's earliest memory is of walking down a dusty path in the heat of summer with her mother and father, her younger brother and sister holding her mother's hand. She is following last, kicking at the dust, feeling hot, cranky, and miserable. They are going to their house in Cushing, Oklahoma for the first time. This house on the corner of East Oak Street would be their home for many years. A melancholic disposition contributes to Hope's introspection, her way of trying to find the source of her unhappiness. "I wish I could be a jolly person," she says to herself.

Cushing is a boomtown where oil explorations are accelerating; middle and upper income people are seemingly content. The Great Depression of 1929 has not yet arrived. My grandfather, a lawyer known as "Judge Grubbs," a tall distinguished-looking man, is a deacon in the Baptist Church and a leader in the community. His office is within walking distance of their home. The house has been remodeled more than once—bedrooms and baths installed upstairs, new kitchens built at different times, and porches on three sides with a porch swing. Hope often watches her mother carefully training tendrils of vines that shade the porch on the west side of the house, a regular morning ritual that she enjoys all summer. Her father, after walking home from his office each day, likes to sit in a rocking chair on the east porch and watch the shade gradually creep across the yard until darkness settles in. Hope wonders about the pensive, almost brooding expression on his face.

Hope rarely has quiet times alone talking with either of her parents, nor does she think there is any one person who takes a special interest in her.

"I know I'm not neglected in the sense of material things, but I hunger for love and understanding. Mother is so distracted by her duties, the cares of our home, and her own physical problems. I can't say that she is of a happy, carefree disposition, and I expect motherhood is a trial for her. She seldom punishes us physically, but I don't like her to say, "Don't dispute my word," when I want to have my way about something. I would never do that! Possibly she and Daddy don't get along. I never see any tenderness between them. I know they are intelligent and I'm sure they want what is best for us. Daddy demands respect and he certainly has it from us all!"

Hope's mother suffers from chronic osteomyelitis, the result of a childhood injury to her left leg that never healed properly, so she has to change a large bandage on her leg every day. Caring for Hope and her two siblings so close in age is a struggle for her. As a child, my grandmother became a serious student about many topics since she was prevented from playing active games. She read everything that was available to her, including her father's religious material, which exerted a great influence. As an impressionable young girl, she is troubled by the many conflicting ideas there were about God, Jesus, and human salvation. While each church denomination claims to be based on the Bible, they often violently oppose one another. In an effort to reconcile these contradictions, Bible study becomes an absorbing obsession. She believes that by using Bible concordances, she can discern the original meaning of the Hebrew and Greek words, and come to some satisfying conclusions of her own. As a young mother she reads the Bible to Hope and her siblings and teaches them to memorize pertinent verses and recite them at mealtime.

Hope watches her mother sit for hours with her lame leg propped up on a stool, her books in her lap, and writing paper at hand. In order to make their memory lessons easier, she arranges the verses alphabetically, the first word of the verse beginning with a letter from A to Z: *"A soft answer turneth away wrath, but grievous words stirreth up anger."* *"Be not overcome with evil, but overcome evil with good,"* and so on. Hope begins reading the Psalms on her own and often notices references to *"my enemies."*

"Thou preparest a table in the presence of my enemies." "Deliver me not over to the will of my enemies." The verses trouble her. "What does this mean? Who are my enemies?" she asks her mother one day. Hope sees she has her mother's undivided attention, and is never to forget her quiet, but deliberate answer.

"Your enemies are in your own heart—your impulse to say mean things to your brother, to be cranky and quarrelsome, to be cross and disagreeable, making us unhappy when you act like that." Her mother quickly gives her the way out of her natural inclination to be a bad girl. "With Jesus to help you, to forgive you when you say you're sorry, you can overcome your enemies and learn to be a better person." This is the first realization Hope has had of her own inner sinful tendencies. It evokes in her a need to be a good girl—which means overcoming that which is bad inside her.

As a serious child, Hope wants to please her parents—especially her mother and her teachers. She develops an unreasonable fear and dread of breaking any rule, like the senseless rule imposed by the woman principal in her grade school. "No talking after the first bell rings," a way of summoning all the children to line up and march in orderly rows into the school building for classes. Hope is in line with her classmates, when a girl holds up to her face a rock, or maybe it's a small bar of soap with an unusual shape. Hope notices its nice smell. "What is it?" she asks. At that moment her heart breaks with fear and trembling. She is unable to look at the other children around her, and certainly not her teacher. She is sure that some terrible fate awaits her because she has broken the rule. No one speaks to her and in the classroom she sits down at her desk and hides her face in her arms folded on the desk top, not looking up even when the class begins. She is afraid to face anyone and sits there with her head down for the duration of the class. For whatever reason, the teacher doesn't approach her to ask what the matter is. Finally when class is dismissed, the principal comes to her and without any explanation tells her she should take her things and go home. Hope assumes the girl with the soap has told on her and the teacher has allowed her to suffer a long time punishing herself for her thoughtless remark. The incident is never explained.

Much of the time, Hope feels angry and frustrated because her efforts to please are rarely rewarded. No one hugs or kisses her lovingly. Consequently she quarrels constantly with her brother and sister. A defining event in Hope's childhood takes place in relation to her brother Champion (Champ, they call him), a year younger than Hope. The two of them are playing with neighbor children one sunny afternoon, when Champ begins to clown, standing on his head, showing off for the other children. Suddenly he falls off the top step of the porch, twisting his left arm under his body. He lies there screaming on the ground until their mother rushes out the front door to see what the matter is. Hope is transfixed with a mixture of fear and a certain childish glee that Champ has gotten what he deserves, showing off to get attention from her and the other children.

Champ's arm is broken at the elbow and modern methods of setting broken bones have not yet reached small Oklahoma towns, so a simple binding intended to immobilize the arm as it heals fails to restore its functionality or normal appearance.

After this accident, Champ cannot bend his elbow, and a large bone malformation protrudes from the joint. This deformity results in his withdrawal from social situations and exacerbates the quarrelsome relationship he has with Hope. He becomes a moody boy and a voracious reader. For hours he sits reading volumes of a set of encyclopedias, creasing the corner of each page before proceeding on to the next one, thus leaving evidence of all his excursions into learning, but defacing the whole set.

By the time Hope is thirteen, her mother has become more established in her own religious beliefs and has attracted some friends who are studying the Bible with her. She is convinced that the Biblical reference to "hell" does not refer to a place of torment, but simple means the grave, and that death, the opposite of life, is the penalty for sin. She begins to feel hypocritical in maintaining membership in the Baptist Church while not believing Baptist doctrine. Hope is with her mother in a Wednesday prayer meeting and watches her rise from her chair and ask that her name be removed from the church rolls. She hears the emotion in her mother's voice that reveals the courage it is taking to make this declaration. Though her father doesn't openly express his disapproval, Hope senses it keenly, because it leads to a subtle rift in their family.

As a teenager, Hope excels in school, finds comfort in reading good books, but is unable to articulate her feelings of loneliness even to herself, and much less to others. She has not had anyone to point out to her the contemplation of nature as a solace for her sadness. But one summer evening when she is fifteen years old, she is permitted to take the family's Model-T Ford on a drive out into a rural area beyond Cushing. Driving aimlessly west, she stops the car on a hill where she can see a beautiful flaming red and gold sunset in the western sky. The sublime immensity of the sight overwhelms her, dwarfing her puny inconsistencies, and fills her heart with a reverential awe that there is something infinitely bigger than she is, someone who loves her who she can trust completely. In time she finds poetry that mirrors the comforting feelings she has that day.

Hope graduates from high school as valedictorian of her class just before her seventeenth birthday. Since her mother has been a teacher before she married, and her father is also a well-educated man, it is naturally expected that she will go to college. That summer she enrolls in a crash course in shorthand and typing at a local business school in preparation for her enrollment at a prestigious school for girls in Denton, Texas. The College of Industrial Arts (which later becomes Texas State College for Women) offers every opportunity to excel in nearly every field of education to create an incentive to pursue a career, though few careers are open to women at this time. A women's college is the choice of parents who want their daughters to be educated at least for two years without exposure to young men, decreasing the possibility of early marriage and increasing the possibility of their going on to a university.

Hope plunges into her college activities along with nine hundred other freshmen women, working hard to excel in each subject, and is elected secretary of her class. Attending all the lectures and cultural events arranged at the school, she is especially influenced by John Cowper Powys, a distinguished English writer on the visiting lecture circuit, who urges his audience of young women to buy *The Oxford Book of English Verse*, to keep it by their bedsides, and to read at least one poem every day. "This is as important as eating a good breakfast every day," he says. Hope is impressionable; she buys the book and makes this commitment to herself.

Noticing other freshman girls, homesick from the first days of school, crying for attention and sympathy, Hope thinks they are silly and she vows not to be like them. Instead she concentrates on adjusting to her new environment and doesn't let herself think about home and family. She adjusts so completely to the school situation that when Christmas comes, she doesn't anticipate going home and is even glad when the holidays are over and she returns to school. *"Amazingly, I feel more at home at school than I did at home, though I do often feel alone and melancholic."*

Hope enrolls in music in her second term and is assigned to an excellent private piano teacher, whose students practice in a long wooden building of small rooms that run the length of the building on both sides of a narrow hall. Each student is expected to master a difficult classic composition which is to be performed at the annual spring recital. Practicing alongside twenty or more girls playing at the same time is a nerve-racking challenge for Hope, but she works diligently on it in order to give a credible performance.

The weeks pass quickly and spring break is just days away. It is decided that Hope won't make the trip home, and instead her father will come on the train to spend the weekend with her, staying in a hotel room overnight. At the beginning of the school year, Hope was diagnosed with an over-active thyroid condition and rapid heartbeat. Consequently she can't participate in a regular program of physical education. The college physician, a stern and composed woman, is thorough in her work and takes a special interest in the girls who can't participate in the regular gym classes. She makes it a point to tell Hope that she can come to her anytime if she doesn't feel well, but Hope ignores this piece of advice and resents being set apart as a "not-up-to-par" person.

As the days lead up to her father's visit, the college dormitory is alive with excitement and pandemonium as the other girls prepare to depart for the holidays. Once Hope's roommate and her other special friends leave, only three girls remain on her floor. The sudden change to an eerie stillness, coupled with the possibility that perhaps she has been under more strain than she realized, Hope is unable to sleep, and the following day she is unable to eat. She decides to go on a long hike to make herself so tired that she will sleep, fearing that if she can't sleep a second night, she will become really sick. "*What will Daddy think of me?*"

> "*Well, I still can't sleep, and it's the middle of the night. I just went down the hall to the floor counselor's room. I don't even really know or trust her, but she let me in her room, handed me an orange, and asked me what was wrong. I sat there talking and talking and talking, forever it seemed. I don't even remember what I talked about and I think she went back to sleep right away. I didn't cry though.*"

The next day, a Saturday, Hope remembers the woman doctor who told her to come to the infirmary if she needed help. Though she doesn't feel sick, she knows she needs help, and she is obsessed with the thought that her father will be alarmed to find her in the hospital. Finally Hope gathers the courage to walk to the college infirmary, a small building on the campus, and the doctor gives her a sedative. She is the only patient in one of several beds in rows. She notices that the ticking of her watch sounds strangely too loud, so she takes it off and throws it on a bed several spaces away. She sleeps heavily and wakes up feeling normal, but still worries about her father finding her there. Before noon, her father arrives and she is allowed to dress and go into town with him for dinner at a hotel. She is relieved that he doesn't show great concern, and she is comfortable with him.

Later they go back to the campus and stop at the building where the college Dean's office is located. Hope sits in the lounge while her father goes into the office to talk with the Dean. She is uneasy and wonders why no one has spoken with her or asked what she thinks the reason is for her trouble sleeping and eating. Finally her father comes out of the Dean's office and walks over to where Hope is sitting.

"You're going home with me, Hope," he says. "You must go to your room, pack all your things, and be ready to leave on the train with me in two hours." She's dumbfounded. She doesn't want to go. Hope hasn't grown up in a generation of children who question their father. She dares not ask who has made the decision that she must leave school. Do the school personnel not want the responsibility for her? Is her father so ashamed of her? If some of her teachers were here, might they have intervened? The one person her father has spoken to has the authority to decide her fate. Mindlessly she packs her things in boxes or suitcases and reluctantly follows her father to the train station. That night in a sleeping compartment, she is unable to sleep.

The next day Hope stumbles up the front walk of her home into the arms of her mother, who comes running out to meet her. She remains at home that summer and fall, angry and embittered about her situation. She begins to write in her journal again, describing the irrational things she does and says during this time, things that are completely out of character for a well-behaved, always desiring-to-please young girl. Her parents are distraught.

> *"Something important happened today that sticks in my mind. I haven't been going to the piano much, but today I sat down intending to play Wedding Day*

at Troldhaugen, the composition I memorized before leaving school. I stumbled through the first bars, struggling to perform as I had after many hours of practice and help from my teachers. But I couldn't play it. For a few minutes I kept trying, fumbling over the keys. I wasn't aware that Daddy was listening and watching. Pretty soon I felt his hands on my shoulders. He said, 'Play something simple, Hope.' A flood of relief swept over me. He expected nothing of me. I didn't have to perform or try to please anyone but myself. I think maybe I'm beginning to get well."

Hope gradually regains her mental and emotional stability with rest and medication prescribed by a family doctor, and she is able to return to college in the spring, but not to the school in Denton. She enrolls at Oklahoma A&M College in Stillwater, just fifteen miles from her hometown, and this is where Hope will meet my father.

Walter Elmo Barham is experiencing a different kind of growing up. Walt (as he prefers to be called) is the eighth of ten children born to Arkansas tenant farming parents on May 30, 1909. His parents are conscientious, but humble people struggling to keep food on the table for their large family. It is typical for children in poor families, particularly the boys, to leave home in their early teens, relieving parents of their burden of care. Several rich businessmen from a prosperous oil-drilling town in Oklahoma come all the way to Arkansas to watch Walt play football when he is only fourteen and in the ninth grade. Impressed by his athletic skills, they offer him a job driving their school bus if he will come to Oklahoma and play on their high school football team. The offer includes a dormitory-style room that is part of the school gymnasium where he can stay. Though recruitment for high school sports will eventually become illegal, it is common practice in Oklahoma at this time, and Walt's parents encourage him to go. On the day he is to leave, his little sister, Lodema, runs to him and cries, begging him not to go. She's the baby in the family and Walt has always watched out for her. He doesn't want the rest of the family to see, but Walt cries too.

Walt is only a sophomore when he starts high school in Dundee, Oklahoma, far away from his family home. Along with seven or eight other boys on the football team, Walt lives in the gymnasium and does janitor work or drives one of five school buses provided by the oil companies. Every fourth Friday they are paid twenty-five dollars—a lot of money at this time. Two coaches (subsidized by the oil companies) develop a good team, but many of the larger schools refuse to play them, not wanting to be beaten by such a small school. As an incentive, the oil company men offer each large high school in the vicinity fifteen hundred dollars to play them in order to give players like Walt exposure so they can get college scholarships. An article in the local Dundee newspaper (the "Gusher") pays tribute to him at the beginning of his senior year.

> *"In athletics, in popularity, in school activities, and in sportsmanship, Walter Barham's record in Dundee is unexcelled. He is known all over southern Oklahoma as the best pass receiver and one of the best all-around players in this section of the state. The entire community regrets that this is Walter's last year among them."*

Two days before a crucial game with their archrival during Walt's senior year, Walt is called to Beaumont, Texas due to a death in his family. Since Walt is half of the quarterback/pass receiver combination that has contributed significantly to the Dundee Tiger's success, the team and their fans fear that without Walt there is no chance of victory. On Friday, the day of the game, at three o'clock in the morning, having ridden the bus all night, Walt arrives back at the school. By noon word has spread throughout their community—Walt is back! The game is played at two o'clock that afternoon, and the first touchdown is scored by the Tigers running the ball back on the kickoff return. Four more touchdowns are scored by Walt's catching four long passes from his quarterback teammate and Dundee wins the game 32-6. "Just like a Movie" is the title of another Gusher article describing Walt's near-miss game.

After his final year at Dundee, Walt goes to work in the oil fields, hoping to earn enough money to attend a small college in Durant, Oklahoma, without knowing that coaches at Oklahoma A&M College have their eye on him. The assistant coach finds Walt working in the oil fields that summer and recruits him to play football with a scholarship. A photograph of my father in a leather helmet like they wear at this time shows a handsome young man with dark curly hair and blue eyes that twinkle when he smiles. It's easy to see why my mother falls for him.

Hope and Walt meet on a blind date in the spring of 1930. At first they don't really like each other. Walt, an athlete from a small town, having a poor background for college work, is determined to be the first one of his family to go to college. In Hope's family there has never been a question about the possibility of the Grubbs' three children going to college, both parents being university graduates. But in September of the fall semester, Walt and Hope happen to be enrolled in the same English literature class. Hope is a good student, likes to write, and finds college work well within her ability. What is easy for her is an impossible challenge for Walt, who doesn't understand half of what the professor is saying. Football trips take him away from classes, sometimes two or three weeks at a time, as he is a regular on the successful college team. Hope offers to help him with themes and book reports, class assignments that lead to dates at the library and college hangouts around campus, but never movies because Walt has so little spending money.

Shy and lacking the self-confidence to seek sorority membership, Hope is pleased to have a steady boyfriend who is a football hero. Walt has been invited to join a men's fraternity where he is able to live. He washes dishes for his room and board, while working at several odd jobs on the side, all this in addition to the strenuous hours of football practice. But once football season is over and the magic of spring comes on, nature takes its course. They play with fire, neither of them realizing the risk they are taking, but not wanting to stop.

As a serious-minded child, religion has been important to Hope; she considers herself a Christian, but this part of her life has been neglected since she has been away from home. She feels that their sex play is wrong, but thinking Walt is wiser, she trusts him. Summer vacation comes and they write letters to one another until Hope returns to school the next fall. Early in November, realizing something is wrong, she goes by herself to see a doctor, who after the examination, tells her she must get married at once. "You are pregnant."

"But I don't want to get married now! I don't want to marry Walt. He isn't the person I want to marry!"

Hope can't believe this is happening to her, not having really thought of the possible consequences. In that day and time, she has not been taught about the realities of sex. Her main thought is to spare her parents, deeply religious people, active in church work, Bible class teachers, both of them—imagine the shock and disappointment they will feel. As if that isn't enough, she dreads telling Walt. She knows he won't want to get married any more than she does, but she knows she must tell him and she trusts that he will help her decide what to do.

Walt tells her that there are ways to get rid of the unborn baby. "I'll find out about it," he says. He brings her a drug from the pharmacy and Hope prays for the will to take it, but her conscience intervenes.

"I think it would be wrong and God won't help me do something wrong."

Walt sees her anguish. "I'll do anything you want me to do. We can get married. We'll manage somehow."

But Hope is still not ready to consider marriage, wanting to spare her parents. She prays for the courage to just go away, to disappear, so no one will ever know.

Walt decides to talk to the older doctor who is called in for emergency football injuries and he agrees to see and talk to Hope. His kind fatherly manner offers her the first comfort she has felt in weeks.

"There's no way you can escape your situation," he says. "Your parents have to know. You can't run away. I think that marriage is the best solution and in time your parents will also come to see it that way." Hope is convinced and even begins to feel that she can pray for the strength to face her parents.

That night Hope places a long-distance call from a telephone booth ninety miles away from the college town where she and Walt are going to school. She trembles inside, knowing what a shock her message will be to her mother, yet still feeling the inner strength to do the right thing.

"Mama, Walt and I are going to be married tonight ... we have to, Mama. I know it sounds awful, but I know everything will be all right.... Please don't feel so terrible ... I'm fine." Her mother convinces her that they should wait to be married until they both can talk to her father. So, with her parents' blessings, Walt and Hope are married two weeks later in November of 1931. One day soon after, walking on a downtown street in Stillwater, they happen to meet the doctor who persuaded them to marry. He offers Walt his congratulations, but Walt does not respond kindly to his greeting. Hope sees then that Walt feels trapped into their situation. It isn't easy for either of them with Walt going to school, playing football, and both of them preparing for the birth of their child. Hope finishes her fall semester and then continues to help Walt with his schoolwork while he delivers papers, makes and sells brooms, and continues to wash dishes at the fraternity house to make ends meet.

My sister, Bonnie, is born on June 7, 1932, a perfectly natural event that proves to be too much for Hope. Experiencing what doctors call a "nervous breakdown," she has to leave Walt in Stillwater and go home to her parents with the baby so Walt can finish his schooling. Hope experiences nightmarish delusions during the long days and nights that her mother stays by her bed, having made the decision not to let her be admitted to a mental hospital. Slowly, once again, with rest and freedom from responsibility, Hope regains her health. During the months of Hope's recovery, Walt makes frequent trips from Stillwater to Cushing to see her and their new daughter. A photograph of Walt on one of his trips to Cushing shows him proudly holding Bonnie.

A significant conversation occurs between Walt and Hope's father sometime during the weeks that follow Bonnie's birth. Though my grandfather has good intentions, and one must consider the lack of understanding people have of depression, anxiety, and mental illness at this time, the effects of the conversation will be painful and long-lasting for Hope. In an attempt to prepare Walt for his future responsibilities, my grandfather explains Hope's emotional collapse in terms of something permanent that will prevent her from living a fully responsible life. He describes it as similar to the previous episode that occurred during her first year in college. Because of this propensity, my grandfather warns, Walt should protect her from taking on too many obligations.

Then my grandfather reaches for a check in his desk drawer. "This check is for you."

"No, no. I can't take your money," Walt says. "She's my responsibility now—and I'll take care of her."

My grandfather shakes his head. "This is money I set aside for Hope's education. She won't need this now. I want you to have this in reserve for any emergency that might arise. I insist that you take it."

Lesser men may have bolted at hearing such a dire prediction about the young woman he has taken as his wife and who is the mother of his first child. Fortunately for Hope and Bonnie, it does not weaken Walt's commitment to his fledgling family. It does, however, affect how Walt perceives Hope and how Hope perceives herself.

Walt is one of thirty young men out looking for coaching jobs in high schools the year after he graduates. Having promised his support, my grandfather loans Walt his car so he can apply in person for a job in Haskell, Oklahoma, a little town southeast of Tulsa known for its enthusiastic football fans. Walt makes the trip and through inquiry learns that he can rent a cot over a drug store for fifty cents. He interviews with the school board members for two days and is hired for the 1933-34 school year. To Hope and Walt it's a miracle. The Great Depression is at its lowest point in 1933 when some thirteen to fifteen million Americans are unemployed and nearly half of the country's banks have failed. Considering all the other young athletes who are out desperately looking for jobs, they are thrilled.

On a hot day in August, they load onto an old trailer, a stove, an icebox, a small settee for visitors, and a folding bed for Bonnie, all loaned to them by my grandmother. A bed is purchased for one dollar. On the morning Hope and Walt move into the small house they have rented for eight dollars a month, a group of young boys gather around to watch, and they call out warm greetings to Walt, the new football coach. With twenty dollars a month allotted for groceries, they consider themselves well off with a starting monthly salary of eighty dollars. The kitchen has no cabinets for storage, so dishes and cooking utensils are kept in tubs and boxes on the floor, just right for fourteen-month-old Bonnie to get into. But several weeks later on the way to the post office, Hope spots a cardboard and wood reinforced cabinet with shelves and drawers on display in a store. It's exactly what she needs, and on the first payday after Walt's first month of teaching, they buy it for six dollars.

Walt proves to be an effective coach, winning most of his games the first year. As any football fan knows, the reputation of a good coach travels fast, and in Walt's case it includes him being a strong disciplinarian. One of their first games in the fall is scheduled on the day after Halloween, so the starting tailback, the team's star player, has good reason for a late celebration. A pre-game meeting has been scheduled at the school the following morning and the boy is late showing up. He suits up but Walt won't put him in the game. In the last few minutes, the score is still 0-0. The assistant coach can't stand it and pleads with Walt to allow the tardy tailback to play. Walt relents and the boy runs for a fifty-five yard touchdown to win the game.

When Bonnie is eighteen months old, on December 31, 1933, in Haskell, my brother John is born prematurely, a sickly baby who suffers from colic and poor nutrition. At this time in Oklahoma, teachers are only paid for nine months a year, making a summer job a necessity. The family moves to Cushing, Hope's hometown, larger than Haskell, where Walt has been hired to teach and coach. That summer interval, before he begins his new assignment, is one of record-breaking heat. The only temporary job Walt can find is with an oil refinery, digging deep holes, throwing dirt up on a platform, and then climbing up on the platform to throw it again to the top of the hole. To make matters worse, they still don't have a car, so he has to walk to and from his work.

Concerned about John, Hope has consulted a doctor, who gives up trying to find a milk formula he can tolerate and starts him on solid foods. He prescribes frequent feedings even once or twice during the night. Walt expects a hearty breakfast to face his arduous day, while Hope is up with the baby all night, unhappy about getting up again at five in the morning to fire up the oven for his toast. This wakens Bonnie and she never gets back to sleep. They quarrel over who is having the harder time. The climax comes one morning when Hope leaves the house and walks home to her mother for three days. There she can put the children down on the floor with wet towels over them in front of an electric fan. When my grandfather offers to loan Walt his car, Walt comes and drives Hope to a park where they can hopefully make up. Hope writes, *"We both came to appreciate the other's difficulties and real suffering."* Baby John, too, begins to thrive on his new diet.

By now Champ, Hope's brother, has finished high school and college, graduating in civil engineering, and is employed by the Oklahoma State Highway Department. Hope's sister, June, is also married with one child and lives in Chicago. Champ and Hope no longer quarrel and he occasionally comes to visit Hope and Walt and their family. He learns to love Bonnie and John and enjoys playing with them, and this becomes the only tie between him and Hope. Still, Champ is a loner and appears to those who know him as shy, retiring, and uncommunicative. Eventually Hope and June learn that Champ is drinking, causing much grief to their parents. No one in the family knows if he has ever had a close relationship with a friend or if he has ever hurt anyone or had cause for remorse. But on a gloomy cold day in February, Champ walks into a wooded area and hangs himself from a tree with his belt. This tragic event is devastating to Hope, who holds herself responsible. *"We never developed an affectionate brother and sister closeness. I don't remember ever saying a kind word to him."*

Deeply regretting her lost years with Champ and wanting to prevent, at all costs, anything like Champ's death ever happening to her family, Hope vows to do all she can to prevent her children from quarrelling. *"When a dispute arises, I will send both children to separate rooms and forbid their coming out until they can resume amicable relations."* Hope keeps this promise to herself.

Both Haskell and Cushing are good towns for Walt to start a coaching career because of the enthusiastic fans that follow his every move. He is popular as both a coach and science teacher and is able to make contacts in Cushing that help him find better summer jobs. He begins to sell cars on a part-time basis the second summer, and the third summer he is hired by the city to start a summer camp for boys and girls in the city park. Then later he manages a swimming pool, hires lifeguards, and teaches swimming lessons.

Hope enjoys being the wife of the well-liked coach in their community and getting to know some of Walt's football players. Harvey is one of the best, but during one game, Walt calls Harvey to the sidelines to ask him why he isn't running and blocking as he knows he can. "Coach, I'm not getting any grub," he replies. Harvey's mother died early and he's living with his father who is thought of as a slacker. Harvey becomes a member of the family for two meals a day and happily helps Hope with the dishes. One evening after supper, he says to her, "Do you know what the cheapest food is that stays with you the longest?" Hope has never gone hungry in her life, but Harvey has followed the wheat harvest in the summer and knows how to survive. "A can of pink salmon and a five-cent box of crackers," he says. Walt persuades a restaurant owner to give Harvey a job washing dishes for his meals, but is outraged when he finds out the owner denies Harvey a piece of pie for dessert.

Bonnie starts school in Cushing and Walt is paying the bills by selling cars on the side. Hope is thrilled when he trades a Chevrolet for an old Essex, a heating stove, a radio in a cabinet, and a piano. Noticing his productivity, a school teacher friend approaches Walt about beginning a fund for Bonnie's future college education, an insurance policy whereby a parent can pay six dollars a month every year, beginning the child's first year of school. By the time she graduates from high school, it will have accrued in value, enabling her to go to college.

"What a great idea!" Hope says.

"Where do you think we'll get the extra six dollars?" Walt asks.

She knows he's right; nothing is left over after buying all their necessities. But Walt does make a promise to her. "I will always be able to provide whatever our children will need. When the time comes for college, there will be a way." This motivates Hope to be a frugal homemaker in whatever house they live—and there will be many—four different rental houses in Cushing until they are able to buy a little square house for three hundred dollars and have it moved across town to a lot Hope's father owns.

After six years in Cushing, Walt submits his resignation in order to accept a coaching job that offers a substantial salary increase in the Oklahoma town of Bartlesville. They only stay there for one year, the year I am born on December 8, 1941. Then Walt has the opportunity to move to Tulsa, reportedly the best place in Oklahoma to teach and coach. They rent a house until they are able to sell the little house in Cushing and make a down payment on a bigger house in need of repair on the north side of Tulsa. The house costs $1500, and with a lot of paint, wallpaper, and floor sanding, they make it livable. It has four small bedrooms, a room for each child, and it is close to Walt's school, important because they still don't own a car. Eventually, however, Walt realizes this house isn't a good investment because of the neighborhood, so they begin to look for a house they really like that they can settle in permanently. By this time, my mother is tired of moving. So in 1943, my family move to the house I will grow up in on Madison Place. Their payments are thirty dollars a month with a mortgage to pay off in eleven years.

INSIGHTS: How Our Earliest Relationships Shape Our Capacity to Love

John Bowlby believed that the earliest attachments we form with our parents are crucial, in that those relationships become the foundation on which the rest of our emotional life is built. Something like a "blueprint" develops in our minds as children, Bowlby explains, which impacts our capacity for giving and receiving love in any future relationships. Bowlby's thinking, which has become known as "attachment theory" and its growing body of research, is applicable to my parents' lives. An understanding of his theory provides a foundation for explaining and accepting the choices I have made in regard to my past relationships.

Bowlby's critical work was launched in 1939 when he introduced the term "attachment" to apply to the powerful emotional bond that normally develops between infants and their mothers. He was the first theorist to explain why a child needs a reliable ongoing attachment to at least one adult, and why the child will suffer emotional damage if that attachment is threatened, interrupted, or lost.[1] Bowlby was the first modern psychologist to follow Darwin's example of looking to our primate ancestors for the origins of our earliest desires, fears, needs, and capacities. For more than thirty-five million years, primate infants stayed safe by remaining close to their mothers. To lose touch could mean death. This is not true of many other animal species that emerge from the egg fully capable of feeding and protecting themselves. Humans and other primates emerge so immature and helpless that they need constant attention and protection if they are to survive.

It was plain to Bowlby that both the parent and the child must have instinctual bonding behaviors that have evolved over time to maximize survival and reproduction. Even in utero the fetus responds to the mother's chemistry, memorizes her scent, and recognizes her voice, the beginning of a tenderly vulnerable relationship that continues after birth, when the infant becomes acutely sensitive to signals of her maternal commitment.[2] Though human infants cannot feed or protect themselves, no one has to teach them how to cry or smile. Behaviors such as clinging, sucking, babbling, and smiling, all have an instinctual goal of keeping the mother close by. Young and vulnerable infants also react following separation from a stronger, older, caregiver. Immediately after separation, infants often protest vehemently, crying, screaming, and throwing temper tantrums as they search for their caregivers. Bowlby reasoned that strong protest when separated from a caregiver is a good initial strategy to promote survival, particularly in species with developmentally immature and highly dependent infants.[3]

Parents, in turn, do not have to learn how to respond to their children's cries. Sensitivity to a crying infant is also evolutionarily adaptive because when infant behaviors are met with positive responses from the parent, by the end of the first year, the child will have developed a repertoire of "attachment behaviors" that are relied on to keep the mother close. Protesting her departure, greeting her returns, following when able, are satisfying to both mother and child and elicit feelings of love, joy, and security. If mother-infant bonding is an inherent necessity, then, Bowlby believed, that would explain why a rupture in that process could have severe results.[4]

Bowlby believed there were two overriding environmental factors that would predict early childhood problems. The first and most obvious is the death of the mother or a prolonged separation from her. He and his followers produced abundant evidence pointing to the causal relationship between loss of maternal care in the early years and disturbed personality development—from delinquent character formation to a personality prone to anxiety states and depressive illness. The second factor is the mother's emotional attitude toward the child, as it is observed in how she responds to her child and how she handles the everyday aspects of maternal care. This fact has emerged since childhood problems became linked to the parents. Is there unconscious hostility toward a child, such as unnecessary deprivations, impatience, bad temper, or lack of understanding which is usually intuitive in a loving mother?[5]

I think there is evidence in my mother's writings as a child that she missed the kind of warm connection Bowlby describes as being important between a mother and child. My grandfather's distant work role in the family and my grandmother's chronic illness may have limited the amount and quality of time my maternal grandparents were able to spend with their children. Conditions of poverty in my father's large family were factors that may have contributed to feelings of uncertainty and self-doubt.

Bowlby explains that by an infant's first birthday, ideally she can quickly discern between familiar people and strangers, and among those who are familiar, she chooses one or more favorites. She has also developed a set of attachment behaviors and reactions that monitor and regulate the distance between her and her attachment favorites. She is always keeping track of one or more caregivers. If a caregiver is near, responsive, and available, she can relax and engage freely in other kinds of behaviors, like exploring the environment. The presence of an attachment figure serves as a secure base—a safe environment in which she can learn, play, and interact with others. If the attachment figure is absent or unresponsive, however, she will abandon all other activities in order to restore proximity to her caregiver. Her loss causes anxiety and distress, and the recovery of her loss brings a sense of relief and security. On this foundation, the rest of her emotional life is built; without it, there is risk for her future happiness and health.[6]

Bowlby clearly believed that different kinds of childhood experiences lead to different expressions of attachment security. Developmental psychologist, Mary Ainsworth, shared Bowlby's interest and worked with him for a time compiling data for a study on children who were left homeless by World War II. Rigid and punitive methods of child rearing were popular at this time, and parents were cautioned about "spoiling" their children. Bowlby fiercely opposed these ideas because they led to the deprivation of love and affection that children sorely need. He insisted that the enduring nature of needing others we can depend on is not "*a childlike quality to be outgrown, but rather an essential aspect of human nature.*"[7]

Both Bowlby and Ainsworth knew that in order for any scientific discipline to take root, it needed some valid means of measurement. In 1963 Ainsworth received a grant to further their research comparing parenting styles and their effects on a developing child. Her goal was to devise a standardized assessment procedure for human mothers and their children which could be carried out in a natural environment and could be reliably rated. The result of this work was the "Strange Situation" experiment, an invention that has carried attachment theory into its central position within developmental psychology today.[8] In the Strange Situation, mothers and infants are first observed spending time alone in a room containing interesting and novel toys. Then a stranger enters the room and begins interacting with the infant. After a few moments, the mother is instructed to quietly slip out, and the infant is observed reacting to being left alone with the stranger. Then the mother is instructed to return, and the infant is observed reacting to being reunited with her.

The entire twenty-two minute session is videotaped and rated, focusing particularly on the response of the child to separation and reunion. Three minutes alone in a strange situation can be an eternity to a child. The experiment elicits all the many individual differences in behavior the child manifests while coping with the stress of separation. After observing a number of infants as they experience the Strange Situation, Ainsworth and her colleagues identified three distinct patterns of responses that they thought characterized three distinct styles of infant attachment:

Secure attachment characterized infants who had the most responsive and available attachment figures. These infants confidently explored the new toys when their mothers were present, were upset when left alone but easily soothed when their mothers returned, and were willing to socialize with a stranger as long as mother was near.

The second group of infants appeared to be more distant from their mothers. They concentrated mostly on the toys, insensitive to whether their mothers were present or not, and they were uninterested in socializing with the stranger. This pattern was labeled *avoidant attachment* and seemed to characterize infants whose attachment figures were mostly unavailable or unresponsive.

A third group of infants were unwilling to explore the novel environment. They were terrified when left alone, and upon reunion with their mothers, paradoxically appeared both relieved by her return and resentful at the separation. This pattern, labeled *anxious attachment*, seemed to characterize infants whose attachment figures had been inconsistent—available sometimes and intrusive or dismissive at other times.[9]

So what does all this work with infants have to do with intimate relationships between adults, like the relationship between my parents? Although Bowlby's work focused on attachment in infancy, he believed that the attachment behavior system was a central part of human functioning "*from the cradle to the grave.*"[10] Repeated experiences with caregivers form the basis of enduring beliefs and expectations about how others are likely to respond to our needs. Will they be there for us most of the time, only part of the time, or perhaps never? The answer to that very important question leads us to our beliefs about ourselves. How worthy am I of other people's attention and support?

> *"In other words, people who develop the expectation that attachment figures are likely to be available and supportive are also likely to believe they are worthy of that support. Conversely, people who have grown to doubt their attachment figures are also likely to doubt themselves."* [11]

I don't think my mother enjoyed a facet of parenting that Ainsworth identified as *sensitivity*, a crucial element in determining whether a child develops a secure or insecure attachment with a caregiver. The fact that four children were born in four years would certainly reduce the number of simple acts that Ainsworth describes as characteristic of a sensitive caregiver: responding to a baby's cry, holding her close, and uttering comforting sounds that then elicit a calming effect on a child. It is these behaviors that begin the attachment process that is so important in later emotional development.[12] My mother's writings as a child also reveal that she had very little heart-to-heart conversation with either of her parents, especially intimate talk about her feelings. As a child develops language skills, a parent can further the attachment process by mirroring back feelings with words that put names to the child's emotions and convey acceptance. These may be feelings of happiness and contentment, but even more important is the parent's feedback of negative feelings such as hurt, anger, or sadness. Are these negative feelings treated as justified and is the child helped to understand them? My grandmother's description of my mother's negative feelings being her own worst enemy being embedded within her as something bad does not exemplify this kind of nurturing. If that component is not there early on, a child may begin suppressing those feelings that can emerge later in some form of dysfunction.[13]

Armed with Ainsworth's research and the Strange Situation tool, Bowlby could now argue with greater force against the unfeeling style of child care that he deplored, particularly the idea that a somewhat depriving upbringing fostered autonomy, self-reliance, and strong character. He believed the very opposite was true—self-reliance both in childhood and later life did not rest on stern discipline, but on secure attachment to a trusted caregiver. In the 1970s and 1980s, research attention turned to fathers, a person who is often overlooked because he is less available for observation. It was no surprise that the percentage of children strongly attached to mothers was about the same as that for fathers, but no correlation existed between the two. A child could be securely attached to one, both, or neither of her parents, but while one secure attachment was better than none, children who were found to be securely attached to both parents tended to be the most confident and competent.[14]

From my own experience with my paternal grandparents, I think my father had a more secure attachment with his parents than did my mother with hers. My father was more comfortable and confident in his relationships with people in general than was my mother, but he also had cause for his own insecurities. The stress of growing up poor in a large family and having to leave home at such an early age must have had some detrimental effect. For as long as my siblings and I can remember, our father had an irrational fear of saying goodbye, and he would use almost any means to avoid partings with loved ones. His fear was so pronounced, that it was absorbed by the three of us children until we were able to recognize and talk about it sensibly as adults. This fear stayed with my father all his life, a scar undoubtedly resulting from his premature separation from his family.

Other attachment researchers have looked at the overall emotional tone of individual family dynamics as being a factor in determining a child's level of attachment security. Some writers have speculated that John Bowlby's early upbringing could have contributed to his keen sensitivity to the suffering of children. His parents were described as *"conventional upper-class people of their day, with a belief in intellectual rigor and a stiff-upper–lip approach to all things emotional."*[15] This description may have fit that of my maternal grandparents. My mother's early acknowledgement of the lack of tender affection between her parents may have contributed to her insecurity as a child. I don't know how solid my grandparents' marriage was, or how their conflicts were managed, or if there were family secrets and covert family alliances that needed to be brought into the open and dealt with. Any of these issues can have a bearing on family dynamics. I do know that my mother's view of herself as being flawed and inadequate was reinforced by the conversation that took place between my father and grandfather after my sister was born. The transfer of monies to my father that had been set aside for my mother's education was also a blow to her self-confidence and a source of great resentment. Another severe setback occurred when her brother, Champ, committed suicide, an event that exacerbated her guilt about their childhood relationship.

Bowlby once said that he came from a *"stable environment,"* but this didn't mean a warm, emotionally responsive environment. He did not enjoy happy relations with either of his parents, but he remembered fondly a much-loved nursemaid, Minnie, who left the family when John was four. Possibly it was from Minnie that he learned what a loving mother might be.[16] My mother didn't have this kind of an example. The perception of herself that she acquired as a child set the stage for a family dynamic that repeated itself throughout my parents' marriage. Without understanding, patterns of relating get passed down from one generation to another. In his earliest writings, even before empirical data existed on this transmission process, Bowlby made an insightful comment:

> *"Thus it is seen how children who suffer deprivation grow up to become parents deficient in the capacity to care for their children and how adults deficient in this capacity are commonly those who suffered deprivation in childhood."*[17]

While a fundamental respect of each other was present in my parents and enabled them to accomplish their roles as well as they did, when facing disappointment and discouragement, like many couples, they found reason to blame either themselves or each other. They had next to no insight into my mother's tenuous attachments to both her parents and little support in how to nurture a better foundation for a secure attachment between themselves. These two factors were at the root of many of their future struggles, and had a significant impact on the nature of my own challenges in relationships. There is no justification for blame on anyone. It is part of the human condition that we have to make do with the degree of knowledge and understanding that is available to us at the time. In comparison to many parents, mine adapted as well as they possibly could have, considering their limitations.

References:

[1] Bowlby, J. 1967. Foreword. In M. D. S. Ainsworth. *Infancy in Uganda: Infant care and the growth of love*. Baltimore:

Johns Hopkins University Press: p. v.

[2] Polan, H. J. & Hofer, M. A. 1999. Psychobiological origins of infant attachment and separation responses. In *Handbook of attachment*, eds. J. Cassidy and P.R. Shaver. New York/London: The Guilford Press.

[3] Simpson, J. 1999. Attachment theory in modern evolutionary perspective. *In Handbook of attachment*, eds. J. Cassidy and P. R. Shaver. New York/London: The Guilford Press.

[4] Karen, R. 1998. *Becoming attached: First relationships and how they shape our capacity to love.* New York/London: Oxford University Press.

[5] Karen 1998.

[6] Bowlby 1967.

[7] Holmes, J. 2014. *John Bowlby and attachment theory.* London/New York: Routledge, p.19.

[8] Ainsworth, M. D. S., Blehar, M. C., Waters, E., & Wall, S. 1978. *Patterns of attachment: A psychological study of the strange situation.* Hillsdale, NJ: Lawrence Erlbaum.

[9] Ainsworth et al 1978.

[10] Bowlby, J. 1979. *The making and breaking of affectional bonds.* London: Tavistock, p. 129.

[11] Bradbury, T. N. & Karney, B. R. 2010. *Intimate relationships.* New York/London: W. W. Norton & Co., p. 108.

[12] Ainsworth, M. D. S. 1982. Attachment: Retrospect and prospect. In *The place of attachment in human behavior*, eds. C. M. Parkes and J. Stevenson-Hinde. New York: Basic Books, Inc.

[13] Holmes, J. 2010. *Exploring in security: Towards an attachment-informed psychoanalytic psychotherapy.* London/New York: Routledge.

[14] Karen 1998.

2

MY CHILDHOOD

Mama refers to me as an "*afterthought*," an ambiguous term that leaves the matter of a planned birth in question. Nevertheless, I'm received by a welcoming family—two dedicated parents, a brother soon to be eight, and a sister who is nine. It isn't an ordinary day, not because it's my birthday, but because I'm born the day after Pearl Harbor is bombed, December 8, 1941, the event that brings the United States into World War II. Perhaps it's the trauma of this catastrophe that sends my mother into labor.

I'm named Mary Kathleen—Mary, after my maternal grandmother (Mary June), and Kathleen, because Mama loves the Irish ballad, "I'll Take You Home Again, Kathleen." The song is about a woman who has emigrated from Ireland to the United States, but longs for her home country. An accomplished pianist, Mama enjoys playing all the Irish ballads, "My Bonnie Lies over the Ocean" being the inspiration for my sister's name, also a song about missing someone who is left behind in their homeland. I don't know why Mama loves these songs so much, because she lived only fifty miles from her parental home, but perhaps it's an emotional distance that haunts her. Daddy calls me Mary and Mama calls me Kathleen, setting a precedent for being flexible in what I prefer to be called. Having a name with many derivatives is a great advantage, and in time I will have used three more: Kathy, Katie, and Kate.

Though I am born in Bartlesville, Oklahoma, the only home I remember is the one my family moves to in Tulsa when I'm three years old. The pale yellow stucco house with its flat roof resembles some southwestern-style homes that are built today, though it is located on a rural dirt road called Madison Place in the outskirts of Tulsa. There are other homes around us, but ours is on one of two lots so we can have a milk cow, raise chickens, and even have a horse named Ribbon that we can ride. Mama loves flowers and she plants several rows of yellow jonquils on both sides of the walk leading up to our front porch. Other flower beds bordering our yard are filled with iris, roses, peonies, dahlias, nasturtiums, zinnias, and four-o'clocks, all flowers I learn to recognize and favor because they are the flowers that Mama loves. Artistically arranging flowers for bouquets in the house is her forte, so during the spring and summer months, there is always an exquisite bouquet on top of the bookcase that you see when you first walk in the front door.

Every spring Mama and Daddy plant a large garden on the lot next to the house. "We're very lucky to have such good, fertile river-bottom land," my father frequently reminds us, since the Arkansas River runs parallel to Madison Place about three blocks away. One summer Mama loses her diamond ring in the dirt, not a ring my father bought for her, but a ring passed down to her as a gift in her family. It's very special to her. They search and search for the lost treasure and never find it. Years later, when my parents finally sell the lot next door, I grieve that Mama's ring is gone forever under the new house to be built there.

Before I am old enough to go to school, our neighborhood is undeveloped, and the dirt road we live on ends at an open field just a half block away, tempting Daddy to plant a large watermelon patch there. My earliest memory is of walking hand-in-hand with him from our house to the watermelon patch. When we reach our destination, Daddy pulls a large watermelon from its vine, undoubtedly the first one to ripen in the patch, and places it in front of me. I can't be more than three or four years old, because I'm stretched out on my stomach, my face propped up with my elbows implanted in the dirt, watching him carefully as he kneels down beside me and prepares a smooth place in the ground. I watch him take the melon in his large hands, raise it up above his head, and suddenly thrust it hard against the earth, causing it to burst open, revealing a most glorious sight. Having never seen such a thing, I look up at him smiling at me, wondering what I am to do. "Go ahead, eat it!" he says, so I slither close to the melon and take one big bite from its choice red heart, burying my face in its crisp, sweet juiciness, as Daddy tosses his head back and laughs, clapping his hands with pleasure. I have never tasted anything so good. When I've had my fill, we leave the bulk of the melon uneaten in the patch and walk together on the dusty road back to our house.

Our home consists of a living room and dining room with walls of textured stucco and a floor furnace between the two rooms that heat the whole house, a kitchen, one bathroom, and two bedrooms. My parents sleep in one bedroom and Bonnie and I share the other. I don't know where my brother John sleeps before Daddy builds on another bedroom at the back of the house for him. We have an "ice box" for our food and I often go with my father to an ice plant to buy ice. Later, a truck comes by regularly to deliver large blocks of ice, and milk is also delivered to our door by a man driving a panel truck.

The bedroom that Bonnie and I share is on the front corner of the house, with double windows on two sides, one facing the south, so our bedroom is usually bright and sunny. Bonnie chose the décor before I was born—wallpaper of delicate pink roses arranged in wreaths, filmy, ruffled, white organza curtains on the windows, a double bed with pink rosebuds carved into its white headboard, and a soft green quilted bedspread to match the stems and leaves of the roses. Our room is one befitting daughters of sovereigns, and Bonnie is my princess. Sometimes at night before we go to sleep, she asks me if I will gently rub her arm. I always do because it's a privilege for me if it helps her go to sleep.

By 1945 everyone is affected by the war in one way or another. The terrible death marches are occurring in Germany as the Nazis move prisoners away from the concentration camps to hide evidence of the atrocities being committed there. Thousands of prisoners are killed before the marches begin and others, too weak or ill to keep up, are executed. When Daddy, Bonnie, and John leave for school each weekday morning, Mama stays home taking care of me. She reads accounts of the war in the newspaper and is disturbed by stories of misery among the men in battle areas. Some of Daddy's friends enlist or are called up, and he is classified 1-A three different times for the draft. It's a terrible worry for our family each time he has to go report to the draft board. Fortunately for us, since he has three children and is in charge of a physical fitness program for boys soon to be eighteen and subject to the draft, he is deferred each time, and this brings immense joy and relief.

Mama begins to feel that our family isn't doing enough for the war effort, not making any sacrifice, while so many others are suffering and dying. "I want to do something to help," she says. She knows many women are working in the war industries and, from the newspaper, she learns about the Lanham Act nurseries which are set up by the government to provide childcare for these working women. She is qualified to be a childcare nurse or teacher, so she applies and is accepted in one of the nurseries. The plan is that Bonnie will take some responsibility for the evening meal; John will walk to the high school where Daddy works and come home with him; and I will go to the nursery with Mama. Daddy doesn't object to her plans, perhaps feeling some guilt about his three deferments, but he also doesn't strongly encourage her. Nevertheless, her plans go awry from the beginning.

First she learns that it's against the rules for a mother to bring her own child to the nursery where she works, so I am taken to another Lanham Act nursery. Then Bonnie needs a costume for a play at school so Mama stays up all night making it. John doesn't like having to go to Daddy's school in the afternoon because he wants to come home and play with his friends in the neighborhood as always. By then we do have one car, but everyone has to get up early to get to their schools or nursery and Mama to her job. It's February and a heavy snowfall leaves the streets icy. I contract chicken pox at the nursery and have to be separated from the other children. These obstacles are all met, and though Mama feels pressure, she is determined to continue on. At the nursery she copes well with the children and gets along with her co-workers, but gradually more and more tension begins to build until one day, after a trivial difficulty with a child, she reaches her limit, sinks into a chair, puts her head down on her folded arms and cries, realizing she can't make a decision about anything.

The nursery contacts Daddy and he leaves Bonnie in charge so he can take Mama to her parents' home in Cushing. The trusted family doctor prescribes a liquid concoction of bromide, commonly used as a tranquilizer, but dangerous if over-ingested. Too much bromide replaces chloride in the blood, which has a toxic effect on the brain resulting in psychosis, seizures, and delirium. In some people doses of 0.5 to 1 gram per day of bromide can cause this toxicity known as bromism. Her recommended dose was 3 to 5 grams, thus explaining why my mother develops bromism. The family is terrified by Mama's deteriorating condition and the doctor is so alarmed that he makes arrangements for my father to take her to Oklahoma City and admit her into the Coyne Campbell Mental Hospital.

Mama is locked in a bare room that has a large drawing on the wall of a dressing table, undoubtedly drawn by a former patient to take the place of a real piece of furniture. One morning she wakes up to find herself tightly bound in wet sheets, unable to move. With a frantic struggle, she frees her naked body from the wet sheets and she realizes she is in a room directly across from the first room she was in before, only this one contains a bed and a glass window facing the hallway. The room doesn't have a solid door, but one with horizontal bars across the entire length of it, and for a short while, a man stands outside the window staring at her; she feels ashamed and degraded.

Another day she wakes up from a deep sleep in a room that seems to be on a lower floor—a kind of room where treatments are given. A large woman doctor is sitting beside her and asks her for her name and when she complies, the doctor gives her a glass of sweet sugar water. Gradually Mama begins to understand that the doctors are giving her insulin shock treatments, a form of treatment that is used mainly for schizophrenia. Patients are repeatedly injected with large doses of insulin in order to produce daily comas over several weeks. After the insulin injection, patients experience various symptoms of decreased blood glucose, and as the injections increase, a coma accompanied by seizures follow. The wet towel wrap is to protect her from rolling, tossing, and thrashing. Each coma lasts up to an hour and is terminated by intravenous glucose. Whether Mama recovers this time because of the treatments or in spite of them is a fair question. For whatever reason, she is no longer locked in a bare room, but is put in a room with two beds, sharing it with another woman. As patients improve they are moved down the hall with other roommates, free to go anywhere on the third floor and assemble in a large lounge type room at the end of the hall. One day to her surprise and joy, my grandmother appears on the third floor. "Why have you not come before?" Mama asks as she eagerly hugs her mother.

"We were not allowed to come before now," my grandmother explains to reassure her.

I've not seen Mama in over a month, the longest time I've been separated from her. Bonnie sees my distress when I frequently ask about her. She comforts and reminds me, "Mama will be home soon." During the day I've become accustomed to the nursery when Bonnie and John are at school, but there are times when I need overnight care, and Daddy relies on the families of the coaches he works with to take care of me. One night I sleep in bed with two older children I barely know. In the middle of the night I'm squeezed out of the bed and spend what seems like the whole night sitting on the floor leaning up against the wall. Another time Daddy takes me to spend a weekend at my grandmother's house, where I sleep alone in the upstairs bedroom. Windows line one wall and I sit on the bed looking out the row of windows waiting for Mama and Daddy to come to get me. Surely they know how lonely and frightened I am. I know they love me, so why don't they come?

Eventually Mama is given a room on the first floor that is like a nice hotel room, and she is allowed to go for walks outside. It's during this time that Daddy, Bonnie, John, and I come for a visit on a Sunday and we are permitted to take Mama to a park. Bonnie and John, thirteen and twelve, are reserved and uncertain as to how to respond to her, but I greet her joyfully, just happy to be with her again in a normal situation. Because of my mother's long illness, and because the treatments have blanked out the events leading up to her treatment, she is simply quiet and not as responsive as we expect her to be. But a week later, Daddy goes to get her and brings her back home to Tulsa. Slowly she regains her full senses and is able to be my mother as I remember her before she became ill. But my fear of being separated from a person I associate with safety and security will stay with me the rest of my life.

One day I am with Mama when she is shopping in a downtown department store. Not yet tall enough to see over the counters, I pay close attention in order to keep her in sight. But something distracts me and before I know it, I can't see Mama anywhere. I run quickly around every corner in hopes that she will come back into view. I'm crying now and a sympathetic clerk must observe my fright. She takes my hand and reassures me that she will help me find my mother, and she does.

I wish I could say this was the end of Mama having to suffer from harsh treatments for mental illness. Episodes of her illness will occur again at intervals, one when I am six, another when I am twelve, and another not long after I am married. Each of these times, she will receive electroconvulsive shock therapy, a process of placing electrodes on her head while she is completely awake to deliver powerful shocks to her brain in order to produce convulsions, a terrifying procedure. Mama wrote this in her journal:

> *"I know that shock treatments do help some people, but to me they are horrible, like going to the electric chair every other day. I am forcibly made to undergo a violent convulsion, after which I am mercifully taken back to my room on a gurney where I fall into a deep sleep from which I awake, glad to be alive again, but then enduring the ordeal again and again on successive days."*

I understand that shock treatment induces seizures that alter many chemical aspects of the brain associated with a mental disorder. Their purpose, as Mama understands them, is to jolt an abnormal pattern of brain waves into a more normal one. To her, and consequently to me, it is like throwing a deck of cards up in the air, in hopes the cards will fall neatly into separate stacks of hearts, diamonds, clubs, and spades. A series of these treatments, usually one on alternate days for three to four weeks, are needed to end her depressions. She spends the first few weeks in the hospital, and then is allowed to come home, returning to the hospital during the day for the remaining treatments.

I'm in the first grade when my mother is ill again. I awaken early one morning by the sound of her crying and pleading with Daddy not to take her to the hospital. I imagine the horror that awaits her. I also feel a deep sympathy for Daddy, because I sense his feeling of helplessness in his efforts to console her. "The treatments are what the doctors recommend," he says. "They will help you." What else can he do?

It's Christmas Day when Mama comes home to celebrate the holiday with us. I can see that she is better—happier and more relaxed, but still subdued and weak. I'm not yet aware that memory loss of events leading up to each treatment is an expected side effect, so there is nothing from Mama under the Christmas tree. I'm not so troubled by that, but several weeks later, she discovers my previously-bought gifts on the shelf in the top of her closet. With utter joy and excitement, she calls me to the bedroom to share her discovery. "Look, Kathleen! Look what I found! Here are your Christmas presents!" I'm barely able to respond to the doll and coloring books because of the assault to my awareness. What happened to her that she forgot all about my Christmas presents?

My favorite times with Mama are when she reads to me. A six-volume set of books called *My Bookhouse* are my favorites. The first volume, "In the Nursery," contains poems, nursery rhymes and simple stories that have my scribbles on their pages from when I was younger. The second volume, "Story Time," contains the stories I love most ("The Little Engine That Could," "Tales of Peter Rabbit," and my most favorite, "The Wee Wee Mannie and the Big Big Coo.") The remaining four volumes contain stories that are progressively longer and more advanced with fewer pictures. I think a peaceful state of mind eludes Mama much of the time, causing her to seek out anything that calms her unsettled mind. She derives a great deal of comfort from reading good, inspiring books, and I have acquired a love of books from her. I sense contentment in her when she reads to me; this is pleasant and reassuring.

I am much my father's child during my grade school years, playing on the bleachers in the high school gymnasium while he keeps score at basketball games, riding with him in the car to scout out-of-town football games, and swimming every summer at the country club pool where he works. Daddy is

MY CHILDHOOD 47

patient and never raises his voice in anger at me, nor has he ever spanked me, but there is one time when I learn there is a limit to his tolerance. To supplement his salary as a high school coach, Daddy manages a swimming pool and teaches swimming at an elite Tulsa country club. The job entitles him to some privileges, one of them being that I can attend the day camp along with the children of the country club's affluent membership. The camp director teaches girls' physical education at the same high school where Daddy teaches and coaches, so they are good friends. One afternoon another seven-year-old camper friend and I decide to sneak off from the camp activities and hide somewhere on the spectacular golf course where children are not allowed without their parents. Celebrating our freedom, we scamper about the rolling green hills from one clump of trees to another until we find the perfect hiding place. We spend most of the afternoon out there before Daddy, a country club official, and the camp director find us. I know instantly that Daddy is furious at me for embarrassing him with my ungrateful behavior. I'm not punished, but his cold withdrawal of affection is enough. I learn then how important authority is to my father, and if I am to retain his love and affection, I will do well to respect authority in my own life. I trust my father and having his approval gives me confidence and a sense of security.

On the country club swimming pool premises is a small snack bar that serves delicious hamburgers, French fries, and chocolate chip ice cream cones. These are treats my camper friends can buy just by signing their parents' names as members. Daddy and I have lunch privileges, but not at this snack bar. We eat in the kitchen at the main clubhouse with the other hired help, all males, both Caucasian and African American. Still bare-footed and in my swim suit, I complain one day on our way up to the clubhouse.

"I hate walking on that greasy kitchen floor, and I don't like having to eat with all grown-ups." I see he's displeased with me, but I continue to pout. "I want to eat with my friends at the snack bar."

Daddy takes my hand and we turn to go in a different direction. "I want to show you something," he says with determination as he steers me toward the main front entrance and he continues to talk. "We are getting a far more nutritious meal in the kitchen than we would at the snack bar. The food we're eating is the same food that's being served to club members in the main dining room." We enter the front door, and walk down the hall to two wide double doors that Daddy opens for me to see inside. It's an impressive large room full of round tables covered with white tablecloths, a thick red carpet on the floor, and giant chandeliers hang from the ceiling. "See? Today in the kitchen, you're going to be eating the same food that will be served here." Daddy smiles at me with satisfaction assuming my attitude has undergone a change having witnessed this demonstration. I still don't like it, but I accept my fate, and occasionally Daddy buys me a chocolate chip ice cream cone at the snack bar.

Along with every child of country club members, I learn to swim from my father, and if you learn to swim from Coach Barham, you learn to swim well. Daddy never hires anyone else to teach swimming, and every lesson is a private lesson— one child at a time. When we are not tall enough to touch the bottom of the pool, he holds us in his strong arms until we learn, first to float, then kick, and then use our arms to swim by ourselves. He wears a hard safari-type helmet to keep the sun off his face, and every summer Daddy spends most of his time standing in the water teaching children to swim.

Daddy doesn't forget the promise he made to my mother years ago that he will find a way to pay for our college education. John is fourteen, Bonnie fifteen, and I am six when Daddy gets the idea to start a firewood business. He's chatting with one of the country club members one day after he's just given the man's son a swimming lesson.

"I know you're a successful business man," Daddy begins, "so I wonder if you might have a suggestion as to what I could do to earn extra money for my children's education. I won't be able to do it on my teaching salary. Do you know if there's a need for some service I could provide?"

The man takes Daddy's question seriously and promises he will ask around the country club and get back to him, and it isn't long before Daddy has his answer.

"You may be surprised at this, Coach Barham, but we've all agreed on one thing. None of us know where to get good firewood. We don't know the difference between a rick and a cord of wood, let alone how much we should pay for each. Guys knock on my door peddling firewood, but they could load four ricks on the truck and sell it as five or six, and I wouldn't know the difference!" This makes immediate sense to Daddy, because he knows that all the luxury homes are built with large dens and fireplaces; probably every club member has one.

"We also don't know the best kind of wood to burn—oak, hickory, pecan, ash, elm? If I answer an ad in the paper, what should I ask for? Should it be green or seasoned, and if seasoned, for how long?"

This is all it takes to arouse Daddy's interest. By coincidence, he has observed a boy in his biology class who continually falls asleep. "Why can't you stay awake in class?" Daddy finally asks him.

"I'm sorry, Coach Barham—I'm worn out—I cut and sell firewood after school and on weekends." From this boy, Daddy gets some valuable information. The next Sunday afternoon, Mama and Daddy take a drive out in the country, stopping at farmhouses where stands of trees are on nearby land, asking if there's anyone willing to cut the wood and how much it would cost to buy it. Finding some ready takers, he buys an old flat-bottom truck, a monster truck that will hold five or six ricks of wood. (A rick is four feet high and eight feet long; a cord is twice as much.) In order to advertise his new business, Mama suggests they have double postcards printed so that a buyer can easily mail back half the card indicating whether they want oak or hickory (both hardwoods, hickory the most expensive and it smells better), twenty-four or thirty-six inches, green, seasoned, or half-and-half (which Daddy recommends—seasoned to get the fire started, green to make it last longer), and which Saturday they want it delivered. The country club manager is happy to provide their membership mailing list, and as September days get cooler, the orders start pouring in.

On Saturday mornings, sometimes as early as 3:00 a.m., Daddy and John get up and drive to the farms, load up the truck, drive back to Tulsa, deliver orders (some requiring wheelbarrow transport to be nearer the house), and then go back for another load. Some Saturdays they deliver over twenty ricks of wood (eight dollars for twenty-four inch and twelve dollars for thirty inch). Daddy's reliability and honesty are already known by the parents whose kids learn to swim from him; his firewood business thrives.

After Daddy gets his firewood business going, John rarely has a free Saturday to spend with his friends. One Friday night he goes to a midnight preview at the drive-in movie theater, the most popular place to see movies. He doesn't get home until two o'clock in the morning and at five-thirty Daddy wakes him up to start the day's work. That is the last of his midnight previews. John learns what hard work is. One year the Arkansas River floods south of Tulsa and over one hundred ricks of wood wash down the east bank of the river. Daddy and John are able to recover most of it, but every stick of wood they sell that season has to be brushed to remove the sand.

The printed postcards are only needed for two years; after that all of Daddy's customers know our phone number. Mama stays home every day during wood season to take orders, and all of us kids learn to take orders when we're not in school. By its third year, the business is so successful, Daddy and John alone can't manage all the orders. With a loan from the teachers' credit union for four thousand dollars, Daddy leases acreage less than two miles from our house and hires someone who will not only cut the wood, but also bring it into the town lot and stack it. The most dependable man, Mr. Remington, only has one arm, and he isn't young either—I can't imagine how he operates a chain saw. Of small stature, always scruffily dressed, wearing an old dilapidated hat and speaking in a gravelly voice, he comes to our front door at the crack of dawn to be paid. Since I sleep in the front bedroom, I'm often awakened by Mr. Remington's loud cackle as he jokes with Daddy.

Daddy also begins hiring other people to help him deliver wood—John's friends, young coaches, and athletes who need extra money. One man, who owns his own truck, but can't read, brings his wife with him to read the names of streets. Another boy from a rural area spends three months with us, sleeping in our laundry room and working for Dad during the week. Mama makes huge bowls of oatmeal or corn meal mush for him every morning, and he is one of the best workers we have. These are some of the best years for my parents, working alongside each other to ensure that we will get a college education. Mama points out to us that many professional men won't go to the back doors of wealthy people's homes delivering firewood. "Your dad has not an iota of false pride," she says. "He makes friends with every man or woman he works for or with—the poor men needing work and the wealthy people who appreciate the good wood, the honest measure, and prompt service. He's doing this for you."

When I'm ten years old and spending more time with my school friends, Mom decides to volunteer as a teacher's assistant in a school for mentally challenged children. She has a keen intelligence and she wants to use her abilities in a productive way. After doing this for a while, the director recognizes her ability and offers her a full-time job. She's very excited about this prospect, but Dad fears the responsibility will be too strenuous for her, both mentally and physically. Whether she lacks the confidence to challenge him, or harbors similar fears herself, I'm not sure, but she turns down the offer.

Not long after this, Mom hears a religious message over the radio that she recognizes as being similar to the viewpoint held by her mother—that hell is not a place of torture, but only represents death, the grave. She is overjoyed to hear her mother's beliefs affirmed over the radio. This perspective brings her far more comfort than the fundamentalist view of salvation taught in the Baptist Church that we attend. She learns that these Biblical teachings are contained in a set of more than twenty books, the first six of which she orders. A woman, just the age of her own mother, soon contacts her, introducing herself as "Sister Louise," one of a small group of people in Tulsa who meet in one another's homes for Bible study and worship. Sister Louise begins to visit Mom frequently to study the lessons contained in these books. It's a scholarly approach to studying religion that appeals to Mom's intellect. Followers see themselves as independent thinkers and set themselves apart from other religions of our day, while still espousing Christianity as the foundation of their teachings. Most appealing to Mom is their teaching that the masses of mankind are not on trial for their salvation in this age, but are only here to experience suffering as the natural consequence of evil. They go on to explain that there will come a time when all will be resurrected from a sleep-like death, righteousness will prevail, suffering will end, and Christ will reign on Earth a thousand years. This prediction becomes a panacea for Mom, applicable to every conceivable misfortune anyone might encounter—the ultimate solution to every problem. Every morning she gets up early to go into the living room, where she sits in a comfortable chair next to a bookcase containing several Bible translations and her new set of Bible study books. She reads, studies, and makes notes about their precepts, lessons, and symbolism.

Mom's new interest, along with the support she is receiving from her new group of friends, especially Sister Louise, help to calm an inner frustration. It also seems to provide a mental stimulation that she needs. Gradually she becomes more and more grounded in the scriptures that support her new perspective and more compelled to share it with others, including the wives of the men who work with Dad, our neighbors, and the mothers of my friends. She hangs a large chart above our table in the dining room that illustrates the chronology of the teachings, thereby creating opportunities to respond to anyone posing a question about it. Her newfound resource, however, is unsettling to Dad, who is more comfortable in a conventional church setting. He fears the unorthodox nature of my mother's new religion, thinks it extreme, and clearly has no desire to dig into its dozens of books. I often wonder, if Mom had had a successful work experience, the religious studies might not have become so consuming.

I sense Dad's disdain for Mom's new religion, and I must want some reassurance and direction from him. With little thought one evening, when our family is seated at the dining table, I speak to him.

"I don't like Mom saying 'Sister Louise' in front of my friends. Why does she have to call her that?"

Mom bursts into tears, shocked I suppose that I appeal to Dad in this way, hurt that I am so critical of her dear friend, and maybe even angry that I am betraying her. I wait and watch Dad carefully as he keeps his eyes riveted on his plate and continues to eat without saying a word. Clearly, I am placing him in a dilemma. To censure my unkindness will be to condone Mom's religion; to empathize with me will risk further hurting her. By saying nothing, he leaves us both unaided. I take this to mean that I am on my own in dealing with Mom and her religion, and this event becomes a pivotal point in my relationship with her.

I deeply regret hurting her and I begin to show an interest in her religion, seeing that it reassures her. She confides in me, sharing feelings of disappointment in Dad's lack of interest in Bible study. I learn that I can be a support to her in a way Dad can't, a peculiar temptation to a child. From this time on, it is as if I can only watch Dad out of the corner of my eye as he models a cheerful and steadying influence in our family, because I believe my primary responsibility is to my mother, to monitor her moods and be there for her.

Thus begins my indoctrination in the teachings that the "brethren" call "The Truth." Mom explains to me why I should stop attending Sunday school at the Baptist Church in order to go to the weekly Bible classes with her in the homes of the brethren. I'm well prepared the afternoon my Sunday school teacher arrives at our house to inquire about my absence. Mom listens proudly as I explain why I can no longer believe in hell as a place of torment, and I cite pertinent scriptures to support my position. By this time Bonnie has left home for college, John is still attending the Baptist Church and enjoying its youth program, and Dad has stopped going to church altogether, probably the only way he knows how to exert a neutral influence. Perhaps he can see, as I have, that her religion is meeting some important needs, so he never openly criticizes it. When she hosts the small Bible class in the den at the back of our house, he sits in the living room reading the Sunday paper, and then amiably visits with the brethren when they stay for coffee in our dining room.

Every fall the Bible class hosts a weekend convention in Tulsa, to which "elders" come from various places around the country to expound on scholarly Biblical topics with a gathering of people from Oklahoma and neighboring states. A church sanctuary is rented if anyone wants to be baptized, a ritual that signifies the surrendering of oneself into the will of God. I decide to be baptized when I'm twelve, the age when children are considered mature enough to make this important decision. It so happens that Mom is hospitalized with another bout of depression at the time of the convention, so a couple in the Bible class takes me to the baptismal ceremony. I sit in the front row alone as the presiding elder explains to me the significance of what I'm doing. It's as if God is handing me a blank piece of paper, he says. The baptism, only a symbol of my dedication to do God's will, is akin to signing my name at the bottom of a contract, thereby agreeing to do anything which God might ask of me. His metaphor makes a strong impression, though it's not clear to me how I will recognize the specifics of God's directions. Nevertheless I believe that if

I'm faithful to my promise and earnest in my desire to please God, I can trust that whatever happens in my future will always result in something good. If only Mom was here to see me, I think, as I lean back onto the elder's hand while he lowers me into the water—this would make her very happy.

My baptism and Mom's emotional breakdown move me to be more sensitive to her needs and eager to please her. I learn that two of her earliest symptoms of illness are an inability to sleep and a need to talk, both evidence of anxiety to which I respond. Mom becomes a trusted confidante; we often have what she calls heart-to-heart talks, not just about her concerns, but about my own worries and desires. When she agrees to my taking the costly tap and ballet lessons I want so badly, I know she will do most anything for me. The dance studio is on the opposite side of town, making it even more of an extravagance since she has to take me there.

Although I'm learning important relationship skills—how to express my feelings and listen to hers, there's a downside to our intimacy. If our discussions occur late in the evening, as they often do, Dad becomes anxious. Already in bed himself, he gets up frequently to remind us of the late hour. This is confusing to me and I struggle to understand it. Does he fear that our talking late will overstimulate Mom, causing her to have difficulty sleeping, the dreaded warning sign? Or could he be trying to protect me from Mom's religious zeal? It even occurs to me that he might be jealous, without being totally aware, because Mom is confiding in me instead of him. I'm really not sure what his motivation is, but I'm beginning to feel torn between the two of them.

My sixth grade school teacher is helpful. Mrs. Bostick is Greek, a stoutly built woman with neat, short, salt and pepper hair, bright red lipstick, and a pleasant, but no-nonsense manner. I tell Mrs. Bostick about Mom being in the hospital and I think that's why she's taking a special interest in me. She even comes to our house to visit after Mom comes home, and I think this is to make me feel better. I truly love her! She is quite different from Mom—more confident in herself and assertive.

I have two special friends in Mrs. Bostick's class this year, both of them are named Patricia, but one is called Pat and the other Patsy. Pat and Patsy get into a quarrel one day and stop speaking to one another. This upsets me because it makes it impossible for me to enjoy being with either of them, so I tell Mrs. Bostick about Pat and Patsy's disagreement.

"Why don't you write up a "peace treaty" for Patsy and Pat," she suggests.

"A peace treaty?" I'm intrigued. "What would it say?"

"A peace treaty is a promise to agree to something. What is it that you want your friends to agree to?"

"I want them to say they're sorry to each other, and agree to be friends again."

"I'm sure you can write something that says that and then include a place at the bottom for each of them to sign—if they are willing." Then she gives me a big smile of encouragement.

I do what Mrs. Bostick suggests and it's working—Pat and Patsy are talking to each other again and I'm glad. When two people I love aren't getting along, I don't like it, and I never will.

I know that Dad has his own fears and insecurities to deal with and that he needs to be the strong figure in our family, especially during the times Mom falters. Though warm and accepting in many ways, he isn't generous with affection, and rarely do we get a glimpse of him being openly emotional. One thing we are clear about, however, is his dread of saying goodbye. Sometimes Mom and I take a bus trip to visit her parents in Cushing. When I go to Dad to say goodbye, I notice that it's hard for him to speak, and I feel a tense resistance to my hug. When I see his lips tremble and his eyes glisten with tears, I feel afraid. I see the same response when we bid his parents farewell after a visit to their farm in Texas. I sense a deep hurt that Dad can't reveal to us—a hurt so deep that all three of us kids are growing up fearing to say goodbye and believing we mustn't cry about it because it will only make things worse.

This is the day my brother John is to leave for Baltimore, Maryland, where he will be stationed in the Army. It's a long way from our Oklahoma home, and I'm dreading it. Dad, Mom, John, and I get in the car to go to the bus station. Mom and Dad are in the front seat; John and I are in back. On the way there, the tension is unbearable. No one is saying a word. With little understanding of why we are so afraid, John and I are terrified Dad will cry, and we believe it will only take one peep for the floodgates to open. I hold back my tears until the pressure makes my head throb. Mom seems immune to our burden, but is also silent. Stoically and hastily we hug John before he boards the bus, and I watch him sit down in a window seat, hoping he will look back at me so I can wave, but his eyes are fixed on a point straight ahead. After the bus leaves the station and rolls out of sight, my parents and I walk back to the car—still in silence—a silence that lasts all the way home. It isn't until late that night, alone in my bed, a pillow pressed against my face to muffle any sound, that the release of tears dissolves the pain behind my eyes.

Since Bonnie graduated from college, married, and moved to San Francisco to live with her new husband, the only long trips my parents and I make are to see Bonnie or John. Our first trip to San Francisco takes us within one hour's drive of the Grand Canyon. "It's one of the Seven Wonders of the World," Mom hints in hopes that Dad will make the detour, but his heart is set on California; he isn't much interested in sightseeing. After a good four-day visit, Dad loads our suitcases into the trunk as Mom and I get in the car for our return trip home. From the back seat I see Bonnie standing at the big picture window inside her apartment waving goodbye to me. As I stifle my tears, I watch my sister point to her eyes and then make a falling rain motion with her hands to indicate, "I'm crying." Her silent admission comforts me and I feel less alone.

INSIGHTS: The Effects of Maternal Depression on a Developing Child

My siblings and I have all been deeply affected, though differently, by the separations and emotional distress that accompanied our mother's periodic bouts of mental illness. The fear of her illness hung over our family like a cloud of dread that has remained a significant factor throughout our adult lives. We all have admitted to long-term forms of anxieties and acknowledged that we've each had to confront the fear of mental illness in ourselves. Bonnie and I share the particularly painful memory of hearing Dad having to coerce our terrified mother into going to the hospital for shock treatments, though our memories occurred at different times when we each were five or six years old. John's most painful memory was of drawing picture after picture for our mother when she was crying, hoping his artwork would cheer her up. Our experiences, however, took different forms. Bonnie felt little confidence in our mother when she was a child, which can be explained by the fact that our grandmother was her primary caregiver when she was an infant, as a result of our mother's breakdown after Bonnie's birth. Bonnie relied almost entirely on our father as her mainstay. I think I may have bonded more easily with Mom than did Bonnie or John, both of them born at a time when she was less emotionally reliable. By the time I came along, Dad had settled in his work as a teacher and coach, our parents' marriage was better established, and my mother's mental health had improved. However, the vivid memories I have of her hospitalization when I was three may have set the stage for compounding anxieties later.

John Bowlby's attachment theory teaches that the greatest disruptions to a child's level of attachment security occur before conscious memory, that is, before one is three years old.[1] If my mother was displaying symptoms of depression during my first three years, I could expect that research on the early effects of maternal depression would yield more information about me. If those effects didn't apply to me, then I could speculate that my own anxieties didn't develop until later. While my exploration didn't yield absolute certainty on this point, it does provide some helpful insight.

Depression is one of the most common mental health disorders among women of childbearing years and is generally associated with higher rates of insecure attachment in children.[2] Children of depressed mothers are also two to three times more likely to develop adjustment problems and mood disorders.[3] Unresponsiveness and irritability are commonly found in depressed patients and can be assumed to be behavior to which the young child of a depressed mother is frequently exposed. As seen in the Ainsworth studies of mothers and their infants, mothers of babies who showed insecure attachment behavior in the Strange Situation measurement tended to be less responsive to a baby's signals, less accepting and warm toward the baby, and less cooperative and accessible than mothers of securely attached infants.[4]

In spite of these statistics, some children of depressed mothers turn out to be well-adjusted and even high-functioning individuals, so it can't be said that maternal depression causes negative outcomes in children. While children of depressed mothers may be at greater risk, other contributing factors may be marital functioning between the parents, availability of other nurturing figures in the child's environment, and even unique temperament characteristics in the child.[5]

When depressed, a mother's tendency is to withdraw her interest from the outside world and become increasingly preoccupied with an inner world in which her loved ones are lost to her or have become unsatisfying. Consequently she feels abandoned and unloved. Her mood can therefore fluctuate between sadness and anger, and her emotional state may change quickly from one state to another. She may give up engaging in her children's lives, communicating with them, or showing affection toward them. Other mothers may desperately try to control their children in order not to risk further loss. In either case, whether she is withdrawn or intrusive, she is less aware of the realities in her environment and less responsive to the people in it.[6] If her young children are dependent on her for their survival and cannot escape a distressing situation, the effects of her negative mood and impaired capacity for relating may undermine the attachment bond between her and her child.[7] If, however, there are alternative sources of nurture such as an attentive father, an aunt, or older sibling, these available caregivers may buffer the effects of the mother's depression.[8]

It is also known that children are affected not only by their direct interaction with parents, but also by their observations as bystanders to the interaction of their parents. Maternal depression affects children when it contributes to marital discord, which in turn may increase the effects of maternal depression on the child. In some cases conflict between the parents may be a stronger predictor of child outcomes than the mother's depression itself.[9] I am aware that the conflicts between my parents, whether or not they resulted from Mom's depression, had a profound effect on me. For as long as they were alive, I felt responsible for their relationship. (This was a significant factor in my becoming a marriage and family therapist.)

Harsh forms of treatment, like those my mother was subjected to, can have a significant effect on a child's perceptions of a parent's difficulties. Bromide, the medication my mother was given when I was three, was eventually banned from clinical use in many countries and severely restricted in others. Insulin coma treatment was used very inappropriately, as evidenced by the severe side effects my mother suffered from bromism. Fortunately it fell out of favor in the 1960s and was replaced by antipsychotic drugs. Recent articles about insulin coma treatment now say that it was embraced in psychiatry not because of any scientific evidence, but by a few dramatic recoveries that had been seen in some patients. *"Today those who were involved are often ashamed, recalling it as unscientific and inhumane"* wrote Deborah Doroshow in the *Journal of the History of Medicine and Allied Sciences* in 2007. Electroconvulsive therapy, as it is now called today, is still being used as a last line of intervention, but only with informed consent, and under controlled circumstances. For example, patients are now thankfully anesthetized.

Studies that investigate the effects of maternal depression reveal that children respond to depression in their mothers in strikingly different ways, explaining the differences between my siblings and me. Some, like Bonnie, needing to protect themselves from possible rejection and finding it difficult to detect the mother's changes in mood, may retreat into avoidant behavior. Other children of depressed mothers, who are not as inclined to withdraw from their mothers, may instead become more determined in their efforts to obtain a positive response from her. I think this applies more to John and me, less so with Bonnie, who did not feel so responsible for her.[10] John and I felt more conflicted between our parents. John remained in Tulsa all his life, never married, and cared for both our parents until their death.

Andrea Pound describes a third group of children, who observe their mother's helplessness, and choose to take control, thereby freeing themselves from identification with her helpless state. This description may apply to me. There is an obvious attachment between these children and their mothers, but it is of an unusual kind. Both mother and child may feel safer if the child is in control. I can relate to Pound's following explantion:

> *"It is intimate, even intense, but not warm; continuous but also continuously threatened; and the only satisfaction seems to be that somehow the relationship is preserved intact. Some of the unusual features of the relationship can be seen as arising from reversals of the balance of power and resource that normally prevails between mother and child. Instead of the mother holding the child in her concerned attention, the child watches her, ready to respond to her need as it arises.... While the healthy mother sees herself as responsible for the child's survival, in depression the child may feel responsible for the mother's."*[11]

I'm inclined to believe that my mother's symptoms were at a minimum during my infancy. Letters that she wrote to her mother or sister at that time indicate that she enjoyed taking care of me and that I was the lucky recipient of adoration from my two older siblings. If she was experiencing symptoms of depression during my first three years, I suspect that my attachment to my father may have helped to make up for that distraction. I also know that Bonnie filled in many times as a surrogate mother to me, and I still have a strong attachment to my sister. I believe that the descriptions of children who form an intense and watchful attachment with their mothers do apply to me. The propensity to be discerning of her moods may have begun early on or emerged after I experienced my mother's first serious illness. Whichever the case, the episode at the family dining table in regard to Sister Louise had the effect of bringing this propensity into full bloom and I began to look for more effective ways in which to respond to her. I can well understand children who learn to feel more secure when they find that they can be of comfort to their mothers.

In this case of "role reversal," the cost to these children is that they have to look after themselves and their mother with the internal resources they already have. In short they are *"forced into a precocious maturity and have to become an attachment figure before they have had sufficient experience of being attached."*[12] Some children in this situation develop surprising capacities by observing their mother closely, making accurate assessments, and finding their own sources of satisfaction and enjoyment. They may also have social and cognitive skills that help them receive positive attention from adults other than their parents.[13]

Another helpful concept pertaining to my relationship with my parents has come from the work of Salvador Minuchin and Murray Bowen who were influential in the development of what is known as *family systems theory*. This approach considers human behavior being fundamentally shaped by how people function in relationship to their family as a whole. Most family therapists believe that in order to function effectively, all families need to have a hierarchical structure with parents who are in charge of their children. It's also important that parents work together to raise children, lest differences between them undermine authority.[14] All families are sometimes challenged when the emotional intensity between two family members becomes difficult to manage. When this happens, it is common for a third person to become involved. Bowen called the three-person system a triangle and said that it occurs whenever there is tension or anxiety. He explained:

> *"The twosome might reach out and pull in the other person, the emotions might overflow to the other person, or the third person might be emotionally programmed to initiate the involvement. With the involvement of the third person, the anxiety level decreases."*[15]

Imagine a two-legged stool becoming unstable, but with the addition of a third leg, stability is restored. The formation of triangles is a natural human tendency and triangles can be helpful if they are flexible and able to change according to need. But problems arise when a child becomes a part of the triangle and is rigidly used (or puts himself or herself in the position to be used) to regulate the stress and conflict between two parents.[16]

It's reasonable to me to think that a triangle began to form in my family after my mother chose not to take the job at the school as a teacher's assistant. Perhaps my father's unwillingness to support her in this new opportunity revived earlier resentments regarding her father's transference of money for her education to my father. Her immersion into her religious studies further divided my parents, producing intense emotions neither of them knew how to manage. Sensitive to the rising tension between them, I appealed to my father at the dinner table to take charge. But without the resources or support to know how to handle a difficult situation, he wasn't prepared to respond in an effective way. To reduce the tension between them, I initiated further involvement with my mother, and was partially successful, but not without an accompanying anxiety. I think John played a similar role as the third leg of the stool with our parents, and his role was intensified to fill a void when I married and left Oklahoma.

Both Minuchin and Bowen believed that the formation of triangles in families is probably influenced by preceding generations, and no doubt influence succeeding generations. It was no accident that both my mother and grandmother pursued a religion that was not favored by their husbands. They both relied on a daughter with whom to share that religion. To complicate matters ever more, my grandfather suffered a stroke soon after the suicide of their son, Champ. The stroke affected his speech, which may have limited him and my grandmother in their need to express intense feelings of grief. My mother's new discovery of religious tenets similar to her mother's beliefs, was a way she could reconnect with her mother and together mourn the loss of Champ, consequently reducing the tension between my grandparents. The pattern of a mother relying on a child for something she is not getting through her marriage is one that has been passed down from one generation to another in my family. I subsequently succumbed to the same pattern myself in my first marriage. It doesn't mean we can't change these patterns with awareness, but no matter how we analyze the function of modern families, and despite the form our family of origin happens to take, like it or not, our identity as an individual is greatly influenced by our family.

References:

[1] Bowlby, J. 1953. *Child care and the growth of love.* London: Penguin Books, p. 11.
[2] Kessler, R.C. 2003. Epidemiology of women and depression. *Journal of Affective Disorders,* 74(1):5-13.
[3] Beardslee, W. R., Versage, E. M., & Bladstone, T. R. G. 1998. Children of affectively ill parents: A review of the past 10 years. *Journal of the American Academy of Child and Adolescent Psychiatry* 37(11):1134-1141.
[4] Ainsworth, M.D.S, Blehar, M. C., Waters, E & Wall, S. 1978. *Patterns of attachment.* Hillsdale, New Jersey: Lawrence Erlbaum Associates.
[5] Cummings, E.M. & Davies, P. T. 1994. Maternal depression and child development. *Journal of Child Psychology and Psychiatry* 35(1):73-112.
[6] Pound, A. 1982. Attachment and maternal depression, in *The Place of Attachment in Human Behavior,* eds. C. M. Parkes and J. S. Hinde. New York: Basic Books, Inc., Publishers.
[7] Pound 1982.
[8] Bernard-Bonnin, A. C. 2004. Maternal depression and child development. *Pediatric Child Health* 9(8):575-583.
[9] Cummings, E.M. & Davies, P. T. 2002. Effects of marital conflict on children: Recent advances and emerging themes in process-oriented research. *Journal of Child Psychology and Psychiatry* 43(1):31-63.
[10] Pound 1982.
[11] Pound 1982, p. 125.
[12] Pound 1982, p. 126.
[13] Cummings & Davies 1994.
[14] Minuchin, S. 1974. *Families and family therapy.* Cambridge, MA: Harvard University Press.

[15] Bowen, M. 1978. *Family therapy in clinical practice.* New York: Jason Aronson, p. 400.
[16] Minuchin, S., Rosman, B., & Baker, L. 1978. *Psychosomatic families: Anorexia nervosa in context.* Cambridge, MA: Harvard University Press.

3

MY ADOLESCENCE

In the 1950s and 60s, Tulsa, Oklahoma is a city dominated by the oil industry, a phenomenon which creates almost a caste system of wealth, or lack of, among its population. Clear demarcations exist between old wealth families, new wealth families, middle class, and poor families. The neighborhoods that people live in are strong indications of where they fit in the social order. Our neighborhood on the southeast side of the city has developed since Dad bought the property, and our residential area is made up of working class people and middle income professionals like Dad. Northeast of our neighborhood is an old residential area inhabited by the second or third generation wealthy families, many of whom belong to the country club where Dad works in the summer, and consequently they are also his firewood customers. Further east are the younger generation newcomers just beginning to make their way up the income ladder.

When I'm in elementary school, attending summer camp at the country club, I'm not aware of the differences between these socio-economic classes and their significance. No junior or senior high school has yet been built on the south side of

Tulsa, so Bonnie, John, and I are all attending large schools downtown when I begin the seventh grade. I have to ride the school bus for the first time and I'm shocked and intimidated by the bullying of younger boys by older ones on the bus. Having left the security of an elementary school made up of children from my own neighborhood, it's an adjustment to be thrown in with hundreds of new kids from all parts of town. It's also my first encounter with social clubs, which are a visible part of teenage activity in Tulsa junior and senior high schools. Organized much like college sororities and fraternities, they sponsor social events, but their most salient feature is that social club membership serves to identify the socio-economic status of a student's family. Membership is selective and exclusive.

On Monday morning the third week of school at Horace Mann Junior High, I observe quite a number of students wearing little ribbon pins of different colors on their clothing. What could that be, I wonder? Eventually I learn that each color represents a different club, and the students who are wearing these colored pins have been chosen as new pledges. "Rush Week" has just occurred, the process by which one's membership is determined, if you're considered for any club membership at all—and some, like me, are not. Large groups of boys or girls are invited to an initial rush party by one or more clubs, depending on how much in demand you are. This gives existing members a chance to look you over to see if you measure up to their standards. Then the process of elimination begins for smaller follow-up parties until the very select few who are left at the end of the week are invited to become junior members. Those left out can quickly identify the chosen by the different colored pledge ribbons they sport on that first Monday after rush week is over. I don't understand how these junior high kids know how much money their parents make, but it seems to be a determining factor as to who gets into which club, and everyone seems to know the ranking: old wealth at the top, new wealth second, newcomers on their way up third. Sometimes physical attractiveness, special talent, or athletic prowess can help a boy or girl exceed their rank of family income, but more often than not, the rich kids are better looking too. Why is that?

This first experience with social rejection is buffered by my tomboy self-image, which is still intact. I hear that all these rich kids take social dancing lessons at a place called Skelly's, but I'm not interested in that. Dad has just leased a ten-acre parcel of land in the country for his firewood business. On the property he's raising a few head of cattle that he can fatten and butcher for meat for our family. I like to ride with him in the big truck to the rural area to check on the cows and bring a load of firewood back to town. I've seen young people showing their animals at the county and state fairs in Tulsa, and I think it would be fun to raise a calf of my own that I can show at the fair. Mom finds out there's a 4-H Club that meets at the leader's home not too far from us on the outskirts of Tulsa, and she drives me there for an initial meeting.

I'm welcomed by the club's leader, a warm matronly woman who introduces me to a group of about twenty boys and girls of all different ages. Then I hear the club members recite the 4-H pledge: "*I pledge my head to clearer thinking, my heart to greater loyalty, my hands to larger service, and my health to better living, for my club, my community, my country, and my world.*" After club officers conduct items of business, the group divides according to gender, and a professional male and female Cooperative Extension Agent present a pertinent educational lesson. Today's lesson for the girls is to introduce a series of workshops on "Meat Judging and Identification." Any girl who is interested can meet weekly at a local grocery store in the meat department with the agent and a butcher who will cut up a portion of a carcass of meat. After six sessions they will have learned how to distinguish between beef, pork, and lamb, name the cut of meat, identify which portion of the animal the cut comes from (the shoulder, loin, or rump), recognize why some cuts are better quality and more expensive than others, and know which cooking method is the best in each case. This topic does not interest me in the least.

"I would like to have a calf project," I tell Ms. Stringer, the agent, a kindly pleasant and soft-spoken woman.

Ms. Stringer nods encouragingly and says, "Mr. Sharkey can help you with a calf project, but every girl who's in 4-H must also have a cooking, sewing, and home improvement project. Other projects are for both boys and girls, like gardening. You begin with something that's easy, and gradually work up to projects that are more difficult."

I'm just about to give up the idea of 4-H altogether when a pretty high school girl notices me. "Hi Kathy, my name is Susan. Welcome to our club! I'd like to help you get started in 4-H if you decide to join. I think you'll find all the projects fun and interesting, and I'll be happy to help you anytime you need it." I'm flattered by Susan's interest in me.

On my way home from this meeting, I complain to Mom about girls having to sew and cook if they want to raise a calf. She doesn't try to persuade me, but the warm reception that I receive from the parent-leader, the club members, and the special acknowledgement that I receive from Susan, convince me to return for another meeting the following month. I even sign up with a small group of girls to learn about meat. At our first gathering with the butcher at a grocery store, I find out that after our period of instruction, there will be a local contest to determine who will comprise the four-member meat judging team that will represent our county in a state contest. This competition is held in Oklahoma City at a large meat packing plant, and the trip there includes an overnight weekend stay in a nice hotel, a special dinner sponsored by a meat company for all the participants, and some fun activities for the team while they're there. This sounds exciting and motivates me to pay close attention to what the butcher is saying, which pays off and I win a place on the county team. I've never gone on a trip out of town without my parents, so I'm excited about going with Ms. Stringer and my three teammates to Oklahoma City. Once I get there, I'm dazzled by our luxurious hotel rooms. I don't yet know that in the 1950s, agriculture throughout our country is developed by privately owned farms and ranches, so a lot of government funding goes toward encouraging young boys and girls to pursue careers in agriculture and home economics.

On Saturday morning, the first day of the contest, my teammates and I, along with seventy-seven other county teams, walk into the huge freezing-cold room at the meat packing plant, bundled up in our coats, hats, and gloves. Individual cuts of meat have been placed on each side of four rows of long narrow tables. We are to identify each cut, what part of the animal it comes from, propose the best cooking method, and rank order the quality of four groups of the same cut. I have so much fun on this weekend, I am totally sold on the 4-H program. Susan keeps her promise and coaches me through my first sewing, cooking, canning, and home improvement projects, and I win a few blue ribbons at the county fair. The calf project, too far from my home to meet the requirements, falls by the wayside.

Meanwhile, I'm not invited to join a social club in the eighth grade either, but by then I'm finding a safe environment to explore social relationships and learn practical skills through 4-H work. When I'm in the ninth grade, a new combined junior and senior high school is built closer to our neighborhood, and Dad is hired there as its new athletic director. Two social clubs from the old school migrate to the new school, but a new social club is formed at the new school and I'm invited to its first rush party, a swimming party which is held at one member's home. I suspect that I'm invited because someone from the country club knows my dad. I hope that I will be invited to join, but I feel uncomfortable being so scrutinized, and it's a big disappointment when I don't receive a second invitation. Some of the members are nice, but others are snobbish, brazenly rude, and even cruel. I'm outraged when one or more of them cut into the cafeteria lines at school to boast their superior status.

In my first year of high school, some of the middle class girls decide to fight back and create a club of their own. Among them are several friends of mine from grade school, so I'm able to experience belonging to a club and I get to wear its specially colored pledge ribbon after rush week. Never mind that my club is the last of three in level of prestige. And never mind the poor kids who never get to wear any colored ribbons at all.

Near the end of my sophomore year, I make friends with two girls who are new to the area. One of them lives in my neighborhood and the other lives across the river on Tulsa's less prosperous west side. I know it will please them if they are invited to pledge a social club, so I submit their names for rush week at the beginning of my junior year. The club meeting is held one night at a member's home, where the guest list will be determined for the first rush party. I'm driving now, so I take the family car to the meeting, confident and excited to think about my two friends receiving their invitation. One by one, a vote is cast for each girl, and neither of my friends receives the minimum number of votes. Angry and disappointed, I leave the meeting early, drive home in tears, and vow that I will never go to another meeting, and I don't. I hate the social club system that makes so many kids feel inferior and left out. Apparently there are enough parents in Tulsa who eventually recognize the destructive effect of social clubs because in time, Tulsa city schools ban them.

I understand that teenagers are a peculiar sort, self-conscious to a fault, and most of us are desperate to feel that we belong somewhere. If we haven't had strong family support, it's easy to understand why we are vulnerable to joining gangs and using drugs, anything to lessen the excruciating pain of feeling left out, deficient, and rejected by our peers.

I come to love and admire the girls' 4-H agent, Ms. Evelyn Stringer, who is conscientious about finding projects and contests in which I can excel. She has a strong influence on me and it is because of her that I gradually learn there are rewards for doing well in various projects that often include wonderful trips to places I have never been before. My parents, especially my mother, fully support me in my project work, which includes time and effort to assist me when I need it, money to pay for materials, and transport to meetings and events.

On a trip downtown to the Brown Dunkin department store, Mom and I make our way up to the second floor to buy the nice dress fabric I need for my sewing project. While there we make a quick detour down to the bargain basement where Mom purchases a brassiere for herself from a pile of them on sale in a hamper. The contrast is clear; I know she will do anything, sacrifice anything, for whatever my projects require. Mom sees that 4-H is good for me.

Each year a week-long, state public speaking and demonstration contest is held at Oklahoma A & M College in Stillwater, and every summer I look forward to the three-day county 4-H campout. The summer of my sophomore year, I'm included in an older group of boys and girls who plot the mischief of ransacking Mr. Sharkey's cabin for a pair of his boxer shorts, so we can run them up the flagpole in the middle of the night. I'm so excited about this naughty adventure I'm to be a part of that I can hardly eat or sleep. Later on there are two thrilling trips—one to Kansas City and another to Chicago, where 4-H members from all over the nation are treated with lavish dinners and entertainment to reward them for achievement in their project work. The life skills I learn in 4-H are as significant in building my self-confidence as is my experience in public education. 4-H enables me to make most of my own clothes, decorate a home inexpensively, prepare nutritious meals, plant a garden, and preserve the food produced. It's also where I learn leadership skills, and why I decide to major in home economics when I go to college, to prepare myself to be a Cooperative Extension Agent, like Ms. Stringer.

Though I'm very fortunate to have a father who values the education of his daughters as much as he does that of his son, Dad is conventional in his reasons. "Even if you have a husband who's a good provider, you can't always depend on that. You and Bonnie should be prepared to provide for yourselves. You can be a secretary, a nurse, or a teacher," he says. He's distrustful of my hope to be a 4-H agent, not being familiar with that career field. I want his support so I enlist the help of my high school Dean of Students, Dr. Roy, who I know Dad admires. I schedule an appointment for both Dad and me in Dr. Roy's office to discuss my future college plans. In order to work for the Cooperative Extension Service, I must have a degree in Home Economics Education. Dad prefers that I major in something that would prepare me for a broader selection of career opportunities, like Elementary

Education or Business, but I'm determined to do something I know I will enjoy. Dr. Roy is knowledgeable about high school teaching jobs, and he convinces Dad that should I not find work as a 4-H agent, opportunities to teach Home Economics in a high school would be plentiful if I have that degree.

Throughout high school, I remain cognizant of the religious consecration I made when I was twelve. I try to make it a priority in every decision I make and it's this commitment that maintains the strongest part of the bond I have with my mother. I want to do God's will, but I still don't understand how I can always determine just what that is. If only God would write it in the sky—then I could be sure. But he doesn't, so I devise an expedient strategy. When there is something I want, I pray for direction about it in advance, trusting that I will receive the guidance I seek. If it isn't God's will, he will make it known to me, I believe.

I'm using this strategy when Ms. Stringer suggests I apply for the Danforth Award, a scholarship for a two-week summer camp program located on the shore of Lake Michigan at a site called Camp Miniwanca. Owned and operated by the American Youth Foundation, it offers high school and college students an experience in character development, leadership, and group effectiveness while nurturing balance within one's life. This sounds very exciting to me, so I pray about it, apply for the scholarship, and then entrust the outcome to God's will. Near the end of my senior year, I learn that I have won the award. I'm a ready little vessel, open to learning about new possibilities.

The scholarship is funded by the William H. Danforth Foundation, named after an ambitious entrepreneur who gained fame and wealth as the developer of the Ralston Purina Company, maker of a whole wheat cereal that is still sold in grocery stores today. He builds his life on a principle, which he explains in a small book he authors entitled *I Dare You.*

> *"I search for those of you who will go on a great adventure. I am looking for you, one of the audacious few, who will face life courageously, ready to strike straight at the heart of anything that is keeping you from your best; you intrepid ones behind whom the world moves forward."* (Danforth, 1953)

Danforth explains that we have four hidden resources within us—*"four sleeping giants"* waiting to be realized—the physical, mental, social, and spiritual. *"How dare you have within yourself these four-fold capacities and not use them?"* He believes that each capacity is equally important and no one capacity should be developed at the expense of another. The Camp program and curriculum puts Danforth's four-square philosophy into practice and our activities are organized around a Native American theme. We *run* everywhere we go—to meals, classes, and all group activities, a strong message that our physical fitness is important. At 6:00 o'clock each morning, we jump out of bed, put on our swim suits, and run down to the beach, plunging into the ice-cold water of Lake Michigan for our morning bath. The water is so cold, my head aches when I duck under the water to rinse soap out of my hair. Now wide awake, we run back to our cabins to put on dry clothes and then run to breakfast, after which we run to our morning classes, which include topics from each of the four areas of development: I Dare You to be Strong; I Dare You to Think Creatively; I Dare You to Share; and I Dare You to Develop Character.

Our afternoons are spent in competitive sporting events between "tribes" to which each camper is assigned. A beautiful inland lake is used for swimming, sailing, and canoeing. In the evening, we enjoy sing-alongs and storytelling around the campfire. I make a special friend from Ohio to whom I write after I come home. I'm inspired to make the four-square philosophy I learn at Camp Miniwanca a part of my life.

INSIGHTS: Identity Formation in Adolescence

Who am I? What do I believe? What is my place in the world? Will I be able to make it on my own? These are the questions that begin to emerge in the minds of young people between the ages of twelve and eighteen. We call this stage of life adolescence. Child analyst, Erik Erikson, best known for his lifespan model of eight psychosocial stages of human growth and development, considered this stage the most crucial in a growing child's search for a sense of self and meaning. A young person who is able to move successfully through this stage will have a sense of commitment and well-being, a sense of being at home in one's body, a sense of direction in one's life, and a sense of mattering to those who count. A strong identity is what makes one move with direction; it is what gives one reason to be.[1]

Up until this time, children will have measured their self-worth within the first group to which they belong—their family. Young children take on characteristics of their parents in a process Erikson called *identification*, whereby they build a set of expectations that they learn from their environment.[2] These expectations may vary from culture to culture. Yurok Native American boys have succeeded when they achieve the engineering feat of bridging the river with a dam that yields a whole winter's supply of salmon. American boys and girls are successful when they make good grades in school and find healthy activities in which they can excel. What the two groups have in common is that both have achieved a standard that has been established by their culture and promoted by their parents.[3]

But something very significant happens in adolescence. Children lose interest in merely adopting the roles and personality attributes of their parents; this no longer provides satisfaction. What emerges is a desire to shape one's world in unique ways. When identification is no longer useful, the formation of one's sense of identity begins in the fullest sense. Regardless of the outcomes of developmental steps that were faced before in childhood, all the components of the growing child's identity are questioned once again. This is due to the rapid body growth that occurs during this period and the new addition of sexual maturity. Newly found cognitive skills and increased independence and autonomy allow the adolescent to explore vocations, political and religious ideologies, and relationships. Changes may involve a passionate interest in ideological values of all kinds as the need for guidance transfers from parental figures to mentors and leaders.[4]

Though I wasn't aware of this at the time, the intensity of my relationship with my mother increased during my adolescence which slowed my efforts to begin forming a unique identity of my own. I would be in college before I attempted any kind of emotional separation from her. I don't think Bonnie, John, nor would I have considered "rebelling" in the sense that rebellion is associated with teenagers. The stability in our household was fragile due to the fears we all had of my mother's depressions; any form of challenging authority would have been risky. Our need to please both Mom and Dad was intertwined with our own need for security. We avoided doing anything that would change tranquility into a state of worry and turmoil.

Had I not felt my mother's fragility so keenly, I might have experimented much more fully with different religious and philosophical ideas. But when I was twelve, the time of my consecration and baptism, I began to internalize completely my mother's perception of religion as being the only safe and secure source to draw on when I was afraid or anxious. Our earliest fear responses stay with us for a lifetime, like my fear of being lost or separated from a source of safety and security. Without understanding, our fear responses can become irrational and disproportionate to the stimulus that evokes them. I was beginning to become aware of this when I was a teenager. Part of my reliance on religion was useful in helping me steady my mother, and there was also a part of it that served as a buttress against anxiety for me. The "pray and wait for direction" strategy I developed as a means of decision-making enabled me to go after what I wanted without compromising my need to please my mother and meet her expectations. I remember having a lot of worries when I was in high school, worries about my relationships, my sexuality, my parents, and how they were getting along. Sometimes my feelings of inadequacy would keep me awake at night. To relieve my distress, I wrote a poem that I could easily recall as a means to comfort myself and help me go to sleep. This verse was a part of it:

> *Am I remembering the fruits of God's love—*
> *power, peace, a sound mind,*
> *recognizing confusion and fear*
> *as sin to abandon behind?*
> *Am I often reminding myself*
> *that feelings may come and go,*
> *that the basis of faith will always be*
> *never "I feel" but "I know?"*

I was using my religion not only to calm myself, but also to differentiate my thoughts from my feelings, a skill that still serves me today. It was the beginning of my recognition that I could change how I was feeling by changing the way I thought or interpreted something. I had a choice. As young children, we are unable to do this. Our behavior reflects immediate, uncontrolled expression of emotion. We *are* what we feel. We laugh, cry, strike out, jump up and down, or throw a tantrum, depending on what kind of emotional arousal we are experiencing. As we grow older, we learn that in order to get along with others, some of our emotions have to be subdued, especially unleashed feelings of anger that can get us into so much trouble. The fears we keep to ourselves that surface in the night also have to be confronted. It begins with an awareness of the feeling, then an examination of its likely origin—the thoughts we are having or the interpretations we are making in regard to our experience. That process of separating my feeling from the thoughts that evoke them help me step back from an overwhelming feeling of anxiety long enough to recognize that there might be some other way of looking at a perceived threat. But even as an adult, this is not always easy.

Themes of confusion and alienation during Erikson's own adolescence help to explain the emphasis he placed on teenage development during his academic studies and career. His uncertainty began with dubious circumstances surrounding his birth. Erik was born in Germany in 1902, though his parents were Danish. His mother, Karla Abrahamsen, was Jewish, but her religious heritage was Lutheran. After Karla married and became pregnant, her husband discovered that the baby she was carrying was not his, but was from an extramarital union, and for this reason he left Karla before Erik was born. Erik never saw his birth father or his mother's first husband. Karla raised him by herself until he was three, when he became ill and was seen by a local Jewish pediatrician. Dr. Theodor Homberger cured the child and fell in love with his mother. They were married and the fact that Homberger was not Erik's biological father was concealed from Erik for many years. He was raised as a Jew throughout his youth, so was known as Erik Homberger. In school he was rejected by anti-Semitic German schoolmates because of his Jewish background, but at the Jewish synagogue, he was teased for being a tall, blue-eyed blonde, Nordic-looking boy who stood out among his peers. When, as a teenager, he finally learned the truth about his birth from his mother, he was left with a feeling of confusion about who he really was.[5] After graduating from high school, Erik wandered around Europe for seven years "trying to come to grips with himself."[6]

At twenty-five, while working as a tutor to four children of an American woman studying with Sigmund Freud's growing psychoanalytic movement, Erik underwent psychoanalysis with Freud's daughter for more than three years in conjunction with his tutoring. *"My analysis, which gave me self-awareness, led me not to fear being myself ... so the process of self-awareness, painful at times, emerged in a liberating atmosphere."*[7] By 1933, when Hitler came to power, Erik and his Canadian-born wife and two sons left Europe for the United States. When he became an American citizen, he took the surname Erikson (son of Erik), suggesting that his identity was his own creation. His experience of rootlessness and immigration as a young adult convinced him that personality development doesn't stop at puberty, as Freud believed. He believed that identity continues to be shaped over the entire lifespan and that experiences later in life might help heal the hurts of early childhood.[8]

When examining both the pluses and minuses of my adolescent experience, I was surprised to realize how critical my 4-H activities were to my personal growth. They provided a social experience that was free from any personal rejection and an environment where I felt I belonged. Research reporting that caring adults outside one's family can help to compensate for an insecure attachment was certainly true for me. My 4-H club leader and Ms. Stringer were both women who were confident in their adult roles and generous in their support of me. I thrived under their tutelage. The opportunities they provided for me to achieve, along with their praise and encouragement, helped to strengthen my sense of self so I was better able to support my mother. The skills I learned, the friends I made, and the recognition I received supplanted what was a less pleasant experience in high school. 4-H also gave me a way of differentiating myself from my high school peers. Though I lived in the city, most of my 4-H friends lived in the rural communities outside Tulsa, so I was the only 4-H member in my school. Though my experimentation with work role aspirations was challenged somewhat by my father, my relationship with Ms. Stringer strengthened my commitment to be a 4-H agent, which turned out to be a good fit for me. While the over-identification with my mother, especially as it involved religion, was a psychological deterrent, it was she who encouraged me most in my 4-H work. Without her support, I would have accomplished little, and failed to develop the confidence that I did.

Adolescents are primarily concerned with how they appear in the eyes of others as compared with how they see themselves. Any confidence I had accrued in childhood was matched against the way my peers saw me. This was reflected in my own self-consciousness when I became aware of social clubs in junior high school. I was obviously apprehensive about how others viewed me. Like any scientific theory, my own self-theory was open to refuting data, and when I learned that I didn't "measure up" to others' expectations, it was disturbing. Consequently I was searching for any new data that would support my own self-theory that I was okay.

I can understand how children of minority groups would be particularly vulnerable at this age because they have to deal with an additional dilemma. Our preschools and elementary schools are somewhat successful in meeting the challenge of helping minority kids develop a spirit of self-reliance, because children of this age are remarkably free of prejudice. But sometimes those successes in grade school lead to a shock in adolescence when young people, so in need of acceptance from the common group, encounter a cruel intolerance of differences.[9]

The danger in adolescence is when one's emerging personal identity is unable to withstand a barrage of disconfirmation. Young people bewildered by a standard forced on them to which they don't fit may seriously question their essential personality characteristics, their view of themselves, and how others see them. Consequently they may doubt the meaning and purpose of their existence. Troubled teens desperately seeking a satisfactory sense of belonging may resort to aberrant behavior. To keep themselves together, they may run away from home in one form or another, leave school or a job, stay out all night, or withdraw into depression. Erikson didn't underestimate the intensity of this stage.

> *"Should a child feel that the environment tries to deprive him too radically ... he will resist with the astonishing strength encountered in animals who are suddenly forced to defend their lives. Indeed, in the social jungle of human existence, there is no feeling of being alive without a sense of ego identity."*[10]

Nearly all adolescents go through some kind of "identity crisis, and some are able to resolve the crisis more easily than others. A lot will depend on the support they receive from their parents. If at least one adult in a child's life accepts their unique personality and recognizes that learning to discipline oneself should be the goal, then the teenager's trial and error attempts may lead to a pleasant outcome of action and self-expression. Unfortunately some adults will cruelly exploit their child's dependence, seek to exert tight control, making the child pay for their own psychological errors, victimizing the child with faults they dare not correct in themselves. An adolescent needs time for experimentation with sex, gender, and work roles and a deeper exploration of moral values and ethical principles. This requires a playful, even daring kind of motivation that only flourishes in an atmosphere of freedom.

"We have learned not to stunt a child's growing body with child labor; we must now learn not to break his growing spirit by making him the victim of our anxieties. If we will only learn to let live, the plan for growth is all there."[11]

One important aspect of identity formation is a shift in how a young person begins to reason about moral issues. Due to their newly acquired cognitive abilities to think hypothetically in abstract terms, adolescents are able to develop a more mature type of moral reasoning. These changes were studied critically by Lawrence Kohlberg, a young Jewish man who developed an interest in morality when he was helping smuggle Jews from Europe into Palestine to protect them from persecution and death. He himself was captured, placed in a concentration camp, and escaped. His interest in what was morally right or wrong reached a turning point when he was working in the psychiatric ward of a hospital and he observed what he determined was unjust treatment of a paranoid patient. The patient was subjected to electric shock treatments by the clinical director for expressing a fear that the director didn't like her. Kohlberg's outrage led him to shift his career focus to social psychology, specifically to study how people developed their moral viewpoints. During his graduate studies, he devised a twelve-year longitudinal study of seventy-five boys between the ages of 10-16, who were tested at 3-year intervals until they were 22-28 years old.[12]

The results of this study became the basis of a three-level theory of moral development, each level representing a different type of relationship between the *self* and *rules and expectations of others*. To very young children, the physical consequences of an action determine what is right or wrong. What is punished is bad and what is good is rewarded. Rules and expectations are external to the self, and moral decisions are based on the avoidance of unpleasant consequences. As children grow older, the expectations of their family are internalized and conformity to the majority behavior is important. Good behavior is that which pleases others and is approved by those in authority, a concern that expands into the larger community of schools, churches, and laws.[13]

Adolescence brings a major social-cognitive advance that allows an individual to more away from one's own self-interest toward a perspective that reflects concerns with fairness, social justice, equality, and openness. An individual has differentiated himself from the rules of others and defines his values in terms of self-chosen principles. These are not concrete rules like the Ten Commandments, but are shared principles that are not only reciprocal, but are open to scrutiny, debate, and tests of logical consistency. Thinking at this level requires that one first questions the view of morality he inherited from his past. Then he needs to have acquired the ability to think in abstracts, consider different viewpoints, and interpret the thoughts and feelings of others—all advanced thinking skills. Often it's a matter of weighing one principle against the other and making a judgment about which one should take priority in a given situation. There are still wide disagreements between the wisest of thinkers.[14]

When I recall those events that took place between the time I was fourteen and seventeen, I like to think that I made some progress in becoming a more principled thinker. Moving from a frightened and timid young girl who was destroyed when she didn't get the second invitation to the rush party to a much stronger emerging young adult who was able to take a stand in regard to the exclusiveness and unfair treatment of high school social clubs was a big step for me.

I was eighteen when I attended Camp Miniwanca. Differences existed between the Danforth challenge and the religious consecration I had made. My character development should be a fourfold process, I learned, each area of growth being equally important; one was not to supersede the other. It was less austere than the path of consecration my mother was following, one that put spiritual goals above all others, a path she represented to me as being the only safe course. It was not so different, however, that it jeopardized my current belief system; I could incorporate it into my own personal philosophy without betraying my childhood consecration. The practical lessons I learned there may have protected me from pursuing a course that would have been more rigid and emotionally restrictive. Consequently I was better able to remain open to other resources of information to which I would later be exposed. I didn't experience a "crisis" element in my identity formation until my senior year in college, and it re-emerged again when I was in my thirties. Understanding what *ideally* occurs in a healthy resolution of identity formation in adolescence has helped me to understand better the changes that occurred later when I was a young adult.

References:

[1] Erikson, E. & Erikson, J. 1997. *The Life Cycle Completed.* New York: W. W. Norton & Co.
[2] Sokol, J. T. 2009. Identity development throughout the lifetime: an examination of Eriksonian theory. *Graduate Journal of Counseling Psychology*: Vol. 1: Iss. 2, Article 14.
[3] Erikson, Erik. 1980. *Identity and the life cycle.* New York: W. W. Norton & Company, Inc.
[4] Sokol 2009.
[5] Obituaries. May 13, 1994. "Erik Erikson, 91, psychoanalyst who reshaped view of human growth dies." *The New York Times.*
[6] Coles, Robert. 1970. *Erik H. Erikson: The growth of his work.* New York: Da Capo Press, Inc. p. 15
[7] Obituaries 1994, p. C16.
[8] Papalia, D. E., Camp, C. J., & Feldman, R. D. 1996. *Adult development and aging.* New York: The McGraw-Hill Companies, Inc.
[9] Erikson 1980.
[10] Erikson 1980, p. 95.
[11] Erikson 1980, p. 106-107.
[12] Schrader, Dawn. 2015. Evolutionary paradigm shifting in moral psychology in Kohlberg's penumbra, in *Kohlberg Revisited*, Boris Zizek, Detlef Garz & Ewa Nowak (Eds.). The Netherlands: Sense Publishers.
[13] Kohlberg, Lawrence. 1976. Moral stages and moralization: the cognitive-developmental approach, in *Moral Development and Behavior: Theory, Research, and Social Issues*, Thomas Likona, Ed.

[14] Gerson, M. W & Neilson, L. 2014. The importance of identity development, principled moral reasoning, and empathy as predictors of openness to diversity in emerging adults. *SAGE Open*, October-December, DOI: 10 1177/2158244014553584, sgo.sagepub.com.

4

DATING, SEXUALITY, AND COLLEGE

What little dating I do in my early teens is stressful and awkward because I rarely like any of the boys who ask me out from my high school. Dad is the athletic director and coach of football and track at my school, so he exerts a strong influence when it comes to my friendships with boys. He's a strict disciplinarian and expects focused attention from his athletes; girls are an unnecessary distraction. Probably because he expects so much, he receives utter devotion from his players and develops winning teams, but any of his athletes would have to have the courage of Beowulf to ask me out—at least that's the excuse I use for not having many dates.

I do enjoy being around boys when I'm in a group, as I am in my 4-H activities, so I am very excited when Jeff, the son of my 4-H leader, asks me to go to a drama production at his high school, where Jeff is a sophomore. Only in the ninth grade of junior high, I'm very nervous about making a good impression with this older boy. Jeff has recently broken his leg, and with a heavy cast, he needs crutches to walk, so his parents drive us to the school and let us out in front. A sidewalk leads to a flight of stairs going up to the front entrance. Jeff is slow in negotiating the stairs with his crutches, so I hang back, not to get too far ahead of him. We make it inside just fine, only to discover there's a second flight of stairs going down to the auditorium. I see that this effort is more difficult for Jeff, so I go ahead and when I reach the bottom of the stairs and turn around to look, Jeff is still struggling midway. Suddenly he misses a step and goes tumbling down the bottom half of the stairs. I'm horrified, and one would think that I would rush to his aid for fear he had hurt himself. But no. So frozen with embarrassment and lack of confidence, I do a terrible thing that I deeply regret. I look away as though I don't notice. Someone else must help Jeff stand up, because ultimately we make it inside the auditorium and sit down, neither of us speaking of the calamity. I'm thankful that he doesn't seem in pain, but mortified because my own insecurity prevented me from being a thoughtful and considerate human being. This is my first date—and last date with Jeff.

When I'm in the tenth grade, a family with two boys lives just four blocks from us, one in the ninth grade and the other is a junior on Dad's track team. Both boys often ride to and from school with Dad and me. I have a crush on Darin, the younger one, and unbeknownst to Dad, Darin and I begin talking frequently on the telephone.

I already know how to drive, because Dad has taught me to drive his big truck on the country roads when we go to get firewood and check on the cows. I'm permitted to drive our old Plymouth coupe in the immediate neighborhood, as long as I don't cross two busy streets, 41st Street going east and west and Riverside Drive going north and south. This leaves me about half a square mile in which I can navigate without a license. School is almost out for the summer, and Darin and I devise a plan. I can only imagine that it must be newly awakened hormones that move me to take such a risk.

A large window fan in my bedroom keeps our house cool at night when it's hot. After everyone has gone to bed one night, and the fan is purring loudly to muffle my sounds, I put pillows under my bed covers to simulate my body. I remove the screen from my window, climb outside, and walk to where the old Plymouth is parked. I put the gear in neutral, allowing me to push the small car easily into the street out of earshot where I can start the engine. I have to venture across 41st Street where Darin is hiding behind a bush in his front yard. He hops in the car and we drive back across 41st Street into my safe zone. We cruise around the neighborhood for about twenty minutes, chattering about our audacious adventure, before crossing 41st Street again to take Darin home. That's it. When I return to our house, I stop the car in front, turn off the engine, and push it back to its parking spot. I climb back through my bedroom window and notice that the fan is now off. One of my always frugal parents must have turned it off to spare electricity. My camouflaged pillow scheme has worked. This is the most fun thing I have ever done with a boy.

It's a year later when my friend Judy tells me she has a friend she wants me to meet. We're eating lunch together in the school cafeteria. "His name is Mike," she says. She reaches into her purse and hands me a small school picture of him.

"Wow!" I say. "How do you know him?" I notice his dark hair, dark eyes and nice smile. "He looks like he could be a football player."

"He is!" Judy laughs with pleasure as her shiny, almost black hair swings freely and her eyes glisten. A very cute ballet dancer in exquisite physical shape, Judy already has a steady boyfriend who goes to another Tulsa high school. "Mike's family lives in Collinsville and he's on the high school football team." Collinsville, a small town northeast of Tulsa, has a 4-H

Club, and I know some kids there. Judy explains that Mike's mother and her mother are good friends. "They both work at Douglas Aircraft. A year ago our mothers introduced us, but I was already going with Jimmy. I think you might like him."

"So how am I going to meet him?" I'm excited. Here's someone who doesn't go to my school, so I don't have to worry about Dad. Judy has it all planned.

"How about this Saturday we drive to Collinsville and go by his house? I haven't seen him in a long time, and we'll just say we're in the area and decided to drop by."

"Sounds good to me!"

So Judy picks me up Saturday morning and we drive to Collinsville, forty minutes from my house. It's a warm fall day and as luck would have it, Mike and two other boys are outside in front of his house working on a car. We park in front and I spot Mike immediately, confirming that he's as good-looking as his picture.

Judy opens the door and gets out of the car. "Hi, Mike!"

Mike lifts his head from under the hood. "Well, wadda ya know!" He walks up to Judy, his eyes glued on her. "It's great to see you! What brings you here?" I sheepishly get out of the car since he hasn't noticed that Judy is not alone.

"Kathy and I were just in the area and I told her I had a friend who lives here. We decided to stop by. Kathy, this is Mike."

He finally shades his eyes from the sun with his hand and looks at me. "Hi there! Nice to meet you."

I inch my way forward. "Nice to meet you too."

He turns around and motions his friends over. "This here is Joey and Leon, my buddies." We exchange nods and Mike turns back to Judy. "So what've you been up to? How's your Mom?"

"She's fine, working too hard, as usual. How's yours?"

"Same with my mom."

Judy points to Mike's football jersey. "Are you still playing football?"

"Yeah! We've started practicing. You ought to come and see one of our games."

"That's a great idea! I'm still going with Jimmy, and I think he'd like that."

I wondered how Judy was going to break this news. Mike looks puzzled and after an awkward moment Judy says, "Kathy's dad coaches football at Edison, our high school."

"Is that right?" His enthusiasm has dropped a notch, so maybe the purpose of our visit is beginning to sink in. "Well, maybe all of you can come and see one of our games then."

Then, to my relief, Judy changes the subject. "Are you having car trouble?"

The conversation shifts to the details of the ailing vehicle, and at last Judy tells the boys that we need to be going. "You have my number, so let me know when your football schedule comes out."

In the car, we wave and drive off. I'm certain Mike is disappointed that it isn't Judy wanting to stir things up, but Judy is optimistic. "I think he got the idea. We'll see what happens."

I want to believe that Mike will call me, but I'm earnest in my desire to make everything in my life comply with my consecration. I tell Mom about Mike, pray about my hope, and then leave it in God's hands. It must be God's will, because very soon Mike calls Judy for my phone number and then he calls to ask me out. On our first date when Mike comes to our house, Dad invites him to eat watermelon outside on our back patio. I've told Dad that Mike is a football player, so Dad inquires about his coach and his team. I notice that Mike isn't spitting out his watermelon seeds as I do. He's swallowing them. Does he want to make a good impression? I hope so. He and Dad get along just fine and I'm so glad he doesn't go to my school. I'm not much a part of the social scene at my school anyway. We begin dating every weekend, most of the time attending events at his school in Collinsville. During football season I proudly sit in the stands with his parents since Mike is a star player on the team. I meet his younger brother, Pat, who's just nine years old, and his maternal grandmother, a warm and accepting lady, who also lives in Collinsville.

In time I learn that Mike's father has struggled with alcoholism and that his parents were divorced for a time, but are back together now, trying to make it work. I experience his father as a gentle, sweet man and for Christmas that year, he gives me a bottle of cologne. Mike tells me that his dad has been abusive with his mother when drinking, and more than once Mike has had to intervene to protect her. In our senior year, his parents divorce a second time and his mother moves into a smaller home in Collinsville. She's embittered about her marriage and one day admits to me that she will always love Jack, though she knows she can't live with him. I see her sadness.

Mike fills my need for a special friend of the opposite sex with whom I can safely begin exploring my sexuality. I feel secure with him and he never puts any pressure on me as our relationship develops—something I appreciate. Before long Dad starts to worry—about my virginity, I suppose. When we park in our driveway some minutes before my 11:30 curfew, Dad's shadowed figure appears through the window of the front door. He stands there long enough so we know he expects us to get out of the car and come in. This is enough motivation to make our goodnight exchanges brief, but it also leads us to find other more secluded places to park.

In previous years Mike has followed the wheat harvest for summer work, keeping him away from home all summer, so we are both delighted when Dad finds Mike a lifeguarding job at another country club that is managed by one of Dad's coaching friends. One summer evening, Dad and I are sitting out on the front porch talking about Mike's job as a lifeguard. "He rescued this little girl who almost drowned," I tell him. "Her parents gave him an expensive sweater to show their appreciation." I want Dad to think well of him.

After a moment of silence, he surprises me, "You know boys will tell you anything to get you to do what they want."

His eyes evade mine as I stumble for words. "What do you mean?"

"I just mean you need to be careful," he says, still not looking at me. I'm too embarrassed to say anything more, but I get the message, and that is the full extent of sex education I get from my father.

Mom also talks to me very little about sex, but she's told me about her out-of-wedlock pregnancy and that she considers it the paramount sin of her life. I'm enjoying the affection that Mike and I share and I'm the one who places his hand to my breast the first time. The next day I'm sunbathing in our backyard, fantasizing about how exciting that has been. I don't feel guilt; after all, we aren't having sex, but I do stop talking to Mom about that part of my relationship.

One evening Mike and I take a picnic meal to the park that adjoins the zoo. No other people are around by that time and we lie down on a blanket enjoying being close. My state of arousal is apparently so strong that when our fully-clothed bodies nestle together, it evokes a soaring release of tension in me.

My body melts and I let out a heavy sigh. "Something just happened."

"What?" Mike sits up. "What is it?"

"I'm not sure—it really felt good, but I just don't feel like making out anymore."

I don't think Mike is any more sexually experienced than I am, but we eventually figure out what happened as our intimacy progresses. We learn how to pleasure one another through mutual stimulation and release without having intercourse, something that neither my conscience, my consecration, nor my heightened fear of pregnancy, could withstand. Without the pressure of mounting sexual tension, we are better able to explore other aspects of our relationship. The summer after we graduate from high school, we're both preparing for college. Mike has a football scholarship to a junior college in southeastern Oklahoma, and I plan to attend Oklahoma College for Women in the southwestern part of the state.

Another girl in my high school class is also going to go to OCW, and though we are not good friends, we decide to be roommates. The college is small, located on the edge of Chickasha, Oklahoma, far removed from the two largest Oklahoma cities, Tulsa and Oklahoma City. It's easy to feel that one belongs here within a close-knit community of faculty and all female students. The campus is built around a large grassy oval in the center, a perfect place to continue my habit of running every morning. A freshman Physical Education major named Pat has the same idea, so we begin running together the first week of school. The two largest dormitories are on one side of the oval, one for freshmen and the other for sophomores, and three smaller dormitories for juniors and seniors are on the other side. Also clustered around the oval are administrative and classroom buildings, a student union, a large cafeteria that serves breakfast and lunch, and a large formal dining room where we eat dinner, served family style around table-clothed tables, each accommodating eight people.

During orientation week, I learn that OCW has three social clubs, not sororities with national origins, but local college organizations, and membership is determined by choice, each one seeming to attract different types of girls, though not everyone fits a certain stereotype. It appears to me that one club has the most serious students, quite a few who are majoring in theater and the arts. Another club has the most Physical Education majors and they seem to have the most fun. A third club has the prettiest prim and proper girls, including the Home Economics majors. Social gatherings are sponsored by each club during orientation and one upper-class girl is assigned to one or more freshmen girls, their role being to influence the new students to join their group. At the end of orientation week, we select the club we want to join, and a girl from that club becomes our "big sister," who will mentor us during our freshman year. I am instantly attracted to a girl named Gloria, because of her laid-back, fun-loving manner, and sometimes boisterous antics. Though a member of the serious student club, she is uniquely a Physical Education major. Tall and lanky, with short red curly hair, freckles, and an infectious laugh, Gloria is an accomplished athlete. I decide to join her club, and at a party for new freshmen members, she becomes my big sister, and we give each other a vigorous hug.

I like my professors, two of them especially—Dr. Burroway, my Ancient and Medieval History teacher, who is nearing retirement, and my Home Economics Tailoring instructor, an attractive, stylish woman who insists that our skirts be fitted only to girdled measurements. The tailoring skills I learn from her I will use the rest of my life, and what I learn from Dr. Burroway is equally valuable. She delivers comprehensive essay tests, the first of which I score a D, the first D I've ever received on an exam. I immediately schedule a conference with her to find out what I can do to improve my performance. We're studying the history of three different civilizations—the Greco-Roman, the Judeo-Christian, and Germanic traditions in that order. Though the histories of all three were taking place at the same time, that fact had escaped me, causing my failure to see important connections between the three. Dr. Burroway suggests that I make a chart with all three civilizations listed vertically and the time frames horizontally across the top, filling in events on the chart so I can see which events were taking place at the same time. This strategy of making a new visual depiction of what I am learning turns out to be a strategy I continue to use in all academic studies or research I do on my own. If I want to remember new information, I either write a summary in my own words, create an outline of what I have read, or make a chart containing notes in visual categories, any of which helps to embed the information in my memory because I can mentally "see" the information on a page.

I'm enjoying my time at OCW more than I ever enjoyed high school. I'm making new friends, swimming with the synchronized swimming club, and taking part in other extra-curricular activities. Many of the girls at OCW date officers stationed at Fort Sill, a nearby army base, but I choose to be loyal to Mike. We each rely on transportation provided by friends to get back home to see each other at least once a month, and we each visit the other's college for one weekend during our first semester.

Frequently I am told that I resemble another freshman student, named Ellen. "You should meet her," they'll say. "You really do look alike!" Once I meet Ellen, she tells me that others have said the same thing to her. We quickly become good friends and make plans to be roommates the second semester. Besides being taller than average with dark hair, fair skin, and freckles, Ellen and I have other things in common. Both our mothers suffer from mental illness, and we both rely on strong religious beliefs. Ellen is from Oklahoma City and attended several Protestant churches. In high school she was active in the Youth for Christ organization, a group I avoided at my own high school. Seriously committed to our different faiths, we find enough common ground to talk about religious issues comfortably, so frequent talks about our life experience bring us very close. We also have fun together. On Halloween night, neither of us have dates. We go to a party on campus, both of us dressed as ghouls in black with nylon stockings stretched tightly over our heads. We never speak and no one knows who we are.

One weekend mid-way through the semester, Gloria invites me to spend the night at the junior class dorm, a common occurrence with big and little sisters. When I go to Mrs. Jones, our dorm-mother, for permission to be gone overnight, I sense some hesitation in her response, though she reluctantly grants my request. I have a fun time that night getting to know Gloria's suite mates, all of whom are as playful and high-spirited as she. Gloria and I share a twin bed and that night I wake up once to find Gloria's arm resting around me. I'm a little uncomfortable, though I have no conscious fear, but I shift my body in such a way that she removes her arm, and there is nothing more to that.

Later that same week, after our run around the oval one morning, my friend Pat asks if we can talk somewhere privately later in the day. We agree to meet in the lounge of the third and top floor of the freshman dorm that afternoon when our classes are over. I'm aware that Pat and Gloria grew up in the same Tulsa community and went to the same high school, but

I have no expectation of what she wants to discuss. A small wiry girl, with straight red hair and freckles, she's waiting for me on the sofa, and I sit down in the large soft lounge chair across from her. She wastes no time getting to the point.

"I think there's something about Gloria you should know."

"Okay. What's that?" I squirm a little.

"Gloria is lesbian. I'm not sure if you're aware of that."

Anything I could say at that moment would be an understatement, because inside I'm terrified. I know nothing about homosexuality. The only exposure I've had—only to the idea of it—was in high school. If you wore green and yellow together on Thursday, that meant you were "queer." I've never known anyone queer, because, of course, no one ever wore green and yellow together on Thursday. I'm shocked by Pat's revelation because it's simply not in my realm of experience. My fear isn't so much of Gloria as it is about *me*. Though I'm not aware of any sexual feelings toward Gloria, *I really like her.* I thank Pat for telling me and I go straight to the bathroom on the third floor to be alone with myself. I shut the door to the stall, sit down on the toilet, and stare down at my feet in a state of panic. I don't know what to do, but I'm so completely preoccupied with Pat's revelation, I decide that I must go home that weekend.

It's my good fortune that my brother, John, is home and present when I speak to Mom about what is troubling me. The three of us are sitting at the dining table when I describe my new friendship with Gloria and the recent conversation with Pat. John reacts first.

"Aw, Sis—that's no big deal. That was so common when I was in the Army, you wouldn't believe it … but I know how you feel. It was a shock to me too, at first. You're at a girls' school, so it's to be expected, but there's nothing to be afraid of." Mom also appears sympathetic. In the past, she has told me about having crushes on some of her female teachers when she was growing up. I'm relieved that they both are relaxed and showing no sign of alarm.

"What worries me is that I really like Gloria." I want to get at the root of my fear.

"Just because you like Gloria doesn't mean you're homosexual," John says. You still like Mike, don't you?"

"Yes." It's good to be reminded of Mike and how much I enjoy the sexual part of our relationship.

John shifts in his chair and appears thoughtful. "I suspect it's as much a choice as anything. It's more apt to happen when people are only around their own gender. Once you're clear about yourself, you'll be comfortable being friends with Gloria. It doesn't sound like she means to put any pressure on you, so it's nothing that you need to worry about."

John's perspective is just what I need to hear, and I return to OCW that weekend with a wisdom and knowledge that gives me confidence. I can be responsible in choosing my preferred sexual orientation, while also enjoying a caring friendship with Gloria. This prepares me to understand those girls who engage in lesbian relationships while at OCW, but later switch to heterosexual relationships upon transferring to a coeducational school.

Ellen and I move into a room together at the beginning of our second semester. I've learned that Ellen sometimes struggles with depression, though she doesn't talk to me about her down times. From the talks we've had about our families, I conclude that, as an only child, she feels responsible for the emotional needs of both her parents, a situation that I understand. But in Ellen's case, both her parents were the only child in their families growing up, so not only does Ellen have no siblings, she has no cousins, aunts nor uncles, and her grandparents are dead. She has no one to talk to about the burden she carries One day I return to our dormitory room after my classes to find a note she has left me: *"Dear Roomie, I have to go home for a few days."* I suspect that Ellen is worried about her parents, and that a temporary reunion will relieve some anxiety in both Ellen and them. When she returns and I express concern, she's her usual cheerful self, assuring me that everything is okay. "You're like a sister to me," she says, and I tell her she's the closest girlfriend I've ever had. We're both certain that our friendship will last a lifetime.

Ellen dates the young men from Fort Sill, so I'm usually up waiting for her on most weekend nights. Bonnie is expecting her first child, so one Saturday night I'm working on an embroidered baby quilt. Ellen surprises me by arriving home early from a date with Sam, a young man she's been corresponding with during the week. She tosses her purse onto the dresser and crashes on her bed, looking straight up from her pillow to the ceiling.

"We broke up," she says.

"Really?" I'm surprised and I put down my embroidery. "What happened?"

"He's too secretive. I think he has a girlfriend back home he doesn't want to tell me about, but he's too honest to lie, so he's evasive. This makes me not trust him. I can tell I'm getting too emotionally invested in the relationship and this is *not* a good risk."

"It must be tempting to these guys from back East, like Sam, to find relationships out here … on the plains of southwestern Oklahoma, of all places. I'm sure they get lonely."

"The Fort Sill guys from New York crack up when I tell them I've been to 'the city,' meaning Oklahoma City. They think they've been sent to hell."

"Can you be content to think of it as temporary and not expect it to develop into anything permanent? He's quite a bit older than you, isn't he? All these officers have to be college graduates."

"Yes, I know. I shouldn't have gotten so involved with him in the first place."

"Don't blame yourself. Sam's been a really nice guy and it's easy to understand why you were attracted to him."

Ellen sits up on the bed and begins to undress. "No, I'm glad it's over. I'm glad I ended it and I think he was relieved too."

"Are you sure?"

"Yes, I'm sure. I think I want to burn his letters."

I laughed. "Would that help to bring closure? We could make a ceremony out of it."

Ellen is in her pajamas now and she looks over at me. "You know, that might be fun. We could invite our friends and do it on a Sunday night when everyone is tired from the weekend, but not quite ready to face Monday morning. Tomorrow night is the sing-along—so how about next Sunday night?"

"Suits me." I pick up my embroidery again. "We'll make a party of it—a good riddance party."

The following Sunday night, six of our friends are in attendance for the ceremony. Ellen and I wear our black ghoul costumes, minus the stockings. The lavatory sink in our room, which is to be the burning place, is decorated with dried flowers and draped with silky head scarves. A sign hanging above the lavatory on the mirror reads, "This flame flickers out as a symbol of his dying passionate love."

The room is dark except for the goose-neck desk lamp that is aimed at a box of letters sitting on the empty desktop. I invite our guests to share a thought or feeling about the broken romance.

"She can do better."

"He didn't deserve her; it's his loss."

"He wasn't man enough."

"Have no regrets."

One by one, Ellen drops each letter into the sink and lights it with a match. After three or four letters have turned to ash, someone bangs on the door and I open it to see a girl from down the hall. "What's burning in there?" she asks. "Mrs. Jones smells smoke and she sent me up here to see what it is."

"Oh! We burned some popcorn. We'll be finished in a minute. Tell her we're sorry," and I close the door.

When the final letter curls up and is consumed by the flame, Becky, a drama major, raises her hands and cries, "Wait! I must spit on the ashes, and at that moment, a pain will pierce his heart." The sizzle from Becky's spittle is followed by a loud crack. Six jagged lines radiate like lightning bolts from the bottom of the sink.

"Oh no! Ohhhhhh! Ellen cries, holding her cheeks in her hands. "We should have known! Now what have we done?"

Monday morning Ellen and I know what we must do. Although the sink is holding together in one piece, it leaks when we fill it with water. After our classes that afternoon, we take the bus to town to price lavatories. Encountering a friendly salesman in the hardware store, we tell him of our dilemma and inquire about the cost of a replacement sink. Seeing our reaction to the price, he motions us to another counter and reaches for a small, neatly boxed tube of porcelain repair.

"This should do the trick, and it's only sixty-nine cents." We purchase this miracle product, take it back to our dorm room, and follow the instructions carefully, waiting the necessary drying time before filling the sink up with water again. It works. This time no leaks.

It isn't until the last week of our second and last year at OCW that Ellen and I, still roommates, but in the sophomore dorm, confess to a school administrator the damage we did in the freshmen dorm the prior year. We offer to pay the price of a new lavatory, but our offer is declined.

INSIGHTS: Compassionate Attitudes about Sex

Richard Hettlinger wrote: *"Everyone has sex before marriage. We're born with it and express it in our relationships from infancy on."*[1] If sex is an integral part of being a person, why is it a source of conflict for almost everyone? I was a graduate student when I first began to think beyond the traditional religious teaching held by my parents that engaging in sexual intercourse outside the context of marriage was wrong. One of my professors loaned me a textbook on the psychosocial aspects of human sexuality written by Richard Hettlinger. Published in 1975, this book was then out of print, but it so influenced my thinking, I copied each of its 315 pages which I've kept all these years in a loose-leaf notebook. Hettlinger recognized that sexual attitudes and behavior are intricately intertwined with morality, religion, and social values that resist rational investigation. His approach wouldn't have been well received in the social climate in which my parents grew up, and his reasoning has contributed to the healthy change we find today that encourages openness, candidness, and honesty when considering sexual matters.

Every society restricts sexual behavior to some extent to ensure that when children are born, they will be born to parents who are willing to assume responsibility for their upbringing. Our society, with its strong Judeo-Christian values, has been overzealous in seeking to instill a sense of caution regarding sex. Guilt-instilling religion is one of the most serious obstacles for young people trying to reach a positive and coherent understanding of their sexuality. Both my mother and my father considered their out-of-wedlock pregnancy as the event that forced an unwanted marriage. What was left over and passed on to their children was a prevailing attitude about sex that evoked fear of something dangerous that had the potential of bringing disgrace and shame to our family. It appears to me that churches have exploited our natural human sex drive as a means of controlling their followers. Christianity especially, by portraying Jesus as one who was miraculously born of a virgin (without sex) and therefore not tainted by sin, keeps people feeling guilty for something that is simply part of being human. Whether one is heterosexual, homosexual, bisexual, single, in a traditional marriage, cohabitating, living in a commune, or whatever, Hettlinger saw these lifestyle variations as secondary. What really matters, he believed, is that one can learn to develop an enjoyment of sexuality as a creative element in personal growth that affects all of one's relationships with people. It also involves learning to distinguish false myths from well-researched information. When expressed with caring and respect for oneself and one's partner, with regard for the rights of others, and with full knowledge and acceptance of one's responsibility, sexuality can be one of the most rewarding aspects of a person's life.[2]

In spite of so much evidence to the contrary, there are still parents who believe that the less their children know about sex, the more apt they will be to avoid it. For the same reason, they may withhold information on contraception and sexually transmitted disease. Facts do not support their assumption. Investigations around the world demonstrate that ignorance, not knowledge of sexual matters, results in greater numbers of illegitimate pregnancies and sexually transmitted diseases.

Adding to ignorance are the many myths that are still spread about the dangers of masturbation to the body or mind, none of which have any foundation in fact. Masturbation is a common phase of early human development, part of a child's first exploration and discovery of enjoyment of his or her body. In adolescence it is probably the first best step of learning to respond to one's full sexual capacity. It does not weaken a person, nor does it lead to moral depravity or cause emotional illness. The only thing it leads to is pleasurable sensations, including orgasm with an accompanying release of sexual tension.[3]

> *"If masturbation were accepted as a normal phenomenon of adolescence, no more reprehensible than wet dreams for boys or the beginning of menstruation for girls, a great deal of anxiety and suffering would be avoided. To condemn it as wicked or sinful is as stupid as to punish a baby for crying when it is hungry or a child for climbing trees. It is part of healthy sexual experience, and in adulthood it may be an appropriate alternative when the person has no suitable sexual partner."* [4]

Much of the conflict suffered by young people who have grown up in a religious environment arises from the tension between religious ideals and the dynamics of sexuality. Religion seemingly has never come to terms with the reality of romantic love, a concept that it accepts as a desirable prerequisite to marriage. If young people are encouraged to be "in love," it is inevitable they will begin experimenting with physical sexual contact. Is it reasonable to limit that to holding hands and kissing? In most fundamentalist religious cultures, most couples marry in their teens or early twenties because they can't wait any longer to enjoy intercourse.[5] However, early marriages are notorious for resulting in a much higher divorce rate.[6] Others, even among the devout, find such restrictive rules irrelevant and use some form of mutual genital stimulation resulting in orgasm as a viable alternative to intercourse. This means of sexual sharing can enable a couple to learn how to give each other pleasure and to enjoy their bodies in an intimate way without violating a religious conviction and without the fear of pregnancy.[7]

But one might ask how different is this from intercourse? Hettlinger sees this technicality as "*getting in the way of a balanced understanding of sexuality.*"[8] He asks, is the mere physical act of coitus more important in our culture than the personal relationships of the couple involved? Rather than to preserve a technical "purity" to satisfy one's own inner sexual guilt, might they have been *more* moral to develop their relationship in an atmosphere of freedom and spontaneity in their choice of sexual behavior, without guilt, shame, or anxiety? What is best for marriage? Might it make more sense to postpone marriage until both partners have achieved economic and educational goals and to accept intercourse earlier? An engaged couple may so concentrate their energies on avoiding intercourse that they never have the opportunity to see each other as non-sexual objects. Their expectation of blissful pleasure in the future may distract them from other important factors that should be considered when choosing a lifelong mate.[9]

Looking back on my early developing sexual relationship with Mike, I think we made a good decision as to how to handle our sexual attraction. In spite of the traditional views of morality we both grew up with, our normal sex drives led us to experimentation that enabled us to enjoy a full sexual response through mutual stimulation without experiencing the guilt that would have resulted had we been having intercourse. I do agree with Hettlinger that it would not have been morally wrong for us to experience intercourse—risky however, without any protection for birth control since neither of us was prepared to have a child.

One of the most significant social changes in American society has been the advent of reliable birth control that provides women with freedom and equal opportunity to pursue education and career goals. For those young people not burdened with religious guilt about sex, it has also had a profound effect on sexual attitudes, so that the pleasures and responsibilities of sex are being applied equally to both genders. Studies indicate that men and women who feel they are treated with equal respect tend to be more satisfied in their sexual interactions and relationships overall than do men and women who feel an unequal balance of power in couple decision-making.[10] Might living our lives according to the Golden Rule lead to more fulfilling sex lives than if we follow the dictates of strict cultural rules? Hettlinger gives priority to the quality and depth of a relationship over the sex act itself, or whom one should have sex with, or under what circumstances:

> *"The fundamental trust that is essential to any deep human relationship is undercut so long as either partner feels it necessary to put on a front or fears that more will be asked than he or she is able to give. Each has to learn to put into words the real meaning of those silent signals and to be prepared to respond to the hesitations, hopes, fears, and joys of the other.... Both partners must escape from the current obsession with sex as a performance, in which the skill or response of the participants is measured as 'success' or 'failure.' For so long as sex is used to demonstrate one's prowess or even one's sensitivity, and so long as one is afraid of being found 'inadequate' in physical achievement, there is no real opening of the self to another, no freedom to trust, no truly mutual relationship.*[11]

Hettlinger's perspective and what I have learned about evolution led me to a more open acceptance of diverse ways of sexual expression, including homosexuality, bisexuality, and transgender decisions. Human sexual behavior is quite different from that of the 4,300 species of mammals, in that the vast majority of all animals engage in no sexual behavior at all during most of the year. Mating is rarely separated from its function of fertilization which generally occurs only when a male and female are fertile and copulation can lead to pregnancy. Humans differ significantly in that they can regularly enjoy sex at times when conception is not even possible, so in light of evolution, sex must have other non-reproductive functions in humans that are beneficial or this characteristic would not have evolved.[12]

To understand how sex might provide a function beyond the desire to have offspring, it helps to understand the role of a neurohormone called oxytocin. Oxytocin provides a biological function of maintaining a balance of water within the body. Sometimes, however, evolution exploits something that evolved for one function and uses it for another purpose, in this case the unprecedented task of promoting intimacy, first between a mother and child during birth and lactation, and later between adult pairs during lovemaking. Oxytocin appears to be a key ingredient in the neurobiological system that promotes feelings of calmness, sociability, and trust, maximizing the development of an intimate bond.[13]

Oxytocin is manufactured in both the brain and the body in female ovaries and male testes, but its effect on females is more dramatic. Manipulation of the breasts or genitals during lovemaking stimulates release of higher levels of oxytocin, and a marked increase in the hormone is detected during orgasm. A good massage can increase oxytocin levels, as can a frequency of hugs. Studies in men have correlated elevated levels of the hormone with lower blood pressure and an increase in the ability to correctly read social information in the eyes. Another study of men indicated that oxytocin is involved in the management and dampening of negative emotions (fear, anxiety, anger), which makes sense, given how it works in females.[14]

It shouldn't surprise us that if oxytocin is about bonding between mother and child, then might it serve a similar function in mating? In a later chapter, I will describe the research that documents the similarity between infant-caregiver attachment (as described by John Bowlby in chapter one) and adult pair bonding. The two share core emotional and behavioral dynamics. Both involve heightened desire for proximity, resistance to separation, and utilization of the other person as a preferred source of comfort and security.[15] The role that oxytocin plays, not only in infant bonding and the formation of attachment, but in pair bonding between adults, helps to explain why humans have evolved to enjoy sex even when it is not functioning as a means to reproduce.

This research also has the potential of reshaping how we think about sexual orientation, because none of the studies on oxytocin restrict its healthful benefits to physical intimacies shared only between men and women, any more than they are restricted to the gender of a child when associated with a mother's bonding behavior.[16] Our need to form strong attachments precedes our need to pair bond as an adult, and our adult attachments are greatly influenced by those earliest bonds with our caregivers. It is no wonder that humans vary so greatly in what attracts them to other human beings. We assume that gender-linked characteristics are most important in determining whether we become sexually attracted to someone. Studies show otherwise, that "*both men and women place as much weight on gender-neutral traits such as intelligence and kindness as on gender-specific traits.*"[17]

Unlike all other mammals, human sexual behavior is determined less by genes and hormones. Our sexual behavior is more influenced by environment, culture, and society. Sexual opportunity and constraint among humans occur in enormously complex social milieus. Most human societies have rigid sexual laws or rules regarding what types of feelings and behaviors are appropriate for different types of adult relationships. Young people are traditionally channeled into the "right" types of relationships. In our own society, "morals" have come to refer almost exclusively to sexual matters, making it even more unlikely to know just how variable sexual behavior can be.[18]

Groundbreaking work by Lisa Diamond that distinguishes between romantic love and sexual desire has further expanded our awareness of the wide diversity we find in human sexual behavior. Her research reveals that although the majority of human adults experience sexual desire and romantic love together, they are two different subjective experiences and each one evolved for different reasons. Wanting to feel close, safe, and secure with another person—even to express romantic love—does not necessarily require sexual desire or sexual involvement.[19]

Sexual desire refers to an interest in sexual objects or activities or a wish, need, or drive to seek out sexual partners and to engage in sexual activities. It is hormone driven, intense, and may emerge for no particular reason. It can be highly motivating and often prompts individuals to seek sexual gratification either through masturbation or having coitus with another person. Sexual desire also refers to a person's ability to become aroused once certain triggers, cues, or situations are encountered, such as a sexual advance by an attractive partner, and reading or watching erotic material. Sexual arousal in either case is directly affected by estrogen and androgen hormones, and it can be reliably assessed by monitoring blood flow to the genitals. These hormones are not involved, however, in the formation of affectional bonds and romantic love. There is no definite means of testing to see if romantic love exists, though a variety of thought processes and behaviors are known to characterize it.[20]

Romantic love begins as a temporary state of heightened interest in and preoccupation with a specific individual. It is characterized by intense desire for proximity and physical contact, resistance to separation, and feelings of excitement and euphoria when receiving the partner's attention. As romantic love develops into companionate love, feelings of security, care, and comfort predominate. All these feelings can be experienced without sexual desire. Even prepubertal children who have not experienced the hormonal changes that take place in adolescence can have intense romantic infatuations.[21]

One can say that romantic love is an adult form of what has been described as *attachment to a caregiver* in infants and children. It is biologically different from sexual desire and evolved originally for an altogether different purpose. Sexual desire ensures the propagation of the species. Attachment and romantic love ensure the survival of offspring and the emotional well-being of all humans at every age. There is another important difference. Attachment and romantic love, as they occur in children and adults, once established, are highly persistent and become more reliable the longer they endure. Sexual desire, on the other hand, is sometimes persistent, sometimes not, and is often less urgent the longer a relationship is established.[22]

While these two systems can be experienced separately by human beings, more often than not individuals end up falling in love with people to whom they are also sexually drawn. This makes good evolutionary sense because it helps to ensure that a human baby will have two parents who love each other and are dedicated to its survival. But this doesn't mean that romantic love evolved in order to augment the reproductive function. While it may have reproductive benefits, that is not its fundamental purpose. Every human being, regardless of one's primary sexual orientation, whether it be for the same sex, the other sex, or both sexes, has the capacity to be attracted to or to become attached to people of either gender.[23]

In order to obtain the most realistic information about sexual activity, Alfred Kinsey and his research team interviewed thousands of men and women about their sexual experience. These studies revealed that sexual behavior, thoughts, and feelings towards the same or opposite sex were not consistent or absolute. Instead of assigning people to three categories—heterosexual, bisexual, and homosexual—their data revealed a bell curve continuum. At one extreme was exclusive heterosexuality and at the other extreme was exclusive homosexuality with a capacity for both sexual orientations being at the highest midpoint of the curve. Sexual experience was so diverse, and the psychological, social, and sexual aspects so varied, that to use the words homosexual, bisexual, or heterosexual to describe anything more than the individual's sexual choice at a particular time would be misleading and inexact.[24]

Dr. David Hull, a gay man, was professor emeritus at Northwestern University and spent much of his life introducing philosophical principles of ethics and metaphysics into scientific debates on biology and evolution. In his essay "On Human Nature," he wrote:

"If evolutionary theory has anything to teach us it is that variability is at the core of our being.... The more usual way to discount the sort of variation so central to the evolutionary process is to dismiss it as "abnormal." Normality is a very slippery notion. It also has had a long history of abuse. Responsible authorities in the past have argued in all sincerity that other races are degenerate forms of the Caucasian race, that women are just incompletely formed men, and that homosexuals are merely deviant forms of heterosexuals.... Certainly nothing that a biologist might say ... is liable to dislodge the deeply held intuitions upon which these theories are based—and this is precisely what is wrong with deeply held intuitions."[25]

I see Dr. Hull's perspective as healthy when it presents variation in sexual expression as being normal. All cultures and societies are made up of individual humans, and no two humans have had the same environmental pressures that might influence their patterns of attraction, sexual desire, and affection. We view the diverse and often weird behavior among animals as miraculous and awe inspiring, but when it comes to us, we seem to be uncomfortable with anything that varies from the norm. What matters most about sexuality is its integration with human relationships which are caring, responsible, honest, and loving. If this is the case, then the adults in those relationships will be more apt to thrive as well as any children who may become a part of their union.

My exposure to homosexuality when I was at OCW and the new insights about the fluidity of what attracts us to others led me to believe that had I grown up in a more liberated culture, I would be capable of having sexual feelings toward people of both genders. Throughout my lifetime I have encountered a few women, like Gloria, with whom I have felt a mutual attraction and they are usually women who have personality characteristics that are similar to those I find attractive in men. I'm grateful for my experience at OCW for giving me that awareness.

I also know that the friendship I formed with Ellen in my freshman year in college became a very strong attachment that has endured to this day. Though I have developed some strong friendships with other women since that time, none of them compare to the attachment I feel to Ellen. I speculate that is because we were both very vulnerable at that time—being away from home for the first time, both having had very close relationships with our mothers, and similar exposure to religious ideas and attitudes. The support we were able to give to each other due to what we had in common became a significant resource to both of us at an important time in our lives.

References:

[1] Hettlinger, Richard. 1975. *Human sexuality: A psychosocial perspective*. Belmont, California: Wadsworth Publishing Company, Inc., p. 57.
[2] Hettlinger 1975.
[3] McCary, S. P. & McCary, J. L. 1984. *Human sexuality*. Belmont, California: Wadsworth Publishing Company.
[4] Hettlinger 1975, p. 12.
[5] Hettlinger 1975.
[6] *Monthly Labor Review*, October 2013. Bureau of labor statistics, marriage and divorce: Patterns by gender, race, and educational attainment.
[7] Hettlinger 1975.
[8] Hettlinger 1975, p. 66
[9] Hettlinger 1975.

[10] Hatfield, E., Greenberger, D., Traupmann, J., & Lambert, P. 1982. Equity and sexual satisfaction in recently married couples. *Journal of sex research*, 18, 18-32.
[11] Hettlinger 1975, p. 116.
[12] Symons, D. 1981. *The evolution of human sexuality*. Oxford: Oxford University Press.
[13] Dunbar, R. 2012. *The science of love*. Hoboken, New Jersey: John Wiley & Sons, Inc.
[14] Dunbar 2012.
[15] Hazan, C. & Zeifman, D. 1999. Pair-bonds as attachments: Evaluating the evidence. In J. Cassidy and P. R. Shaver, eds., *Handbook of attachment theory and research*, pp. 336-354, New York: Guilford
[16] Diamond, L. 2008. *Sexual fluidity: Understanding women's love and desire*. Cambridge, Massachusetts: Harvard University Press.
[17] Diamond, L. 2008.
[18] Diamond, L. 2004. Emerging perspectives on distinctions between romantic love and sexual desire. *Current directions in psychological science*, vol. 13, no. 3, pp. 116-119.
[19] Diamond, L. 2004.
[20] Diamond, L. 2004.
[21] Diamond, L. 2004.
[22] Diamond, L. 2004.
[23] Diamond, L. 2004.
[24] McCary & McCary 1974.
[25] Hull, D. 1986. On human nature. *Philosophy of science association*, vol. 2, pp.5-8.

5

COURTSHIP AND MARRIAGE

Mike and I both transfer to what is now Oklahoma State University for our last two years of schooling to earn our bachelor's degree. Mike rents an apartment with three other boys, while I live in the freshman dormitory as a counselor. For the first time in our courtship, we're able to see each other every day, and our talks together more often turn to our future.

Mike is intent on becoming a military pilot; it's something he has dreamed of since he was a little boy. From the time he was three years old until he was seven, his father was in the navy during the war, and he was raised by his mother and paternal grandparents. His mother and grandmother are strong, assertive women, but his grandfather must have a sadistic streak. Once, while his grandfather held him in his lap, he distracted him with something, and then laughed as he purposely burned Mike's arm with a cigarette. Another time his grandfather coaxed him to go near an unseen wasp's nest in a large bush, then agitated the swarm of insects until one stung Mike.

With this as his only male role model, Mike must hunger to know more about his father. He remembers holding a radio close to his ear when he was six years old, listening to reports of the war, imagining his father being there. These radio reports are the only source of information he has. This helps me to understand why his aspirations to be a military pilot are so important to him.

Usually we spend one evening each week alone at Mike's apartment, often buying a pizza to take there for dinner. After some time together he walks me back to my dorm. On one such evening, he has something important to tell me.

"I've just found out today that the Marine Corps has a new flight training program that requires just two years of college—you don't have to have a four-year degree." Mike is already enrolled in an ROTC program that will grant him a commission in the military when he graduates, usually a requirement for entrance to flight training. "It would mean that I could start earning my wings a year earlier. If I'm successful in the flight program, then I would get my officer's commission the same time I get my wings."

I can hear the excitement in his voice. "But this would mean you wouldn't finish college, right?"

"That's right, but maybe I could do that later on. And getting a degree isn't so important right now. I'd like to make a career in the military, so once I get my wings and a commission, that's really all I need."

"How long does it take?" I've been counting on us both being together while we finish our degrees.

"Eighteen months—and I have to stay single until I finish the program."

"But what if you don't get your wings? Or what if something else keeps you from flying—you could get hurt, lose the required eyesight…?" I know pilots have to have perfect vision.

"Well, that is the risk. If I don't make it through the flight program, then I also don't get a commission. I'd have to finish my military obligation as an enlisted soldier—four years total."

"That's a scary thought," I say. The United States is already involved in Viet Nam with troops on the ground. "Are you sure you want to take that risk? If you get your commission first, you will at least be an officer if you don't get your wings. And we could still get married after we both graduate. We could still be together all that time."

"But look at it like this. While you're finishing school, I can be learning how to fly—and I know I can do it! It's possible that if I apply right away, I won't even have to finish this semester. Then when I complete the program, I'll have my commission too ... and then we can get married."

I can see Mike has already made up his mind to do this. I've not seen nor heard him be this excited about anything else, and who am I to tell him what he should do? He doesn't have any other career goal that he's interested in; his declared major is Military Science. My father has never served in the military and I've been hoping that Mike would get this passion for the military out of his system after he served four years. I hate wars; I think if I were a man, I would be a conscientious objector because I don't think I could kill anyone. But now he's talking about it as a career. What will this mean for my future? My mind is racing. It feels like a rug has been pulled out from under me and I'm fighting back tears. This semester has been wonderful for me, being able to see each other every day. Eighteen months is a long time. I struggle in my mind to find some line of reasoning that will help me deal with this. I see how important it is to him and I want to support him, but it has to be something that I truly believe.

"Maybe there's something for each of us that's more important than our relationship." I say with a mixture of sadness and conviction.

"What do you mean? I didn't say you weren't important to me."

"I've told you how important my religious faith is to me, the consecration I've made to God to do his will. This is a priority for me, just as you're telling me that getting your wings as soon as possible is a priority for you."

"So what does that have to do with our future plans?" he asks.

"Don't you see? Maybe this is creating a balance in our relationship. I'll support you in what is most important to you, if you'll support me in what is most important to me." This is the first time we have encountered a conflict this important to our future. We mutually agree upon a compromise that on the surface seems appropriate, but I'm left with a blur of feelings that is tenuous and unsettled.

Mike applies and is accepted into the Marine Corps Cadet Program. He drops out of school, and I begin to prepare myself for a long separation. For reasons I don't understand, I begin to feel intense guilt about our sexual relationship. For nearly four years, we have avoided intercourse, but the intimate times we have together are important to me. I begin to worry that I'm doing something terribly wrong. One Friday night, just a few weeks before Mike is to leave, I wake up in the night from a bad dream. I feel so frightened that I leave the dorm and walk outside into the dark night, as if to escape my fear. A storm is brewing and I look up at the raging clouds, feeling that the turbulent weather is mirroring my terror. The only thing I can think of that might relieve my panic is to go home and confess to Mom what I've been doing. I want her support. I do wait until morning though to make the hour and a half drive home in the used car Dad has recently bought for me. When I get there, only Dad is at home; Mom has gone to a nearby town to spend the weekend with one of her Bible student friends. Dad can tell there's something wrong with me, but I can't talk to him about it, so I leave to go back to Stillwater. I get hold of myself during the drive back and am convinced that I can wait until next weekend to talk to Mom.

The conversation I subsequently have with her precipitates another pivotal change in my relationship with my mother. We're in the den at the back of the house when I tell her there is something I need to talk to her about.

"I've been feeling some guilt about my sexual relationship with Mike."

"Are you having sex?" she asks.

"Well, not exactly. We've never had intercourse. I'm too afraid of getting pregnant." I explain the intimacies Mike and I share and she opines that they are sinful since we're not married.

"Once you stop what you're doing, I'm sure your anxiety will go away," she assures me.

"But I'm also afraid I'm supposed to break up with Mike. I'm afraid that's what God wants me to do." This brings tears and it's a relief to cry and I can't seem to stop. Suddenly Mom jumps to her feet and suggests that we go for a walk. I follow her outside to the street and we start walking as she continues to reassure me I'll be doing the right thing. She's holding tight to one of my arms with both her hands and I can feel her trembling. I see that my confession has frightened her, thrown her off balance, and I suddenly realize that I can't depend on her for sound support. As we continue to walk, I gradually pull away from her emotionally. I stop crying and I know I can never confide in her this way again.

Back at school I also pull away from Mike physically and emotionally, and he can't fathom what is going on with me. He knows I'm in some sort of crisis, but I'm still too confused to give him any reassurance. I'm back in Tulsa for the weekend just before Mike is to leave to report for his training. I don't want to have to tell him goodbye, so when he comes to see me, I ask Mom to tell him that I can't see him, but that I'll write to him later. I know this must be terrible for him, but it's the only way I know how to take care of myself right now.

I finish my spring semester and go home for the summer to work. I'm also riding the bus downtown once a week to receive treatments from a dermatologist for a rash I've developed from some unknown cause. Each time I get on or off the bus, I walk past a home office belonging to a psychologist; his small unassuming sign in front of the house always catches my eye. One day on impulse, I turn up the sidewalk leading to his front door and I go inside. He's there. Can he possibly see me right then? Yes. How much will it cost? I can pay it … once. I tell him my story about my boyfriend leaving and that I wasn't even able to tell him goodbye, that I've been feeling guilty about our sexual relationship, and even though he is far, far away, I'm still unhappy, and I'm having trouble sleeping. "I think it might have something to do with my relationship with my mother."

I see he's concerned and that he wants to help me, but I also know that I can't afford to see him another time. He asks me a lot of questions, and I'm as honest with him as I know how to be. He doesn't seem alarmed about my report of the sexual aspects of our relationship, and I begin to cry, with relief.

"I think you're suffering from what will be a long separation from someone you care deeply about. That threat may have caused you to return to what was a reliable source of security in your childhood—your mother—but at the same time, you must have taken on her guilt and fear. I think you can trust yourself ... and your feelings ... and I hope you can get back together with your boyfriend."

This is all I need to hear. As soon as I get home, I write to Mike and try to explain my limited understanding of what has occurred, describing the help I received from the psychologist. I want to resume our loyalty and trust in one another and we both begin writing every few days. I haven't completely resolved the sexual issue, but it doesn't matter because we aren't physically together anyway. I'm feeling more stable and sure of myself, which is reassuring to Mom and Dad. They, too, must think that my relationship with Mike is good for me, because late in the summer, they take me on a trip to Pensacola, Florida, where Mike is currently based. Dad rents a little cottage on the beach for a weekend and Mike is able to spend one day and evening with us there. He's doing well in the training command and he enjoys sharing his accomplishments. Though the only time we have alone is during a brief walk we take along the beach, it's comforting to be together, knowing we've weathered a crisis.

I do my student teaching that fall and then graduate at the end of the semester in January. I'm hired as a 4-H agent in Bartlesville, the town where I was born. I love every minute of the nine months I spend working with 4-H kids, but I also look forward to the day Mike will return home. He completes his flight training program and receives both his wings and commission as a second lieutenant in the Marine Corps. We're married by an elder in the "truth" on Oct. 6, 1963, in our house on Madison Place. Only our immediate families are there—Mike's mother, grandmother, and brother, Pat, and my parents, Bonnie, and John. A wedding reception is held at a hotel for other family members and friends.

We load our most valued personal belongings into a used Austin-Healey that Mike purchased after he had earned enough money in the training command. He always wanted a sports car. We make our way to the Marine Corps Air Station in Cherry Point, North Carolina, where Mike is assigned to an attack squadron. Neither of us wants to live on the military base where provided housing is segregated by rank, but there is a small trailer park in town next to the base that we like; both officers and enlisted men and their families live there. Dad loans us eight-hundred dollars to make a down payment on a mobile home with the condition that our payback plan includes the going interest rate. It's important to Dad that we learn about our financial responsibilities.

My first exposure to military social life is a shock. Typically each squadron is made up of about two dozen pilots, the second lieutenants being the lowest in rank. All pilots and their wives are expected to attend the social events usually hosted by the commanding officer, his second-in-command executive officer, or their wives. If it wasn't for a friendship I have with the wife of one of Mike's fellow pilots, I couldn't tolerate the officers' wives' luncheons. Gossip is rampant about affairs going on with the attractive, single flight surgeon attached to the squadron, but it's the first couples' party that scares me to death. I've not been around a lot of drinking. When I was growing up, there wasn't a single bottle of beer ever in our refrigerator. Mike prepares me for the "happy hour" he attends at the officers' club every Friday evening, and he always comes home at a reasonable hour showing no evidence of having drunk too much. When we arrive at the evening cocktail party, however, many of the guests are already reeling under the influence (from my inexperienced perspective), including the commanding officer and his wife, who I later learn set the pace. I'm uncomfortable, especially when approached by an inebriated captain who can't stand up straight or complete a coherent sentence, but wants to dance with me. I decline and seek out Mike to tell him I want to leave. This puts him in an awkward position and he tries to persuade me otherwise, but I'm too unnerved, and we do go home. This becomes an issue between us which we ultimately resolve through compromise. We'll not go to the evening cocktail parties, but we'll attend the afternoon celebrations of a new promotion, the once-a-year Marine Corps Ball, and I'll continue to go to the wives' luncheons.

Our agreement is working well until the executive officer seeks me out at one of the afternoon events. "We missed you and Mike at the party last Saturday night," he says. I smile but don't respond otherwise. "You know these social events are important to your husband's career. I don't think you'd want to do anything that would jeopardize his advancement."

Instead of intimidating me, I'm repelled by his pointed reprimand, but reply. "I appreciate your concern—thank you." I fear Mike's response when I tell him what happened, but am relieved when he seems to resent the intrusion also. We both feel a little more comfortable when we later learn that there's a couple in the squadron who belong to a fundamentalist Christian church and they also don't attend the cocktail parties. I often think about the two priorities that supersede pleasing one another that Mike and I agreed to before he left to join the Marine Corps. He may remember them too and he doesn't pressure me. Eventually we find two couples in the squadron who live in our trailer park and have similar social tastes. They're senior to Mike and have been there for one or two years, each of them with one child. I become the resident baby-sitter and it's from these two sets of parents that I begin to formulate my ideas about parenting. One couple has a book they recommend which I read that advocates treating one child as though you have six ... to prevent spoiling.

For recreation we decide to buy two horses and take advantage of the beautiful places to ride in that rural area of North Carolina. At first we board them at a stable, but the second year we rent a large pasture with a pond for Mike's gelding, Winchester, and my mare, Cherokee. We become very fond of these two animals that provide us with many hours of trail riding. That summer there is an epidemic of equine encephalitis, a virus that attacks the brain and is transmitted by mosquitos. Cherokee becomes ill and goes down at the edge of the pond. Mike and I are afraid that she will try to get up and fall into the water and drown. So the night that she is most ill, we take bed rolls out to the pasture and sleep near her. She does recover, but from then on she is blind in one eye.

I learn that I'm pregnant the beginning of Mike's third year at Cherry Point. Our baby is due in April of 1966 and his squadron will be deployed to Viet Nam the following year. We will at least have one year together with our first child. Mike loves his work, especially the camaraderie he shares with other pilots, all of whom are flying the A-4 Skyhawk, a single-seat attack aircraft being used for support in Viet Nam. I know he's eager for active participation in the war; after all, this is what he's been preparing for the last four years. I underestimate just how impatient he is.

I'm five months pregnant when he arrives home from work one day excited to share some news. "There's another squadron on base that's been alerted for deployment sometime this spring," he says. "Some of their pilots are due to get out before then and they're looking for other pilots to take their place." I can't believe Mike is considering a departure before our baby is due, but the more he talks, the more I know this is his intent. He will have to undergo a short training period to get up to speed in a different aircraft, the A-6 Intruder, and that training will take place right away in Norfolk, Virginia. The realization that he is choosing this new opportunity over being with me the first year of our baby's life is heartbreaking, but remembering our agreement, I don't let Mike know the extent of this blow. I hide my disappointment, even from my parents. A war is going on, so it is easy to let them believe it is happening out of necessity, not from Mike's own decision.

Just before the squadron's departure, we move our mobile home back to Tulsa so I will be near my parents while he is gone. Two weeks after Mike leaves, our daughter, Leslie, is born on April 5, 1966. As part of the hospital's parent support program, I am visited by a representative of the La Leche League, an organization to help mothers worldwide breastfeed through mother-to-mother support, encouragement, and information. I already know I want to breastfeed my baby, and the effect of this woman's visit makes me even more determined. I remember the book I read when I was babysitting the infants of our friends in the military. That author recommended a strict feeding schedule and even encouraged letting an infant cry if necessary. I don't think I can do that, so I make her feedings frequent enough that sometimes I even wake her up to breastfeed to avoid the possibility of her waking up hungry. I'm an anxious mother, so when I take Leslie to the doctor for her two-week checkup, I'm distraught when he tells me she has lost weight, rather than gained!

"You must start giving her supplements," he says and he gives me a starter supply.

"But the lady from the La Leche League said not to give supplements—that that would diminish my own milk!"

"That might be true if you had sufficient milk for your baby, but it doesn't apply here. I want you to continue nursing her, but when she loses interest, that means she's used up your milk and it's time to give her the bottle. She'll continue to get the benefits of breastfeeding."

I can't get home fast enough to feed her, following the doctor's instructions, but to my dismay, after her first two ounces of supplement formula, she throws it up! I'm sobbing over the phone when I call to tell my mother. "I'm afraid she's going to starve."

Mom comes over and wisely suggests that Leslie may need a little time to get used to the formula, which turns out to be the case. At her next checkup, I'm relieved to learn that she's reached her normal weight.

Mike and I are conscientious about maintaining contact during his deployment through daily letter writing, exchange of photographs, and sometimes tape recordings. I worry about him, especially when casualties are reported in the war news. Every evening my parents come over to visit and play with Leslie. I depend on their support, and the year I spend near them again, pulls me deeper into the complexities of their relationship. I have brought a new granddaughter into their midst providing a welcomed distraction from the tensions between them. Their pleasure in the baby grows daily so it is heartbreaking to take her away from them when Mike returns home. The day we leave to go to his next duty station in Yuma, Arizona, Mom follows us to the car to say goodbye. Dad, wrestling with his emotion, stays on the front porch, a safe distance away, and waves.

The Marine Corps Air Station in Yuma is a training facility for pilots, and Mike is assigned to a training squadron as an instructor. His affiliation with this squadron is a very different kind of experience than we had at Cherry Point. The commanding officer and his wife are gracious people and all the social interaction we have there is positive and enjoyable.

Once again we buy two horses and take Leslie with us on trial rides through the desert and orchards that surround Yuma. We also buy a pickup and camper so we can explore more of the distant desert canyons. It is a happy year of becoming unified as a real family.

Mom and Dad come to visit us that summer. We have a joyful reunion as they renew their relationship with Leslie, now two years old. Skilled at finding bargains, Dad checks the classified ads in the newspaper every day, looking for good used items we might need. By the time the week is over, we have our first dishwasher (the kind that you connect to the kitchen faucet with a hose) and a sofa that makes into a bed. He also takes me shopping for a new outfit that meets his buying requirements: the purchase is something he likes of good quality, and it's on sale.

The night before my parents are to leave, we are sitting in the living room. Dad is bouncing Leslie on his knee singing a familiar jingle. "*Ole Dan Tucker was a fine old man, washed his face in the frying pan,*" he croons to the rhythm of his bounce.

"What time are you and Mom leaving in the morning, Dad?" I ask.

"About eight," he says, and he continues his singing. "*Combed his hair with a wagon wheel, died with a toothache in ... his ... heel,*" the anthem ends with a kerplunk to the floor, causing just enough fright to make Leslie shriek with laughter and beg for more.

"I'll have breakfast ready by 7:30 then," I say to Dad, and then to my daughter, "Tell Grandpa goodnight." Amid her protests, I scoop her up in my arms.

I sleep fitfully that night dreading another difficult separation. The clock at my bedside glows 5:15, when I hear rumblings coming from the guest bedroom. A few moments later I recognize the squeak of our front screen door. I leap from the bed and grab my bathrobe. About to rush out the door to intercept them, I stop, wait, and listen until I hear the sound of the car backing out of the driveway, and then slowly fade into the distance. The pounding of my heart subsides and a wave of relief sweeps over me as I hang my bathrobe on its hook and climb back into bed. Dad escaped the painful goodbye.

Our unspoken agreement to avoid goodbyes stays in effect every time my parents come to visit. Breakfast is planned the night before and aborted by a five o'clock departure. Each year it is a little easier because Dad and I both know he and Mom will be eating their bacon and eggs at a diner sixty miles down the highway by six. Though wide awake in my bed as they are leaving, my role in the complicity is to feign sleep as they slip away. Sometimes, while I lie there waiting for the drama to end, I imagine what it would be like to talk about our fear, maybe even cry, and then laugh through our tears. I don't want to be afraid to cry anymore.

INSIGHTS: Attachment Security and Adult Romantic Relationships

In order to better understand my choices and behavior during my courtship and early marriage with Mike, I use the information that has been gathered from studies of John Bowlby's theory of attachment as it applies to adults in romantic relationships. Many mistakenly assume that Bowlby's theory applies exclusively to relationships between infants and their caregivers. Although Bowlby often claimed that attachment was an integral part of human behavior throughout one's life, it wasn't until the late 1970s that researchers began to take seriously the possibility that attachment processes also play out in adult relationships. Adopting a lifespan perspective, researchers identified a developmental path, according to which peers gradually replace parents as principal attachment figures. Parents may serve as attachment figures "in reserve" whenever their adult child passes a developmental milestone or encounters serious difficulties, but close friends and romantic partners often become principal attachment figures during adolescence and adulthood.[1]

From 1975 through 1979, Robert Weiss identified relationships that met the same criteria for an attachment relationship between an infant and caregiver. Weiss found these characteristics within marriages,[2] committed non-marital relationships,[3] relationships between a single parent and an older child, and relationships between women with best friends, sisters, or parents.[4] As early as 1964, the same characteristics of close attachments were found between men and their buddies engaged in military combat.[5] In all these instances, the relationships are recognized as being of central importance and emotional significance. The individuals involved display the same attachment characteristics—a need for proximity in times of stress, heightened comfort and diminished anxiety when in the company of the attachment figure, and a marked increase in discomfort and anxiety when the attachment figure is not accessible.[6]

In 1987 Cindy Hazan and Phillip Shaver[7] went even further by proposing that the emotional bond that develops between adult lovers will resemble the affectional bond that is formed earlier in life between human infants and their parents. This study and many subsequent research projects upheld Bowlby's claim that patterns of attachment established early in life are relatively stable across development. The degree of insecure or secure attachment that was established in childhood with a parent will be reflected in one's romantic relationships. In other words, the attachment style that was established in childhood will affect how safe we feel in a romantic relationship, how comfortable we are with close, intimate bodily contact, the degree to which we share discoveries with one another, and the level of mutual fascination we have with one another.

In order to test this hypothesis, self-reporting questionnaires were designed to reflect the same three major styles of attachment in infancy—on the notion that *a person's adult relationship style is determined in part by childhood relationships with parents*. Participants were asked to identify themselves with one of three statements representing the emotional styles of secure, anxious, and avoidant attachment in adulthood. For example:

"Secure Attachment: I find it relatively easy to get close to others and am comfortable depending on them and having them depend on me. I don't often worry about being abandoned or about someone getting too close to me.

"Anxious Attachment: I find that others are reluctant to get as close as I would like. I often worry that my partner doesn't really love me or won't want to stay with me. I want to merge completely with another person, and this desire sometimes scares people away.

"Avoidant Attachment: I am somewhat uncomfortable being close to others; I find it difficult to trust them completely, difficult to allow myself to depend on them. I am nervous when anyone gets too close, and often love partners want me to be more intimate than I feel comfortable being." [8]

This study found remarkable parallels with the Bowlby-Ainsworth studies of infant attachment using the Strange

Situation measurement tool. In addition, in-depth interviews were developed to explore a person's view of their parents and their experience with separation or loss. By comparing the self-report measures against narrative and interview measures, both types of instruments have been improved for reliability, and the result is a high correlation between the two.[9]

In their comprehensive work *Attachment in Adulthood*,[10] Mario Mikulincer and Phillip Shaver have summarized the research on topics comparing one's attachment style to every possible aspect of adult human experience, ranging from self-image, image of others, emotional regulation, personal growth, couple functioning, sexuality, parenting, dealing with loss and death, and many forms of psychopathology.

Secure attachment suggests that the person, for the most part, has had his or her fundamental emotional needs met through conscientious and caring parents who were probably also securely attached in their childhood, because we know these levels of security tend to be passed down from one generation to another. Secure people are most apt to exemplify resilience, optimism, curiosity, healthy autonomy, capacities for love and forgiveness, tolerance for differences, and kindness. These fortunate ones have learned that support seeking usually results in comfort and relief, so they emerge from childhood with heightened confidence that turning to others is an effective way to cope.

Anxious attachment is characteristic of people who have experienced how good it feels when their needs are adequately met, but in their growing up, this was often not the case, possibly due to family instability, parental addictions or depression, poverty, and the unlimited number of environment situations that can make parenting difficult. Consequently, anxious people have not given up on seeking proximity, comfort, and support, so their tendency is to *hyperactivate* their attachment-seeking behaviors. They will try harder to get attention and care, intensify emotions that emphasize their vulnerability and neediness, and escalate their worries, fears of abandonment, and doubts about their capabilities. They hope to gain the attention they crave by exaggerating their fearfulness.

People categorized with an *avoidant* attachment style have experienced little need satisfaction when they were growing up. They don't expect to get their emotional needs met, so they can't risk allowing emotion to flow freely. Their coping mechanism is to *deactivate* behaviors which might be interpreted as weakness or vulnerability. They want to appear strong and independent. Their efforts are aimed at minimizing closeness and interdependence, regardless of the harmful effects it may have on a relationship.[11] Mikulincer and Shaver summarize:

> *"Avoidant people miss the adaptive aspects of emotional experiences by blocking conscious access to them, and anxious people miss adaptive possibilities by riveting their attention on disruptive rather than potentially functional aspects of emotional experience."*[12]

When I became aware of adult attachment styles, I was able to identify myself as one who adopted an insecure attachment style during my childhood and adolescence, in light of circumstances I've explained so far. Though I think I am primarily anxious, I can also manifest some of the characteristics of avoidant persons, depending on the attachment style of the person to whom I'm attached. This pertinent information has helped me see and understand more clearly the experiences in my life that have either helped or hindered my progress in finding a more secure relationship base.

I believe I was first attracted to Mike because I unconsciously saw him as someone who would be safe, in that he would not expect an intensely emotional connection with me. At the time I met him, I was enmeshed in a symbiotic relationship with my mother that in some ways was satisfying, but in other ways was burdensome. I was learning what a close intimate relationship could be, but also associating the intimacy with feelings of my inadequacy. Mike displayed significant characteristics of my father, with whom I had a more relaxed and contented relationship, though I was not as close to him as I was to my mother. Like my father, Mike enjoyed sports and wasn't too interested in delving into deep philosophical explorations, nor was he in any way religious. Sometimes I worried about this, but the fun we had together, the sexual attraction we enjoyed, and the security of having a steady boyfriend overruled, and I quickly began forming a strong attachment to him.

Mike had his own attachment issues to deal with—most specifically an impaired attachment to his father due to his father's four-year absence during the war. This separation alone was disruptive enough without the anxiety he must have felt in connection with his father's alcoholism. While I displayed more anxious behaviors, Mike, from my observation, was more prone to avoidance. By the time we were able to be together every day when we were juniors in college, we had been in an exclusive relationship with one another for four years, a relationship, however, that had not been tested; we had not yet dealt with any serious conflict. I was confident in the expectation that we would finish our college degrees together and get married soon after. His choice to leave college to join the Marine Corps posed a threat. I could only see that there was something more important to him than our being together and consequently, I experienced it as rejection.

Though I don't question Mike's sincerity, the emotional threat of separation didn't appear to be as intense in him as it was in me. While I was hyperactive emotionally, I believe he was deactivating feelings about us and focusing on a greater need to establish a firm masculine identity among peers he respected and admired. To protect myself from painful feelings, I quickly rationalized his decision as evidence of a more balanced relationship, when in fact, we were both conceding that we each had some unfinished growing up to do that was impairing our ability to make a full commitment to our relationship with each other.

In the 1990s, Judith Feeney did three studies on adult attachment styles and their effects on communication patterns of romantic partners. Secure subjects were less likely to respond to physical separation with feelings of insecurity. They were more likely to use a variety of coping strategies in dealing with the separation, such as confronting the problem directly through open communication and negotiating with the partner. Secure couples also engaged in more support seeking and giving, were better at regulating their emotions, and reported efforts to renegotiate the relationship upon reunion, which led to their viewing the separation as something that ultimately brought them closer.

It was more common among partners with insecure attachment styles to use maladaptive means of coping with the separation, such as escape and avoidance. Feelings of anxiety and despair in regard to the separation were also more associated with insecure attachment. These results support the perspective that securely attached persons are more resilient and able to respond constructively to stress, and insecurely attached persons tend to appraise life stressors as more threatening and less controllable. Furthermore, there is little doubt that relationship conflict is a serious issue for those individuals who are highly anxious about their relationships, particularly when questions of distance and separation are at stake.[13]

I think it was a missed opportunity that Mike and I didn't use his decision to drop out of school as a means of examining our relationship more deeply in terms of our individual needs and the level of our commitment to a future together. My fear of losing the relationship was so strong, however, those practical issues weren't considered. I say this, not to cast blame on either of us, but to point out that both of our insecure attachment styles prevented us from dealing with the issue more openly through communication and negotiation, which might have circumvented the emotional crisis I experienced before he left. As it happened, the fortuitous encounter with the psychologist was useful in its conclusion that the onset of my sexual guilt was a result of a return to my childhood attachment with my mother as a resource for emotional support. When I observed how fragile that support was, however, it helped me to confront the dependency on my mother and assume more responsibility for decisions about my future.

When Mike completed his training and came home, we both were anxious to marry and earnest in wanting to begin a new life together. I think we handled our differences over the military lifestyle fairly well because I was better at owning my feelings. However, some of my doubts and insecurities returned when Mike left for active combat before our daughter was born. Though I was more aware of the loss this time, I still dealt with it mainly through denial, and that subsequently contributed to a marital environment that was based on a weakened trust. At that time, I was still strongly influenced by religious admonitions that a wife should be in submission to her husband, so I was inclined to believe that it was God's will that I accept the sacrifice of parenting our baby alone in her first year. Consequently I didn't harbor resentment about it and I think we did well to maintain a strong emotional connection during his deployment. In fact, Mike was inclined to be more emotionally expressive in his written letters than when we were face-to-face, so his letters were a source of nurturance and comfort. The most detrimental loss occurred in connection with his fathering role. Had I known then what I know now about the importance of early bonding between a parent and child, I would have contended more strongly for Mike to be with us during Leslie's first year. That absence of bonding between them was to weaken their attachment significantly in the coming years, and perpetuate a dynamic that presumed I was the more competent parent.

The scenes I describe regarding my father's difficulties in saying goodbye further illustrate how early traumatic experiences continue to elicit strong feelings throughout our lives. The fear my father experienced as a fourteen-year-old boy having to leave the security of his family were akin to the fear of a small child, dependent on caregivers for survival, when threatened with abandonment. Those earliest feelings stay with us in the most primitive part of our brain, which knows no time or persons; it only feels. Later as an adult, when my father encountered any kind of separation from those he loved, those earliest feelings of despair returned with as much intensity.

References:

[1] Feeney, J. 1999. Adult romantic attachment and couple relationships. In *Handbook of attachment*, eds. J. Cassidy and P. Shaver. New York and London: The Guilford Press, p. 355.

[2] Weiss, R. 1975. *Marital separation*. New York: Basic Books.
[3] Weiss, R. 1978. Couples relationships. In *The couple*, ed. M. Corbin. New York: Penguin Books.
[4] Weiss, R. 1979. *Going it alone: The family life and social situation of the single parent*. New York: Basic Books.
[5] Little, R. 1964. Buddy relations and combat performance. In *The new military*, ed. M. Janowitz. New York: Russel Sage.
[6] Weiss, R. 1982. Attachment in adult life. In *The place of attachment in human behavior*, eds. C. M. Parkes and J. Stevenson-Hinde.
[7] Hazan, C. & Shaver, P. 1987. Romantic love conceptualized as an attachment process. *Journal of personality and social psychology*, Vol. 52, pp. 511-524.
[8] Hazan & Shaver 1987, p. 515.
[9] Mikulincer, M. and Shaver, P. 2007. *Attachment in adulthood*, New York: Guilford.
[10] Mikulincer and Shaver 2007.
[11] Mikulincer and Shaver 2007
[12] Mikulincer and Shaver 2007, p. 194.
[13] Feeney, J. A. (1999b). Issues of closeness and distance in dating relationships: Effects of sex and attachment style. *Journal of Social and Personal Relationships*, Vo. 16, pp. 571-590.

6

CHILDREN

By 1967 the Viet Nam War has heated up to the point that career pilots expect deployment every second year. Mike has served four years in the Marine Corps and now has the opportunity of leaving the military. Viet Nam pilots are sought after by airline companies and many of our friends are getting out and taking good paying jobs. I can't bear the thought of another separation so soon if Mike is to stay in the Marine Corps. Now, it isn't just me, it is Leslie too. We both need him. This time I have the courage to tell him how I feel. Mike lost a dear friend from college in the Viet Nam conflict since he's been home and this has heightened his devotion to the cause. It is difficult for him to leave the Marine Corps, but he does, for us.

We spend Mike's probationary first year with Western Airlines in the Seattle, Washington area, renting a cute little farmhouse on one acre in the little suburb of Auburn. Our yard is abundant with fruit trees and flowering shrubs the summer we move there when Leslie is three. We buy a Boxer puppy, we name her Penny, and our adjustment to real civilian life begins. I hear so much about the beauty of Mount Rainier that I can't wait to see it, but it hides behind clouds for three months before I finally have the chance. I'm returning home across the valley from taking Mike to the airport. Suddenly the clouds split horizontally revealing the peak of this giant, pink, snow-covered mountain. It seems a miracle and is so much higher and more beautiful than I imagined. I shiver with goosebumps and, as if that view was intended just for me, the layers of clouds merge again and what now seems like a mirage has disappeared.

When the frequent rains begin in late fall, we learn the sad truth as to why things grow so well in our beautiful yard. We begin to notice the odor of sewage coming from low places beyond the back patio, so much so that we think it best to keep both Leslie and Penny inside. We complain to the landlord, only to learn that the little farmhouse has never had more than a grease-trap installed for waste water from the kitchen; there is no septic system and sewage seeps out into a ditch that runs alongside the road. He has no intention of doing anything about it, but willingly releases us from our rental agreement. We move to a different rental house in the foothills below Mount Rainier just outside Kent, another suburb of Seattle. This house even has a fenced yard for Penny, and the view of the forested mountainside, especially during the snowy winter months, is spectacular. That spring Mike and I put together a sturdy five foot square red and white cardboard playhouse for Leslie, complete with a door and little windows. The next morning she runs outside to play, but in minutes she is back inside. "The playhouse is gone," she says.

"Gone? It couldn't be gone." I go to the door and look outside. The playhouse isn't gone, but a thousand tiny pieces of it are scattered all over the yard. Penny has utterly destroyed it.

While living in Kent, we make friends with another family who has a little boy Leslie's age. Like Mike, the father is a first-year pilot with Western, and his wife and I, both with three-year-olds, have much in common. But once the probationary year is over, many pilots are transferred to other cities and Mike is to be based in Los Angeles. We both prefer living in smaller towns rather than in a big city, and we know there are pilots who commute with pass privileges from other Western Airlines' destinations. We discovered Prescott, Arizona on a camping trip while living in Yuma, and thought at the time it would be the perfect place to raise a family. A move is risky though because Mike's commute involves a two-hour drive to Phoenix before he can board a plane to Los Angeles. So we take an experimental trip to Prescott and while there we discover a house that is for sale across the road from the National Forest boundary. On an acre of land with a barn, the property means we can have horses again. What better place than this to settle in permanently, so Mike is willing to make the long commute rather than to live in Los Angeles. A pretty yellow house sitting near the foot of majestic Granite Mountain becomes our new home.

Now in this peaceful environment, it seems the right time to have another baby. After an unsuccessful year of trying to get pregnant, and with the encouragement of friends who adopted a baby girl, we decide to investigate adopting a child. I read a magazine article about an organization that facilitates the placement of Native American and Canadian children needing adoptive parents and this stimulates Mike's interest. His maternal grandmother is part Cherokee and he is proud of his native heritage. We send for information and soon begin a process that culminates in our traveling to Quesnel, British Columbia to meet a year-old baby boy who is of the Kluskus Band of Canada's First Nations. He has been living with a foster family since birth and these parents and a five-year-old son of their own have become attached to the baby. Policy is against placing a child with an adoptive family who lives near the child's birthplace, or this foster family would adopt him, so the case worker agrees not to finalize the adoption until the foster family meets and approves of us. It is an emotional time for everyone.

After one day of visiting with the family, they are comfortable with us taking the baby out to a park so that Mike, Leslie, and I can have some time alone with him. He is content to go with us and though his foster mother is reassured and ultimately consents to the adoption, she is still distraught with sorrow the next morning when we leave with him. I promise her I will keep in touch.

I am naïve to think that this is going to be an easy transition until we are in the airport to leave Vancouver. I am carrying my new year-old son, Daniel, when he sees a woman near us who resembles his foster mother. He must think it is her and suddenly he reaches out and lunges toward her, and then cries and cries when she doesn't take him, in spite of my efforts to console him. We soon observe other signs that this separation might have some long-term consequences. For six months or more, when Dan notices we are preparing to go somewhere, he becomes fretful and clingy until we buckle him up in the car seat, reassuring him that he won't be left. Another sign is that Dan becomes anxious and irritable when an unfamiliar woman is in our house visiting us, Mike's mother for instance. Does he fear that another strange woman may take him away? Other than this, Dan is of an easy, calm, and happy disposition, and quickly becomes an indispensable and cherished member of our family. My father isn't enthusiastic about our adopting a child, believing that parenting is difficult enough raising one's own. But when he and Mom come to see us two months after our bringing Dan home, they both are captivated with their new grandson.

The years when Leslie is in the primary grades and Dan is a toddler are some of the happiest years for me. I am aware that the children justify my indulgence in play. Never would I sit for hours making Christmas tree ornaments alone, though I love doing it with them. One year we make all our Christmas gifts. Leslie and Dan pile their red wagon high with presents and deliver their gifts to neighborhood friends. Reading books at naptime is another way the children help me. These are the times I feel most centered and connected with some basic trust in myself. Old favorites such as *Raggedy Ann and Andy* stories and *Tales of Uncle Wiggly* are picked up and read so many times, these characters became imaginary friends. Later as Leslie's appetite for books increases and Dan's attention turns more to cars and trucks, I find a list of children's classics, some of which I had missed as a child, that aren't too difficult for Leslie to understand. We both look forward to summer afternoons when Dan is napping and we lie on the big double bed and immerse ourselves in the lives of Heidi, Tom Sawyer, or Hans Brinker. Later on we read *Little Women* and biographies of Helen Keller, her teacher Annie Sullivan, and Harriet Tubman.

Following a traditional role like that of my mother, I am meeting many of my emotional needs through my children. Mike is settling into a routine of flying commercially, usually four trips a month with two to four days at home in between. Sometimes he has to stay over in Los Angeles until the next morning to make the commute home. It's a strenuous lifestyle and I begin to sense that it will never equal the adventure or the sense of belonging he had in the military. He often tells others that his job is "boring and monotonous, punctuated by moments of sheer terror." He begins to seek out activities to look forward to and that better meet his needs during his time off. For a while he and another airline pilot operate a horseback guide and outfitting business which also serves as recreation for our family. Leslie becomes adept at riding a horse, and we lead Dan on a little white donkey until he is old enough to ride alone. But when the business fails to yield a profit that is worth the amount of work it requires, the men lose interest. Then he and his friend take up hunting, and for several years in a row, they use their two-week vacation from work for deer and elk season, while I stay home and fume because he isn't doing something with us. I begin using his vacation time to take the kids to Tulsa to see Grandma and Grandpa.

Seeking a new challenge and not being afraid to try almost anything, Mike learns how to ride wild bulls and saddle broncs to compete in Arizona rodeos. For three consecutive years, he directs the annual 4th of July rodeo in Prescott, a time-consuming responsibility. Missing the challenge of military flying and the camaraderie he had enjoyed in the Marine Corps, he decides to spend one set of his days off a month flying with the Marine Corps reserves in California. I can't keep from thinking that all these activities would be appropriate enough if his work didn't have him away from home too. He returns home one day after a ten-day absence and I say, "You're gone so much of the time, I feel like I'm parenting alone."

"I've made a commitment to the reserves and I can't back out of it now," he says. His angry response frightens me and the next day I insist on taking him to buy fabric for a new sport coat I want to make for him. When harmony prevails again between us, I'm relieved. I swallow my discontent with our relationship and immerse myself in the innumerable tasks of homemaking and parenting young children. I volunteer as an aide to Leslie's teachers in school and plan all manner of creative activities for the children in her classes. I also reconnect with Ellen, who is working on her PhD at UCLA in Los Angeles. One October I take the children with me to Los Angeles for a convention of Truth brethren and we have lunch with Ellen. I persuade her to come visit us for Christmas. Mike is flying a trip on the holiday and Ellen helps me put together a swing set to be a surprise for the kids. It's a joy to me to see her pleasure in getting to know my children, as she has had little experience with kids. They, in turn, adore her.

I try to convince myself that it will only be a matter of time before Mike will wake up and realize that the genuine satisfaction he longs for is right under his nose. After all, I am happiest when our family is doing things together, going on a picnic in the forest nearby, taking a trip to a Mexican border town, or just going out to dinner together. Why doesn't he feel the same way?

I believe that if I'm living by the tenets of my religion, I will feel at peace in my life, so I try to study my Bible literature every day and provide religious instruction to my children through books and conversation. Mike accepts my religious devotion and tolerates my teaching our children religious values, but he wants no part of it himself. I was originally attracted to his neutrality about religion, knowing that I put sufficient pressure on myself about it. I'm even grateful that there are no people of my faith here in Prescott, because that would make it even more difficult. There are a few elderly brethren in Phoenix two hours away, and I host them in our home when traveling elders come through Arizona for a service. I'm able to minimize the awkwardness of this situation by planning these religious activities to coincide with Mike's airline trips out of town.

My mother has always zealously distributed Biblical leaflets door-to-door, something I forced myself do for a year after I was married, when I could drive to a nearby community where no one knew me. I dread doing it for reasons I'm trying to understand. As a Brownie Scout, I hated selling Girl Scout cookies because I didn't like risking making people uncomfortable. I dislike proselytizing for the same reason. I also don't like its implied arrogance—that I know better what another person needs. It would be one thing if I was asked what I believe, but another to impose my belief on someone else. Mom seems to need others to affirm her own belief, but I see that as a weakness so I recoil at the thought of others seeing me that way. Maybe if I read through the New Testament again, and write down everything in red that Jesus specifically says *to do*, that will help. But even that doesn't relieve the fear that I'm not living up to my consecration.

The only solution I see to rid myself of guilt is to make myself distribute tracts, so one day I force myself to do it in my own neighborhood, reasoning the harder it is to do, the more pleasing it will be to God. Though it's awful and I hate doing it, it brings some temporary relief, but then the build-up of guilt starts all over again.

One afternoon I'm curled up on my bed in a dark depression while nursing a bad cold. Leslie is six years old. Probably sensing my distance and unavailability, she comes to my bedside and hands me a piece of paper. She has drawn a crooked four-pointed star and in the center of the star is a heart with the words "Mama needs" inside. In one point of the star is "love," in another point is "kumfrt," in another point "hapeenus" and in the fourth point "from Leslie." A shockwave goes through my brain. The realization that my inner conflict evokes this response from her jolts me out of the depression. I know two-year-old Dan must also be feeling a similar loss. I reason that this misery I'm suffering can't be from God—not if it is preventing me from being available to my children. I decide I will never distribute tracts again; it is not something I have to do and I won't allow myself to be haunted by this expectation again.

Once a year I take Leslie and Dan to a convention in Los Angeles where we meet with a much larger group of Bible students, but now Leslie is getting old enough to ask me questions I'm not sure how to answer.

"Why doesn't Daddy go to conventions with us? Why do we do Bible lessons when he doesn't?" She has a good point, and it's becoming more of a conflict for me.

I hold Dan back until he is six to start him in kindergarten thinking that it won't hurt him to have one more year to mature. He still sucks his thumb to comfort himself. Afraid that the other kids will make fun of him when he starts school, I suggest a plan. There's a fire truck he has seen in a toy catalog that he wants.

"If you can stop sucking your thumb for these three summer months, we will get you the fire truck before you start school." He's all for it. I notice he's not sucking his thumb. But one morning he comes to me in tears.

"I sucked my thumb last night and now I won't get the fire truck." What have I done?

"That's okay," I tell him and I hug him close to me, "you do the best you can, and you'll still get the fire truck." Have I asked too much of him?

I fear the void that will come when both children are in school, but Dan starts kindergarten in the fall. I don't see him sucking his thumb. I volunteer to help in his class, buying and reupholstering an old sofa for a reading corner in the kindergarten room. Leslie forms close friendships with two girls in our neighborhood who are in her fourth grade class.

We plan a mother-daughter Christmas holiday party for seven girls and their mothers. For three weekends in advance we bake cookies and make finger sandwiches and put them in the freezer. We buy a new dress for Leslie, and the day before the party I order little carnation corsages for each mother and daughter. Everyone comes and enjoys themselves, except Leslie spills cranberry punch down the front of her light blue dress. She's afraid she has disappointed me, and I reassure her. Did I make too much of this party?

One day Leslie comes home from school heartbroken because her two friends are angry and not speaking to her for some silly reason that is important to little girls. I sympathize and encourage her to talk about it. Rather than demonstrate confidence in her to work it out herself, I give advice, and I'm aware it's upsetting me as much as it is her. What am I doing? Who's the adult here? I think I need to find a new goal for myself and stop worrying so much about my kids.

I consider job possibilities. Since I have a degree in home economics education, teaching in a public school is an option. All I need for the necessary credentials is a course in Arizona history, which I can take at the local community college. When I register for the class, I learn that I can take two courses for the same price as one. I leaf through the school catalog and notice a class called "Perspectives for Women" on the fall semester schedule. A woman who has a private psychotherapy practice in Prescott teaches the class. She has been of help to someone I know. It's the late 70s, the dawn of the women's liberation movement and women are encouraged to return to school in order to develop a career potential. Maybe I can learn something useful in addition to satisfying the Arizona history requirement.

INSIGHTS: What Do Children Need?

If there is one thing that is established in the literature on attachment theory, it's that the best guarantee of growing up as a secure person is to have secure parents. Many studies over the years have sought to determine the extent to which a parent's attachment style is transmitted to a child, that is, if the father is insecurely attached to his parents, will his son have an insecure attachment to him? Chances are, he will. Without deliberate reflection and a meaningful awareness on the part of the parent, it is unlikely that change will occur.[1]

Unfortunately, insecure parents often don't realize what is happening to them. I certainly didn't know I was an insecure parent. I wanted more than anything to be a good mother, so I believed that I could be. We may love our baby, talk about it fondly, play with it, compliment it when it is doing well, and conscientiously tend to our baby's feeding, sleeping, and physical comfort needs. But when attachment needs arise—the need to be comforted when in distress, the need to be accepted and understood when frustrated or angry, the need to have the parent close by, the need to feel vital to a dependably responsive human being, the insecure parent may feel an intolerable sense of inadequacy and threat.

> *"To be fully open to a baby's emotional needs is to become reacquainted with oneself as a baby, to re-experience the pain of being totally dependent and desperately in love and yet being shut out and feeling unwanted."*[2]

As children we construct defense mechanisms to prevent being engulfed and immobilized by such feelings. When we become a parent and are faced with the responsibility of caring for a helpless little human being, our defensive walls are broken and more rigorous efforts are required to protect ourselves from buried and unresolved pain. We may become dismissive or overreact to our child's attachment needs, searching for ways to keep our baby and its needs at some distance. Our failure to have insights into ourselves and our parents may cause us to concoct explanations that are self-deceptive or self-serving. We may latch on to belief systems that discourage introspection in favor of early discipline and taking precautions against spoiling. The book I read while baby-sitting for the two Marine Corps couples was an example of this kind of parenting literature that John Bowlby abhorred. I remember my inner conflict, wanting to pick Leslie up each time she cried, but believing that I mustn't.

A mother who has not worked through her own insecure attachment will continue to struggle to find stable love. She may want to love deeply, but it will be hard for her if she has not received enough reliable love to be in a position to give it. She may care for her baby as much as any other mother, but her caregiving may be impaired, making it difficult to be consistently available. I can relate to the descriptions of parents who are frightened at times by their children's needs. Because of my own insecurities, it was difficult for me to acknowledge and cope effectively with any sign of insecurity in my children. Leslie's need to comfort me when I was sick and Dan's fear of being left alone and his prolonged thumb-sucking were unsettling. I interpreted my worry as normal in a conscientious parent, but I had no real understanding that I might be passing on anxiety to my children, nor was I aware of the anxieties I carried in relation to my own parents. The mother-daughter Christmas party and the rift between Leslie and her two girlfriends did give me an inkling that I was having difficulty distinguishing Leslie's needs and feelings from my own, but I wasn't yet able to see how similar my relationship with Leslie was to my relationship with my mother.

In the research literature on parenting, particular attention is paid to parents who have failed to mourn a significant loss, like the death of a parent or losses of a lesser degree. There are probably thousands of ways parents can pass on their own often hidden, separation anxieties to their kids, so that they grow up being terrified of abandonment, fearful about being left alone, or some other variation of this theme. Efforts to understand what makes unresolved parents raise insecure kids underscore all the research data on attachment theory. As much as we love our children and dread harming them, it is difficult to shield them from the damaged parts of ourselves, and we are constantly undermined by our own defense mechanisms that keep us being as we have been for so long. This is true regardless of education levels, intelligence, social or economic status, or ethnic background. Millions of books are sold on child care, and as useful as they may be, none of it will help parents do the one thing they most need to do:

> *"...gain a deeper understanding of their own motivations, conflicts and inner needs. In the self-help literature directed at parents, virtually no attention is paid to the emotional upheavals that the parent is likely to face—the disturbing return of long festering feelings, the sense of being driven to behave in ways that one would rather not think about, the haunting sensation of being inhabited by the ghost of one's own mother or father as one tries to relate to one's child."*[3]

So, if the most important quality that distinguishes secure from insecure parents is their capacity to reflect openly, honestly, and clearly on the inner mental state of themselves and others, how does this capacity help a child? This information would have helped me. Had I been able to reflect on my own mental states (am I happy, sad, angry, hurt, disappointed, frustrated, fearful, anxious?) and then speculate on what it is they need emotionally at any given time, then I would have been better able to help my children understand their own feelings and impulses. Without this capacity, a parent can't provide this function. In the beginning a parent does the reflecting for the baby through verbal and body communication. The simple acts of responding to a baby's cry, holding her close, and uttering comforting sounds that then elicit a calming effect on the child are what begin the attachment process that is so important in later emotional development.

As children develop language skills, the parent can further that attachment process by mirroring back feelings with words that put names to a child's feelings. These may be feelings of happiness and contentment, but even more important is the parent's feedback of negative feelings such as hurt, anger, or sadness. If that component is not there early on, children may begin suppressing those feelings and then fail to become familiar and comfortable with their inner world. If parents are unable to be self-reflective themselves, they are more likely to revert to early patterns of behavior that they first learned when dealing with a rejecting or erratic parent.[4]

In contrast, if parents are comfortable expressing their own negative emotions ("I get angry when …" or "I feel sad when…"), then feeding back the child's negative feelings (I see you are angry, afraid, disappointed, etc.) will convey acceptance of the feeling and an understanding of why the child feels the way she does. She can cry, shout "I hate you," or "You love the baby more than me," and still know she will be responded to in a meaningful way. Her negative feelings do not have to be disavowed. Consequently, this retains the child's integrity and leaves self-esteem intact, thus paving the way to help her be more discriminating about how she expresses negative feelings in her behavior. She can understand that it's okay to be angry, but not okay to be destructively aggressive—to hit or bite. The acceptance of negative feelings continues to be critical in maintaining secure attachment in later childhood.

> *"To be understood instead of punished, to express anger and not be rejected, to complain and be taken seriously, to be frightened and not have one's fear trivialized, to be depressed or unhappy and feel taken care of, to express a self-doubt and feel listened to and not judged—such experiences may be for later childhood what sensitive responsiveness to the baby's cries and other distress signals are for infancy."*[5]

In her work, *Mother Nature*, anthropologist Sarah Hrdy describes the ability of a parent to respond to a child in this way as a quality that differentiates humans from other primates.[6] It involves combining our intelligence and capacity for language with *"articulate empathy"* in order *"to understand cognitively what others are expressing at the same time as we understand at an emotional level what others are feeling."*[7]

As another one of my "book mentors," Sarah Hrdy has helped me put into perspective my past and present role as a mother and grandmother. Hrdy was born in Texas in 1946, five years later than my birth in Oklahoma. Unlike my upbringing in a family with a non-working mother, Hrdy's mother and both grandmothers had delegated the care of their children to governesses. She also had a privileged education and entered graduate school in 1970, almost ten years earlier than I did. Trained in anthropology, primatology, and evolutionary theory, she was exposed to John Bowlby's work much sooner than I was. Because she aspired to being both a mother and a scientist, she had no expectation of having to make major compromises in order to do both, given that she had a supportive husband and other individuals available to help her rear their children.

Still, Bowlby's insights presented a dilemma for any mother who wanted to raise healthy children and also wanted a career of her own. She had learned in college about evolution, and how people studied the behavior of animals to learn more about human nature. Rather than agonize over her two conflicting drives, Hrdy committed to a career in which she studied female nature and motherhood in primates in seven different countries over thirty years in hopes of learning from an evolutionary perspective what human infants actually need from their mothers and why. While continuing to maintain that Bowlby's attachment theory was evolutionary theory's most important contribution to human well-being, her way of observing animals in their natural habitat revealed that motherhood was far more complicated than Bowlby had previously thought.

Hrdy came to believe that Bowlby had overlooked the many alternative modes of infant care found among primates. In his 1969 classic book *Attachment*, he singled out chimpanzees, gorillas, and two species of monkeys, all of whom practiced exclusive maternal care, as examples of how our African ancestors must have cared for babies. Hrdy discovered that exclusive maternal care was typical in only about half of some 276 species, so there was no one universal pattern of infant care among primates. In fact, continuous care and contact mothering is a last resort if she has reliable support from a caregiver who is available, willing, competent, and the mother trusts him or her to return the infant unharmed. It may be the father, a sibling, aunt, uncle, grandmother, or even trusted helpers who are not kin.[8]

Among langur monkeys, babies were passed freely among the mother's female relatives while she foraged for food, while the primary attachment remained to the mother. While not minimizing the importance of a primary attachment, Hrdy explains that infants growing up depending on a cluster of well-chosen caretakers would have to become more adept at "decoding the mental states of others, and figuring out who would help and who would hurt."[9] This would explain why the most outstanding distinction between us and our Great Ape relatives that Bowlby studied is our ability to assess what others are feeling, our impulse to share and cooperate, to theorize about others' intentions, and our eagerness to understand others and to be understood. This is called *empathy*. These are precisely the same skills that children need from their parents in order to feel secure.

This explains why children born into societies that value childrearing and consider it too important to be left entirely to parents do better. It is particularly apparent when there are risk factors such as low birthweight and prematurity due to poverty or when infants are born to teenage or unmarried mothers. Whether parental help comes from older siblings, grandparents, other kin, or other interested helpers, mothers will be more responsive to their infants' needs, and their children will do better cognitively, emotionally, and physically. Just the presence of a grandmother in a household or frequent visits from a grandmother increase the chance that a child will form a more secure attachment to an inexperienced mother. The same is true in those countries where new parents are given extended times of leave from their jobs, and support is provided from trained childcare workers who make home visits during pregnancy and during the child's first two years. In 1999, an ambitious study took place in Israel and the Netherlands to compare children cared for primarily by mothers with those cared for by both mothers and other adults. Overall, the conclusions were that *"children seemed to do best when they have three secure relationships, that is, three relationships that send the clear message 'you will be cared for no matter what.'*"[10]

Research on fathering is mixed regarding the amount of time fathers spent caring for children in our early history, but evidence is clear that father investment and care helps children thrive in both modern and ancient societies. It has already been shown that hormones in women that promote nurturing behavior are more pronounced in mothers than in fathers. There are findings, however, that link such hormone levels in fathers to how much time they spend in contact with pregnant mothers and their newborns. The more time a father spends in actual child care, the higher his levels of nurturing-enhancing hormones are, which then leads a father to engage in more care.[11]

This information prompted Alison Gopnik, a professor of psychology at the University of California, Berkley to suggest that it would be a great advantage to children if females developed a preference for males who are less aggressive and more desirous of being good fathers. In most primates, it has been in the male's genetic interest to father as many babies as he can, which is usually not in the best interest of the female, who is more concerned about the long-term survival of the babies she has. This is especially true with human babies because of the very long time it takes to raise a child to maturity and independence. Gopnik is saying that fathering many babies who share your genes may not be a good strategy for fathers. The more care and resources a child needs to survive and thrive, the more sense it makes to turn out fewer babies and provide them with the resources they need.

"Once women start to develop these preferences, men who engage in paternal investment will also have a genetic advantage. Eventually, males who display this pattern of behavior, and females who develop this pattern of preferences, could dominate over the earlier patterns."[12]

In my first class on evolution, I learned that just because we have evolved in a certain way doesn't mean that our inherited tendencies are serving us well in our present environment. It falls to us to examine what has been handed down from previous ancestors and make choices about what we want to cultivate in ourselves and pass on to our offspring. From my own mother's example, I grew up believing that being a "good mother" meant that my children's physical, intellectual, and emotional needs would take precedence over my own until they started to school. Even then, if I chose to pursue more education or a career, those efforts would be subordinate to my children's needs as they continued to grow and develop.

Unlike Sarah Hrdy, I didn't confront feelings of conflict between my desire to be a parent and to have a career until after both children were in school. I enjoyed my one pregnancy, and even though I was disappointed to learn that Mike would be on the other side of the world when our child was born, I accepted the responsibility of being the sole parent of my baby for her first year, but not without feelings of inadequacy and self-doubt. My parents and brother were a great support to me that first year, and Hrdy's emphasis on the importance of having helpful kin nearby was certainly true for me.

My disappointment in Mike at that time may have intuitively led to my feeling that I was depending too much on my kids for getting my emotional needs met, but this was not a clear understanding. I didn't know at that time that Leslie was forming a comfortable relationship with a teacher at her elementary school, Mrs. Parmet, much like I did with Mrs. Bostick, except that this teacher was not Leslie's classroom teacher. Leslie helped Mrs. Parmet collate papers during recess and the lunch hour, and consequently they had time to talk, Leslie sometimes sharing worries about Mike and me. I was grateful to learn that Leslie had the skills to find a surrogate who was able to help her during difficult times.

My relationship with Dan was different, not so emotionally entangled or conflicted, but no less intense. I think I was calmer, less anxious, due to Mike's presence, though I didn't have the nearby support of my parents or any other relatives. Though Dan was an even-tempered baby, he demonstrated more need for physical affection and reassurance than did Leslie. Attachment theory provides a better understanding of the ruptures that occurred in Dan's early life. We hadn't taken seriously the significance of being taken from one's biological mother shortly after birth. I know now that the unborn child has already begun an emotional attachment to his mother, recognizing the sound of her voice and scent and being familiar with her day-to-day emotional swings which influence her chemistry. Though his foster mother was a caring and affectionate person, she was different, and a bonding process had to begin all over again. One year later, when our family appeared on the scene, the baby they called "Skippy" was most certainly attached to her. She had been a full-time mother to him, along with her own five-year-old son. By the time he was a year old and no qualified family had applied to adopt him, his foster family was hoping to keep him permanently. So both foster mother and child endured a painful separation. "Terrence" was the name on his birth certificate, the name given to him by his birth mother. What happened to Skippy, he must have wondered, and who is this Dan? We named him after a son born to Mike's maternal grandmother, who had died as an infant. We underestimated the adjustment our new one-year-old child had to make.

It was much later that we learned the Canadian government authorized adoption placement of many aboriginal children, many times against the will of the child's family. We were not told the circumstances of his separation from his birth family, only that this was a child who needed a home. Thinking that by forcing assimilation into the dominant light-skinned culture, authorities assumed they were doing these children a favor. This action has since been acknowledged a tragic mistake. Studies done on the adoptions of this group of Canadian First Nations children who were placed with white adoptive families were not generally successful. The damage and pain that was brought to First Nations families has been a blight in Canadian history, no less so than the crimes committed against Native Americans in the United States. Many of the children were unhappy, and as adolescents found their way back to their birth families. We were fortunate that Dan's adjustment was as positive as it was. He was good-natured and fun-loving, and Leslie warmed to her new role as big sister. I think having a sibling was good for both of them in that it provided companionship within our family and may have dispersed the negative effects of having two insecure parents.

Carl Rogers has expressed the opinion that we are probably unaware of both the best and worst things we have passed on to our children. I believe this to be true and the thought is a comfort to me. As parents, we differ in our innate temperament, intelligence, endurance, our susceptibility to diseases, both physical and mental, and many other characteristics influenced by our genes. We each have also experienced different effects from our mothers and fathers, both positive and negative, varying in degrees according to our vulnerability and resilience. It isn't enough just to want to be a good parent when all these influences come into play. What parent hasn't at times felt the lack of a needed skill in dealing with a child? The question is can we apply the compassion we want to show to our children to ourselves? I'm still trying to learn this, lest I pass on guilt and remorse instead of an appropriate willingness to acknowledge my mistakes and take action to undo them whenever I'm made aware and it's still possible.

References:

[1] Fonagy, P., Steele, M., Steele, H., Moran, G., & Higgitt, A. 1991. The capacity for understanding mental states: The reflective self in parent and child and its significance for security of attachment. *Infant mental health journal*, Vol.13, pp. 200-217.
[2] Karen, R. 1998. *Becoming attached: First relationships and how they shape our capacity to love.* New York/London: Oxford University Press, p. 374.
[3] Karen 1998, p.378.
[4] Karen 1998.
[5] Karen 1998, p. 243.
[6] Hrdy, Sarah. 1999. *Mother nature: Maternal instincts and how they shape the human species.* New York: Ballentine Books.
[7] Hrdy 1999, p. 392.
[8] Hrdy, Sarah. 2009. *Mothers and others: The evolutionary origins of mutual understanding.* Cambridge, Massachusetts/London, England. The Belknap Press of Harvard University Press.
[9] Hrdy 2009, p. 66.
[10] Hrdy 2009, p. 130.
[11] Hrdy 2009.
[12] Gopnik, Alison. 2016. *The gardener and the carpenter: What the new science of child development tells us about the*

relationship between parents and children. New York: Picador Paperback, p. 65. (First published by Farrar, Straus and Giroux).

7

TWO YEARS OF PSYCHOTHERAPY

The Perspectives for Women class turns out to be of more help than I ever imagined. We are asked to keep a daily journal, recording our predominating thoughts and feelings and any dreams or fantasies that might provide clues to what we want or need. The teacher's philosophy reminds me of the "unknown possibilities" concept that I learned at Camp Miniwanca. It assumes that we have unseen potential—"the sleeping giants within us" that Danforth described. It includes the recognition that there are factors that may keep those giants asleep and undiscovered, such as deprived childhoods, trauma, unrealistic expectations, depression, or addictions.

We submit our daily writings to the teacher each week for her written comments and questions, an individualized strategy that supplements our class discussions. I'm surprised at how easily my questions and worries pour out in my journal as I begin to trust Clara, my empathetic instructor.

My father is facing retirement and my parents are considering renting a place in Arizona to be near me and my family during the winter months. I'm almost certain that it's this prospect that is causing me to have a recurring headache.

I believe that I have a good relationship with my parents, but I'm also aware that it's a strain to have them visit. I want to support them, but their needs are different. They both enjoy their grandchildren, but Mom looks forward to long talks with me alone and Dad enjoys taking me shopping alone for something we need. It's a challenge to nurture one without feeling that I'm neglecting the other.

One day I come to my Perspectives for Women class, eager to see Clara's responses to my latest journal entries. The first thing she does at the beginning of each class is to return our assignments. At the top of my first page, she has written this question: *"What are the demands you respond to so much on the "outside" of yourself?"* An arrow is drawn to a sentence I wrote that she underlined. "*I'm beginning to unwind and relax and I even took a nap today!*" I'm intrigued by her question and recognize that I hunger to explore the answer because I'm not sure that I understand it myself. Once the class is over, I schedule a session with Clara in her downtown office for the next week.

How I look forward to this session! To think I'm going to have Clara and her wisdom, which I have observed so far in the class, available to me in a private session. Her office is located in an older office building on one of Prescott's main streets. A wide carpeted staircase leads from the entry level up to her second floor office. As I walk up the stairs, my anticipation is so great, I have a sensation of floating effortlessly in air, as if I'm levitating without my feet touching the floor. I smile at myself as I recognize that I'm getting some need met that I don't recall ever having experienced before. After this first session with Clara, I talk to Mike about the possibility of my continuing to see her on a weekly basis at thirty dollars a week, and he agrees.

Over the next few months, through my discussions with Clara, I come to understand the role I play in supporting my mother. I learn how little children are naturally sensitive to their mother's needs (just as Leslie has been to mine) because as children we are dependent on our mothers (or other caregivers) for survival. If our mother isn't all right, then we can't be all right either. The unconscious reasoning is that if I can make her happy, she will take better care of me. There must have been something in my temperament that moved me to take on what was really an adult role with my mother. I could see that my father had no interest in what was helping my mother to cope—her religion, so I could support her in a way my father couldn't or wouldn't.

In Clara's office there is a stack of books sitting on her coffee table. One day she points to them and says, "Just as an experiment, I'd like you to pretend that this stack of books represents all the precepts of your religion—the values it has given you, and especially all the expectations that it has imposed. Can you do that?"

"Yes, I think so," I say, staring at the books.

"Take the stack of books and move them over to the end table there beside you, and begin to imagine what it might be like without them, just for a moment. You can take them back any time you choose."

The simple act of moving the books from one table to another elicits an anxiety that raises the question, *why am I afraid?* Gradually I come to understand that my emotions, particularly those associated with my mother, are hard to let go.

"Even though you're no longer the four-year-old, dependent on your mother for survival, those fears you felt as a child when your security was threatened are still just as strong as they were then," Clara explains. "The process of therapy will help you use the reasoning part of your brain to sort out when those fear responses are rational and when they're not. You'll then be free enough to explore on your own what will best promote a healthy and sustainable self-reliance."

Now that our class is over, Clara wants me to continue writing in my journal, responding, if I would like, to a list of books she has given me to read. One of them, *On Becoming a Person*, by Carl Rogers, makes a strong impression.

> *"I'm reading more of Carl Rogers—I don't want the book to end. I feel free and safe when I'm reading it. It's encouraging to think that someday I may be genuinely myself and aware of the blocks that shut me off. I'm still struggling with some religious concepts, mostly those having to do with things I've always felt I should do. Right now I know that I could throw all the "shoulds" and "oughts" to the wind and still be okay—safe, but I'm not sure if I really want to. Since I've been throwing out so many things that needed to be thrown out, I get my rebellion confused with the things I still want to keep. Right now I'm just taking each day and each situation at a time. I'm not making any blanket rules to apply to the future; I'm just experimenting and seeing how that feels."*

As I become clearer about the unconscious motivations that have been driving me for so long, I want to share my new insights with Mike. One morning, after he's returned home from a trip, Mike is working in the office we've built on to the front of our house. I go in and sit down.

"I've been learning some things about myself in my therapy that I'd like to talk to you about."

He turns in his swivel chair to face me. "Sure," he says.

"I'm aware of why I've used Leslie and Dan to meet so many of my needs. The year you spent in Viet Nam made it easy for me to monopolize the parenting role and it probably set a pattern that has carried over into our lifestyle now—the fact that you're away from home so much—but I know now that it's more than that. I've been following my mother's example, a pattern that felt familiar to me, especially when it comes to religion."

I have Mike's rapt attention, so I continue. "Mom got involved in a religion that Dad couldn't comfortably accept. The same thing was true of her parents. I have made the same religion such an important factor in my own life, it has become divisive between you and me, and I can see now that I've been doing the same thing—with you and Leslie especially."

"I think I understand what you're saying, but go on."

"Leslie's been complaining to me lately that I expect something of her that you don't fully support, and I'm thankful that she's been strong enough to tell me that. It means that she must see me as being stronger than I saw Mom to be. It wouldn't have been safe for me to say that to her. I want you to know that I'm sorry I've been doing something that has created distance between you, Leslie, and Dan." By now my eyes are full of tears.

Mike is visibly touched by my emotions of apology, which encourages me to go on.

"While I've complained about the time you spend hunting and doing things with your men friends instead of us on your days off, I can understand how I've encouraged that. I remember the priorities that we set that night in your apartment before we were married. Do you remember that?"

"I'm not sure that I do. Remind me."

"Well, you had just told me that you wanted to leave school to go into the Marine Corps. That was hard for me to hear because it meant we would be separated for the next eighteen months. While I wished it wasn't so important to you, I realized that my religious faith was probably more important to me than pleasing you. We both had something that was more important to us than pleasing each other. Do you remember that now?"

"Yes, I think I do."

"I know you wanted to stay in the Marine Corps, but you've given up your military career for us, so it's time for me to give up some attitudes that have been preventing me from making a full commitment to you."

Several days later Mike agrees to enter therapy with me, a step Clara has encouraged. The sessions we have together are fruitful and bring a new level of understanding in our relationship.

I have already been sharing the benefits of my therapy with Mom, thinking I might be able to help her and Dad. The psychological concepts, though comforting to her in some ways, are also threatening. I try to reassure her that I haven't completely lost my faith, and that my new explorations are meeting some important needs in me that might also help her. I write to her:

> *"Through some reading I've done recently, I've come to believe that God created us to need love from one another as much as we need good food, ample rest, etc. I think it's harmful to us as Christian wives and mothers to do anything that cuts us off from the very person in our lives who is able to satisfy this need—our husbands. It's very apparent to me that I have more energy to give to Leslie and Dan now that Mike and I are sharing more with each other. You told me about the terrible night when you said hurtful things to Dad and then he suggested separation. All that was painful, but it opened up some new communication between you. You were both saying what you felt at the deepest level. When*

there's been a long period of little communication, most of the feelings that have been suppressed are the negative ones—resentments, anger, and fear. When we begin to communicate honestly and openly, it's those feelings that come out first. This can be frightening enough to stop the whole process altogether. At first Mike hated the confrontations of conflict. But Clara prepared me for this, so I was able to keep my cool until we could come to some sort of resolution. Previously we would have fled in fright, but since we had the strength to see it through, something was accomplished by it, and our courage was reinforced for the next encounter. It's been five months since we started the therapy together and we are just now getting to the point where we no longer have to deal with backlog. Some of the communication has been painful, but our willingness to be more vulnerable demonstrates that we care about each other and our relationship."

I know these revelations will frighten Mom. She has been coping with her conflicts with Dad by seeing them as tests to her Christian faith rather than problems that can be resolved between them. By rejecting her long-suffering as a virtue, I risk her interpreting it as a rejection of her, but I know I can't go on pretending that I share these beliefs with her. The joy I feel about the progress Mike and I are making emboldens me to break off my affiliation with the Truth brethren because I believe this will strengthen the unity in our family. I know my decision may destabilize her. I have nightmares that I'm killing her.

Clara can see that I'm caught in the middle of a triangle with my parents. With her support I try to explain my feelings to Mom in a way that she can hear, but Mom can see now that my new explorations are providing new meaning to my life that surpass the religious faith we have shared. She begins to distance herself from me. I come to see that I can't be true to myself and, at the same time, keep her as close to me as I have in the past. In another letter to her, I acknowledge this acceptance:

> *"I'm glad you decided to mail the letter, because it helped me to see more clearly how you see me. You think I am betraying Biblical concepts while I feel I'm being liberated from some crippling fears. You see me as having come under the influence of others who are leading me astray. I can see why it would look that way to you because I've not revealed my deepest conflicts. It's taken me quite a while just to acknowledge them myself. I'm confronting a conflict between standards imposed on me by others and values of my own. I made a choice—no one made the choice for me. I've gained a strength that I've not known before. I understand your perspective for yourself because it was my own for so long. I want to respect it for you, but I also want the same respect and freedom for myself. My love for you is as strong as it has ever been, but perhaps we have been too dependent on each other. I hope that in time we'll see that this is the best way for both of us, and I hope it won't jeopardize our love for each other."*

Writing this honestly has been an act of courage for me. While I hold to a belief in a personal God who cares for me, I'm able to remove myself from a religious system that has become a burden. I no longer need an outside authority to interpret God's will for me. I'm rejecting a narrow interpretation of what God expects of me, which has been passed down by my mother and the brethren in "the Truth." While I still hold to their perception of a future restitution for the world, my focus has shifted to what I can be doing *right now,* and to an awareness of what I am feeling *right now*. Suddenly I have many more options—exciting ideas for my future I haven't considered before. Surely it is a *good* thing to anticipate new goals that inspire me and bring me joy. I'm trusting that this new path is God's will for me.

Ripples from my therapy spread to my relationship with my siblings. Bonnie calls to see what Mike wants for Christmas since she has drawn his name. I tell her about all the things I'm learning from my counseling and that I'm now able to understand her different way of coping with Mom and Dad's relationship. I'm eager to see her and I feel like we have thirty-five years of catching up to do. I hear new warmth in her voice. She suggests that I meet her in Colorado when she will be there with her husband on a skiing trip, but she won't be skiing, so we can have some time alone together. Mike offers to keep the kids so I can go. I take the bus to Vail, Colorado, and on this trip, I read a book Clara has lent me, *The Believers,* by Janice Holt Giles, a novel about the Shaker religion. It exposes the harm that can come from any uncompromising religious belief, and though the Shaker belief differs from my own history, the impact each belief has on its proponents are the same.

Soon after my conversation with Bonnie, I call John to find out what *he* wants for Christmas because I have drawn *his* name. Sometimes John is open, and other times he's distant. This time he's eager to talk.

"Guess what?" I say. "I'm finding out why we're so crazy!"

"Yeah? Well, tell me about it."

I tell him about my therapy and how I'm coming to understand some of my problems better. "I think they're related to Mom and Dad's relationship and the part religion has played in our family."

"Really? That's just what I'm going through," he says. "Maybe I'd better get out to see you over the holidays!" The connections that result from these conversations with Bonnie and John help me to feel closer to them.

Two years of psychotherapy culminate in a decision to go back to school to get my master's degree. Maybe I can learn to help others in the way that Clara's counsel has so energized me. This goal inspires me more than teaching high school home economics. I learn about a master's program at Arizona State University in Human Development and Family Studies. I can apply to the program with the bachelor's degree I already have; I just have to pass a graduate study entrance exam. ASU is a two-hour drive from Prescott, a long commute, and the program may take me three or four years to complete. But if I can do it in those three or four years, I'll have a credential that will qualify me to teach Child Development, Marriage, and Parent Education courses at the local community college.

I dig up my old transcripts, find several of my former professors who are still alive and willing to write letters of recommendation. I barely pass the Miller Analogies Test, completing the requirements for acceptance into the program. Leslie and Dan are in school all day now and I will make sure I'm home in time for supper. Mike supports my plan and agrees to be more available for child care. Dad even offers to help pay for my schooling, which Mike and I appreciate, but we assure him that we can afford to pay for it ourselves.

I am thirty-seven years old and off to college—again. With a bright new perspective of life and newly found freedom, I'm open and ready to learn. Clara has awakened in me a desire to understand more clearly what it means to grow personally, to actualize my potential, and maybe even learn to teach these subjects to others. As I approach the outskirts of Phoenix on my first trip to Tempe, I notice the smell of orange blossoms with heightened anticipation. I don't yet know I will always associate this fragrance with one of the most exhilarating times of my life. I park my car in the parking lot outside the classroom building where I'm to attend my first class. I'm scared to death. It's been fifteen years since I've been in school. Things will have changed, I know. Will I be able to do this? My feelings of liberation are coupled with flashes of terror.

The topic of my first exam is on inductive and deductive reasoning. I'm clear about the difference between the two, but somehow I confuse the opposing terms, reversing them in all my answers, consequently failing the exam. I'm devastated and fear that my going back to school is a big mistake, but the thought of turning back is even worse. I'm making new friends, learning new perspectives from inspired professors, and exploring new ways of applying them. I look to my new classes for objective lines of reasoning that will affirm the recent changes in my thinking. Positive feelings help to give me confidence, and the fears that accompany them push me forward to seek more knowledge that will shore up my footing. Of the many self-discoveries I make through my graduate work, the insights I receive from the ideas of Jean Piaget are the most strengthening. No other writer was more prolific on the subject of cognitive development, so I am exposed to his ideas early in my program.

INSIGHTS: What Motivates Learning, Growth, and Change?

Have you ever watched an infant learning how to do something for the first time? Imagine a two-month-old baby girl seeing a rattle and being aware of it. At first she tries to reach it, stabbing awkwardly with her little hand, but missing the target. She continues to move her muscles until her hand feels the rattle and she takes obvious pleasure in grasping it. Slowly, she adapts her technique to better organize her muscular actions, so that eventually, when she sees the rattle, she will eagerly hit her target the first time. By her repetition of this newly acquired skill, it is easy to observe that her learning is not only satisfying, it's *joyful*. Through a combined process of using a skill that she was born with, in this case, a grasping reflex, and modifying it into something new, purposely grasping a rattle, she is adapting her grasping ability into new structures in her mind, which is the beginning of intelligent action, according to child psychologist, Jean Piaget.

This scene illustrates the first basic assumption of Piaget's Theory of Intellectual Development: the need to engage in cognitive activity is intrinsic in the normal healthy child—motivation to learn comes from *within* the individual, not from without. The child's mind, if planted in fertile soil, will grow quite naturally on its own.

> *"The infant's world is restricted essentially to practical interaction with objects within her immediate environment which are linked to physical pleasure. Time is now. She neither thinks of the past nor the future."*[1]

Piaget was born on August 9, 1896 and grew up near the Lake of Neuchatel in a quiet region of French Switzerland. He received a baccalaureate degree in biology from the University of Neuchatel in 1915 when he was eighteen, and pursued a doctorate in biology while also exploring philosophical ideas, particularly epistemology, a branch of philosophy concerned with the nature and origin of knowledge. Epistemology asks the question *"How do we know what we know?"* He became more and more focused on this question, wanting to resolve it with some scientific explanation. Unsuccessful in finding any attempts to integrate biology with epistemology, he began formulating his own insights which would eventually become his theory of mental structures and cognitive development.[2]

It was through his work with Alfred Binet and Theodore Simon, developing questions for what have become modern intelligence tests, that his theory began to take shape. His task was to administer reasoning tests on a group of children in a grade school, with the aim of discovering something about their reasoning processes. He began engaging his little subjects in conversations patterned after psychiatric questioning (where there are no wrong answers). By presenting simple tasks and using questions involving cause-effect relations, he could analyze the verbal reasoning of normal children. For example, here is a dialogue between Piaget and Julia, age 5:

> *Piaget: What makes the wind?*
> *Julia: The trees.*
> *Piaget: How do you know?*
> *Julia: I saw them waving their arms.*
> *Piaget: How does that make wind?*
> *Julia: Like this (waving her hand in front of Piaget's face). Only they are bigger. And there are lots of trees.*
> *Piaget: What makes the wind on the ocean?*
> *Julia: It blows there from the land. No, it's the waves.*[3]

In Binet's laboratory, standardized tests usually focused on the correct answers and quantitative results. Piaget was much more intrigued with the incorrect answers children gave and the qualitative differences in their answers between age groups. He recognized that Julia's answers, while not correct by adult standards, are not "incorrect" either. They are sensible and coherent within the framework of the child's way of knowing, depending on the child's age and stage of development. Piaget came to understand that children have real understanding only when they invent it themselves. If we respond to their theories with criticism, they may give up on making up their own theories. The primitive ideas of children are replaced by more mature ideas as they grow older. If we try to teach them something too soon, we keep them from reinventing it themselves.[4]

Central to Piaget's theory is that development occurs by stages and every child progresses through these stages at his or her own pace. Providing children with problems that are in keeping with their maturational level is the most effective way of preparing them to function wisely in a very complex world. By the time Piaget died in September of 1980 at the age of eighty-four, he had left a body of research on how we acquire knowledge that no one since has surpassed. He has been recognized for his contributions to biology, psychology, philosophy, sociology, and especially education. It was left to Piaget's followers and advanced methods of brain imagery to teach us what we now know—that the brain of a healthy individual continues to grow and change perhaps all the way to death if there is adequate stimulation in one's environment. Our minds grow stronger from use and from being challenged in the same way that muscles grow stronger from exercise.[5]

Piaget's theory of how we acquire knowledge helped me to see that the intellectual hunger and discontent that I was experiencing prior to my therapeutic experience was due to an imbalance between two processes that he calls assimilation and accommodation. Assimilation is the process of *integrating new stimuli into existing mental structures,* accounting for a *quantitative* change in our brain. Accommodation is the process of *creating new mental structures or modifying old structures,* accounting for *qualitative* change in our brain. By understanding the difference between these two processes, I could see why my cognitive dissonance and depression had occurred. Ideally, while these two functions are separate, they operate in a coordinated and balanced fashion as a person matures, creating a state of internal stability that Piaget calls *equilibrium*. The stable equilibrium between them characterizes a complete act of intelligence. Without assimilation, there is no sense of continuity, but without accommodation, there is no sense of change, and no way of escaping a repetitive monotony.[6]

> *"If accommodation and assimilation are present in all activity, their ratio may vary.... When assimilation outweighs accommodation, thought evolves in an egocentric or even autistic direction...."*[7] *"Reality is subordinated to assimilation which is distorting, since there is no accommodation."*[8]

These two processes occur as we acquire knowledge. It begins in the infant, by using simple reflexes—sucking, grasping, reaching, crying, following a moving object with the eyes, responding to a mother's voice and face, the infant develops many purposeful behaviors to solve problems. By the time the child is two or three years old, she has developed the needed mental structures capable of *symbolic* thought—that is, using words, objects, and actions as *symbols* to express what he or she is learning in the environment, an example of *accommodation*. The child's brain has matured so that speech becomes possible. Over the next several years, the child will acquire a vocabulary of many hundreds of words, and even learn to put them together and make coherent sentences, an example of *assimilation*.

While Piaget saw these developmental changes as inherent, he also recognized the influence of one's environment. A child growing up with few people talking to her will be slower in learning speech than one who has a rich source of stimulating conversation surrounding her. Ideally, the two functions of accommodation and assimilation will occur constantly in a balanced fashion throughout one's life as new motor and thinking skills are acquired and practiced.[9]

It's easy to see these changes taking place in a growing child, but how do these processes play out in adults? Piaget explains that our emotions serve as self-regulators. They are the "motor" behind any conduct. Feelings of anxiety, boredom, guilt, or frustration can be signals of a need for new challenges.[10] An accommodation may be as major as a career change or a divorce, or it can be as subtle as a change needed in our attitude. For me it was an acknowledgement of the tedium I found in the repetition of the religious study books that were a mainstay to my mother, but forever stayed the same to me. Though there was a security in thinking that we knew and understood a predictable plan for the world and humankind, its instruction for the last twenty-four years was no longer meeting my needs. It wasn't pertinent to my everyday life; it wasn't offering me new ways of looking at my experience; it wasn't encouraging me to discover my own unique truths. My emotions of themselves didn't modify my cognitive structure, but they came into play as motivation to seek a new path toward equilibrium. I believe I had been assimilating too long into a structure of justifying my decisions on an externally imposed dogma for how I should grow and develop. This made every action of my life a matter of urgency that created anxiety. I also felt coerced to do things I didn't really want to do.

Piaget presents our need to engage in cognitive activity as wired by evolution to orient the organism *to bring to balance what is not in balance*. If the capacity is there, we are motivated to use and develop it. A child doesn't need external motivation to crawl or walk or talk. I could trust myself to know what I needed to learn. This was a liberating concept for me. The books my therapist suggested I read were like water on parched ground. All my university courses were exciting to me—even the statistics class that necessitated my hiring a tutor. I felt free to reach out and explore unlimited unknowns. I treasured the metaphor of the plant that is hidden in a dark closet. The vine will seek the light and manage to find its way through the crack of daylight beneath the door.

In Piaget language, I was overdue for an accommodation. But I also learned that the process of accommodation can take time until equilibrium returns. It is often accompanied by feelings of vulnerability—like the moments of panic I experienced during my early stages of graduate school. In this respect, the metaphor of the crab shedding its old ill-fitting shell and growing a new one was helpful. Until the new shell has formed, it is vulnerable without reliable protection. A sense of well-being returns when the accommodation is achieved.

Once I completed my graduate program, I was hired to teach full-time at the community college—child development courses in a preschool education program, lifespan development courses in a nursing program, and marriage and parenting courses for general studies. Most of my students were adults. It was sheer joy for me to share with them the theories I had learned. I designed my curriculum to encourage students to apply what they were learning to their real lives. I asked them to recall their experience of learning to ride a bike or drive a car. Because their brain had reached a stage of development whereby they could learn these new skills, they were sufficiently motivated to endure a period of discomfort while their brain was *accommodating* a new goal. Maybe the beginning was awkward—falling off their bike a few times or stalling their car in the middle of an intersection. Every individual action required their utmost focused attention in order to stay upright on their bike or maneuver their car through traffic. They were willing to devote the time it took to practice this new skill. Before they knew it, they were doing these motions automatically with little conscious thought. Now they were *assimilating*, and had even forgotten the discomfort they felt when first learning a new skill.

We also discussed what happens when accommodation is forced due to unplanned life circumstances, like the diagnosis of a serious illness, the death of a loved one, or being fired from a job. I asked my students to think of times in their life when they were thrown off balance by having to *over-accommodate*. One young woman shared her experience of getting a divorce, moving to a different town, and enrolling in the college nursing program full-time, all within a few months. The first semester was overwhelming for her until she dropped two courses and proceeded on a part-time basis, an adjustment that restored her balance. We discussed how stressful conditions can lower our immunity to disease or create acute psychological problems—symptoms of a disruption in equilibrium.

In the life-span human development course, each student had a self-chosen project. They were to carefully think about something they would like to learn that would be personally beneficial. I wanted them to experience this feeling of self-motivation. They would then design a strategy for gathering pertinent information and perform some kind of experiment or exploration that would reveal qualitative results. Every student project was different. One wanted to stop smoking, another wanted to improve her marital communication, and the most unusual one wanted to understand why someone would choose to sky-dive. He read about it, interviewed others who were doing it, and ended up doing it himself.

In an essay on assimilation and accommodation, Jack Block applies the ability to maintain a balance in our cognitive activity to personality, motivation, the management of anxiety, resiliency, and competence.

> *"... consider that cognitive disequilibration is also an indication to the individual that the world, or a portion of it, does not make sense or have meaning and is therefore not predictable or manageable....It therefore seems reasonable to view a registered cognitive disequilibration as a signal to the individual, an alerting to a survival threat however indirect or far removed."*[11]

He goes on to explain that assimilation, the use of existing mental structures, is the first line of adaption (or defense) for the individual attempting equilibration. If doing the same thing we have always done fails, its inefficiency can be expected to result in intense and agitated anxiety. In this case, the individual must endure a time of unease until a creative accommodation is being worked through. If the unease exceeds one's personal limits or tolerance for anxiety, the individual may return to assimilative efforts to find a way to avoid the problem. Other individuals may shift too readily to a flighty or reckless accommodation out of desperation. Overreliance on either strategy will prove dysfunctional. With intelligent adaptation as a goal, *"the race can be expected to go to the individual who shifts over to accommodation from assimilation neither too late nor too early."*[12] The constructs of "competence" and "efficacy" may be described as a function of an individual's personally chosen changeover point from assimilation to accommodation.

It may seem commonplace wisdom to know when one needs to make a change. But I have found and observed that change doesn't come easy, because I am inclined to want to repeat what is familiar, even when it's not getting me the result I want. It takes a conscious choice to try something new, and courage to endure the temporary discomfort. But it is strengthening to know that by recognizing symptoms of disequilibrium and choosing to act on it responsibly will increase the vitality of my brain. In rethinking all the different stages I am writing about in this book, I see that each change has come about as an effort to restore a sense of balance or equilibrium to my life.

References:

[1] Bybee, R. W. & Sund, R. B. 1990. *Piaget for educators,* Second Edition, Prospect, Illinois: Waveland Press, Inc., pp. 46, 47.
[2] Evans, Richard. 1973. *Jean Piaget: The man and his ideas,* New York: E.P. Dutton & Co., p. 106.
[3] Singer, Dorothy and Tracey Revenson. 1996. *A piaget primer: How a child thinks.* The Penguin Group.
[4] Bybee & Sund 1990, pp. 6, 7.
[5] Cohen, G. D. 2005. *The mature mind: The positive power of the aging brain.* New York: Basic Books.
[6] Piaget, Jean. 1970. In P.H. Mussen (ed.), *Carmichael's manual of child psychology,* Vol. 1 (3rd ed.). New York: Wiley & Sons.
[7] Piaget 1970, p. 708.
[8] Piaget, Jean. 1951. *Play, Dreams, and Imitation in Childhood.* New York: Norton. p. 86.
[9] Ginsburg, H. and Opper, S. 1988. *Piaget's theory of intellectual development,* 3rd ed. Englewood Cliffs, N.J.: Prentice-Hall.

[10] Evans 1973, p. 7-8.
[11] Block, Jack. 1982. Assimilation, accommodation, and the dynamics of personality development. *Child Development*, Vol 53, No. 2 (April), p. 291.
[12] Block 1982, p. 292.

8

LIFE TRANSITIONS

The breach in my relationship with my mother still demands my attention as I seek to find other things we have in common. I sometimes run roughshod over her feelings out of desperation to assert my autonomy. Other times I withdraw emotionally rather than risk a clumsy attempt at support. It's a difficult time for both of us. Dad has retired now, so with more time on his hands, he's looking to Mom more for companionship. I hope that my withdrawal might help them to reach out to one another in new ways, but I don't know if this is happening.

The summer of Dad's second year of retirement, they visit us in Prescott. Dad complains of not feeling well and his appetite is poor, which is unusual for him. He's so rarely sick that even the slightest illness is a worry to him. He isn't able to enjoy the children as he always has. I insist that he see a doctor when they get home and he says that he will. Two weeks after they get home, Dad is diagnosed with pancreatic cancer.

Bonnie and I take turns flying back to Oklahoma to be with Mom and Dad at critical times of his treatment. John lives in Tulsa and visits them every day. Dad recovers from surgery and seems to be responding to follow-up chemotherapy. By Christmas Mike and our family have moved to a different home in Prescott on two acres where we can have enough horses for all of us to ride. I express hope to Dad on the phone that he will be strong enough by spring to make a trip to see us. But over the next few months, his symptoms begin to reappear and my hope for that visit fades. I make another trip home in March. One afternoon Mom is away, so Dad and I are in the house alone. He's resting in the bedroom and I go in to see if he's awake. He's lying on his back with his head propped up by several pillows, and he's looking out the window.

"Feeling any better?" I ask.

"Oh, not too bad."

I sit down on the bed beside him. "Do you feel like talking a little?" He glances at me and then looks away—but he doesn't say no, so I venture further. "There's something I've been thinking about. Remember when you and Mom were visiting last summer? Your stomach was bothering you then, and you didn't have much appetite." He nods without looking at me. "We talked about it and you were worried because you didn't know what was causing it. Do you remember that?" He nods again. "Well, now we know. It's not what we wanted to hear, but at least we know what we're dealing with."

"I never expected it to be this though."

"I'm afraid of losing you," I say, knowing this will evoke the dreaded show of emotion. With tears welling up in my eyes, I continue. "Do you know what I did the day Mom called about your diagnosis? First I curled up on our couch and cried … for a long time. I was afraid for all of us—not knowing how we would ever get along without you. I knew I wouldn't be able to take care of Mom as well as you do. I tried to think of something I could do that would make me feel stronger, give me confidence that I could make it on my own without you. I decided to do something that I've always loved doing with you—something we might not ever be able to do again, but that I could do by myself. I went shopping ... for a new outfit ... something that I really liked, and I thought it would be something you would like too—except that it wasn't on sale." I laugh as I weep and lean over to rest my head with my ear against his chest, feeling the quiver of his silenced sobs. I sit up and seeing the tears in his eyes, I take his hand. He doesn't resist, but he turns his head to the window. "I've always worried that you might have thought that I cared more about Mom than I do you, because Mom and I talk so much. I think you are stronger than Mom and that she has needed me more, but that hasn't meant that I loved you less. I want you to know how much I love you and how much I appreciate everything you've done for me." I don't expect Dad to verbally respond, and I don't want to convey that expectation. I've said what I want to say and it's enough. I kiss him on the cheek and leave the room.

The next day John comes to take me to the airport. "I'll be back real soon, Dad," I tell him before I leave.

Two weeks later, Mom calls to tell me that Dad has had a stroke. He fell while trying to get out of bed and suffered a brain hemorrhage that caused massive damage. He can no longer speak and is totally bedridden. I fly home for the fifth time this year and go straight from the airport to the hospital. Dad is sitting up in his bed with an unfamiliar vacant stare on his face. I greet him, but he doesn't respond. He looks at me, but without recognition. I hesitate to move too close, so I sit down in a soft chair beside him and make useless comments about the room, the flower arrangements, and the view out the window. Still nothing. I lean back and close my eyes and try to get in touch with what I'm feeling. Though there's a heavy sadness, my old fear of saying goodbye is gone. Like his early morning departures after a visit, Dad has once again left early and avoided a painful goodbye.

I'm comforted to think he doesn't know what has happened to him. The doctor thinks he'll die soon because of the stroke. Brain tests confirm the damage is severe, but he lingers on for two more weeks. Finally he's moved to a nursing home and five days later he dies of pneumonia, a merciful end. He was only sixty-eight.

Bonnie, John, and I worry about how Mom will adjust to being alone; she has never lived by herself. At first she avoids being at home alone by doing things for others, using the car Dad left to take her women friends shopping or to appointments, meet with others in a senior citizen's center, teach a little Bible class, visit nursing homes, and play the piano for the people there. But her nights are difficult, so she keeps a radio by her bed and listens to Larry King all night. "*Coming home, there is no one waiting for me or caring if or when I come home,*" she writes in her journal. But then she describes "coming to her senses."

> "*I've learned some good lessons since Walt died.... I used to think, am I just Walt's wife or John's mother? Yes, I was that person and it satisfied me, but now I am someone else. I am Hope, enjoying my independence, deciding how to spend my time, where to go and when to come home. I can be with friends when I need them, but I can enjoy just being with myself.*"

❦

Leslie is fifteen and Dan eleven the year I complete my master's program, but I am working on some additional credits

I need in order to enter a certification program in marriage and family therapy, a goal I've set for myself. I'm wondering if Mike and I discontinued our therapy too soon because we're drifting apart again. Our work with Clara helped us for about two years, but apparently neither of us has learned how much time and conscious effort it takes to stay in touch with another person. We're both busy getting our needs met by doing the kinds of things that feel familiar, activities that don't involve each other. But maybe this isn't such a bad thing at this time in our lives. Perhaps I'm depending too much on Mike to meet my relationship needs, playing the victim instead of taking more responsibility for myself. Delta has bought out Western Airlines, changing Mike's operational base from Los Angeles to Salt Lake City. Missing his military flying, he's joined a reserve helicopter squadron in Utah. One weekend a month he doesn't commute back home, but stays over in Salt Lake City to fly with this reserve unit. Right now he's excited about coordinating some "war games" with a Marine Corps jet training squadron in Yuma, Arizona. I'm still teaching and taking classes to learn how to help other people with *their* marital problems, while struggling with my own.

A year goes by and Mike is flying as an airline captain now with enough seniority to get his choice of schedules. He's also purchased a small airplane that he houses at the local airport where he's become acquainted with a group of other pilots. Each with their own aircraft, they enjoy flying together to attend air shows within range about the country. The friendships he's developed from this activity are important to him.

Meanwhile I've begun working on a clinical internship at the local mental health clinic, forming new friendships with other therapists. Once a week I travel to Tempe with recordings of sessions I've had with clients to play, discuss, and receive instruction from my academic supervisor. At this stage I'm seeing individual adults at the clinic, not yet couples or families. Each person presents a unique kind of distress that results from an earlier damaged relationship, usually with a parent or other family member. I'm seeing firsthand how deep-seated anxieties from early experiences will inevitably create dysfunction later.

One young man is fearful his wife is going to leave him. His closest relationship as a child was with an older brother who protected him from an abusive father. When my client was nine, this brother died from an illness, leaving the boy to fend for himself.

Another is a homely middle-aged woman, adopted as an infant by a mother, who grew so ashamed of her daughter's physical appearance that she confined the adolescent girl to her room when company came for dinner. Her closest relationship is with her pet dog.

A lonely elderly woman, estranged from her husband, shares a childhood memory: She wrote love notes to herself on little pieces of paper, folded them up tightly into tiny little wads that she hid inside petals of flowers. Later she would retrieve them, pretending they were messages from fairies who loved her. Each relationship with a client provides meaning that moves me one step further toward developing a philosophy about my work.

Mike and I are on two separate tracks. When there's tension between us, it's usually over conflicts about time allocated for family. We're also having problems with Leslie. She took the family car out late one night to meet her boyfriend without permission, failed to engage the emergency brake on her return, and the car rolled off an embankment. Mike is furious and I try to protect her.

This morning I wake up feeling weighted down by a sadness about Mike and me. I cry for a half hour. He seems unavailable, but he probably feels the same about me. The difference is that I am losing the hope I had before—I thought we were making a connection and now that's not there anymore. I'm afraid we aren't going to keep growing together. It's so sad because I think we both have what it takes, but it feels so hard. A part of me wants to be alone. That feels easier, but then I'm always encouraged when he acts like he cares. I believe that when we are loved as children, we grow up loving ourselves and being receptive to the love of others. If we are not sufficiently loved, we will never be quite sure of ourselves. Either we seek that acceptance from others or we're so afraid of being hurt, we'll do almost anything to keep others from getting too close. This makes for many kinds of imbalances in relationships. I think Mike and I are on opposite ends of a continuum. I'm so desperate for acceptance that I'm inclined to give love without regard for myself. He, on the other hand, is so afraid of being hurt that he withdraws and even alienates those he loves. We both need to move closer to the center in order to find a balance. I don't want to give up on my marriage.

After my student internship is over, my next step is to complete a period of supervised clinical work with a licensed marriage and family therapist, in this case a woman who maintains a private practice in Phoenix. I am working with Anne as one member of a small group of other therapists seeking certification. At first we watch her work with a couple or family through a one-way mirror and then discuss the session with her later when it's over. When we're ready, each of us takes turns working with Anne as a co-therapist while the rest of the group look on. Finally, when we're prepared to work on our own, Anne and the group are there for support, watching us behind the one-way mirror. It's an interesting and exciting process as we learn from each other.

    Anne recommends that each of us have at least one family session with her to identify any dynamics in our personal lives that might undermine or have bearing on our work. Mike agrees to several sessions in which we discuss our struggles over time allocated for our family and the difficulties we have dealing with Leslie. Anne suggests that Leslie might be a reliable barometer for some strain going on in our marriage, so we follow up with a session that includes the children to give them some reassurance. I'm not sure if it's because we lack confidence in Anne, or maybe ourselves, but we decide not to continue. I sense that both of us are reluctant to confront any conflict between us.

    I do invite my mother, Bonnie, and John to join me in a "family of origin" session with Anne. Mike is able to get free airline tickets for all three of them to come. The main outcome of this session is an affirmation of John's new role as the man in the family. In our discussion about our family's dynamics, Mom is dismayed at the implied magnitude of her influence, but this provides an opportunity for the three of us to assure her of our love and support.

    Once certified, I begin working at the local mental health clinic part time in the afternoons, scheduling all my classes at the community college in the mornings. In less than a year, I open my own office in a newly built complex in downtown Prescott. It's near the back of a building, away from the noise of the street, and I enjoy furnishing and decorating it into a pleasant and peaceful working environment for my clients and me.

    I know that I'm fortunate to be doing what I consider the most important work in the world—helping people enrich and strengthen their relationships, a crucial source of human happiness. I want this to help me be compassionate, understanding, and less judgmental—to see people struggling to do their best with what they have.

Sometimes I get frustrated and I have to remind myself that I can't be all things to all people. The courts are referring mediation cases to me when there's a child custody disagreement. Those are the most difficult. I can be an influence, but I can't control anything when there's no will to change. I want to believe in the power for good in every family I see, and I have to trust that good things are happening. My practice is picking up and the TV parenting classes are going well at school. But deep down, when I'm in touch with the part of me that's the most real, I know that Mike and I are deriving little emotional nurturance from one another.

※

Leslie is in her first year of college in New York and Dan is in his last year of junior high. Needing a new challenge, I've undertaken a new doctoral program at Northern Arizona University in Educational Psychology in Flagstaff. It's December 8, 1984, my forty-third birthday, and I've just gotten out of the first class I'm taking this fall semester. Mike is spending the day at the airport and Dan won't be home for several hours, so maybe just for fun, I'll stop by the shopping center I've noticed on my way out of town. I'll have lunch and do some shopping to celebrate my birthday. Maybe that will perk me up. By 2:30 I start the hour-and-a-half drive back to Prescott, still fighting back some disappointment that this class I'm taking isn't what I'd hoped it would be.

I pull into our driveway and notice that Mike's pickup is there, so he's home. I open the front door and go in, when suddenly, Mike, my good friend Sally, and six of my former work colleagues at the clinic jump out in front of me from in the hallway where they were hiding, screaming "HAPPY BIRTHDAY!" Stunned, I notice the dining room table set beautifully for a fancy meal—obviously all Sally's doing.

"WHERE HAVE YOU BEEN?" she asks with some undisguised irritation in her voice. "We've been waiting for hours! You were supposed to be home by noon!"

"I'm so, so sorry! I had no idea! Why didn't you go ahead and eat?"

"We couldn't do that!" someone says. "It's *your* birthday!"

"I didn't know, so I stopped in town after my class and had lunch and did some shopping. I am so, so sorry. I really appreciate what you have done." I see Mike in the background and I realize that he's been stuck at home most of the day with my party guests, all but Sally he hardly knows, waiting, waiting, and waiting.

Well, I guess we were too good at keeping a secret," Sally says, laughing. "Let's eat, everybody!"

The mood becomes a little more jovial once everyone has food in their stomachs, but I still cringe when I think of how difficult this afternoon has been for Mike. He has little in common with the group of people he has hosted for what has been a very long afternoon. This experience accentuates our separate and diverging paths.

Three months later, I'm hoping a week-long Caribbean sailing trip with two other couples won't be another calamity in reverse. I'm not looking forward to it. Mike and two other men in his military reserve unit have come up with the idea, and the boat is already rented. I'm worried about being cooped up on a sailing yacht with four other people I don't know very well, and Mike and I aren't getting along famously ourselves. We're in the car on our way to Phoenix to shop for sailing gear and clothing we'll need for the trip.

"Sometimes I wonder if you and I will really have anything left in common when the kids are gone." I say. He looks over at me, but doesn't comment.

The sailing trip never happens. One week after our conversation in the car, Leslie is diagnosed with a malignant brain tumor, and our lives change forever.

INSIGHTS: Deceiving Ourselves to Avoid Growth

I turn now to the writings of a philosopher, two psychologists, and two family therapists for perspectives that help me understand the period of resistance and avoidance that Mike and I experienced during the time this chapter describes. The philosopher, Martin Buber, believed that humans need confirmation from one another because few of us are so firmly grounded in our self-concept that we can withstand an environment in which our needs and feelings are ignored.[1] Most of us hunger for a love that will stay intimate and secure while also encouraging our individual fulfillment. Mike and I were no exceptions. After Leslie went off to school, I became more aware of how much I had depended on her for emotional affirmation. Instead of turning to Mike to make up for that, I relied on the interactions I was getting from my work, even though I was aware I was wanting something more from him. I don't think either of us understood that in order for a relationship to flourish, trust and intimacy must be expressed between two people, if possible, every single day, so whether we are aware of it or not, we are constantly measuring how safe it is to think, feel, and speak without being rejected by the other.[9] I know I wasn't aware I was repressing those fears, and I don't think this is uncommon with insecure couples who haven't seen real trust and intimacy being exchanged between their parents. We have learned in our childhood that it isn't always safe to let another person know we are afraid. We become accustomed to pushing those feelings out of our consciousness, not knowing that to express them openly to our loved one is the key to making a connection, because that is when we are the most vulnerable, and the most lovable. One reason children are so lovable is because they haven't yet learned to mask their feelings. In order to reach a level of security in a relationship, it is essential that we can trust one another with our deepest fears.

Our self-concept comprises everything we believe to be true about ourselves, including all the assumptions about our strengths and weaknesses. Our self-concept is especially vulnerable to negative attitudes from others, which may include disapproval, invalidation, or just indifference. Unfortunately disconfirmations are common in family life, where family members are completely ignorant of one another's hopes and fears, likes and dislikes, problems and joys. It's difficult to feel deeply loved if we don't know these things about one another, and that can only happen through honest self-disclosure. Without it we are not contributing to each one's sense of identity, except to make one another feel unloved.

I think the tendency to deny the significance of our differences began before Mike and I married. His desire to pursue a military career at a time when I hoped we would both complete our college education was an opportunity we missed to explore and learn more about our core values. Our relationship was obviously meeting some security needs, but the strength of our attachment wasn't strong enough to overcome our fears of conflict. Neither of us was willing to risk its loss.

is continued. Occasionally the system clogs from a bubble in the line, setting off an unnerving alarm that continues until I'm able to troubleshoot and locate the problem.

Every six months we drive to Phoenix for an MRI to confirm the cancer isn't coming back—additional cause of acute anxiety. The only time I find some measure of relaxation is when Bonnie flies from her home in Maryland every three months to visit. I can trust her to take care of Leslie and Dan so Mike and I can get away, usually to Phoenix, for a weekend. This is the only time I'm able to draw comfort from sexual intimacy. Ellen, my close friend from college, makes two long-distance air trips to be a support to me during two different times of crisis. Visits from Prescott friends, however, become less and less frequent, so my ongoing telephone contact with Ellen and Bonnie is an indispensable source of support.

Once Leslie's chemotherapy regimen is finished, she begins to gain some strength, and our family even takes a short vacation to Durango, Colorado the second winter of her illness. She wants to explore going back to college. We learn of a program for severely disabled students that is available at the University of California in Berkeley. Though participants can hire their own full-time aides, I worry whether or not this will be adequate to meet all of Leslie's needs. Still the prospect of going back to college is giving her hope.

In May of 1987, two years since Leslie's diagnosis, an MRI and CT scan reveal the return of the tumor. We learn the bad news on the same day that Leslie receives her notice of acceptance into the Berkeley program. This leads to our selling our home in Prescott and moving to Salt Lake City, Mike's current work base, so he doesn't have to commute. Now, at least, we can all be in the same city where Leslie will receive follow-up treatment. We make the move in August when Dan

We both had reason to fear conflict. Barriers to relationship growth emerge from the way we have learned to respond to conflict, and most of us learn that from our families of origin. I grew up in a home environment where it wasn't safe to acknowledge a conflict between family members. Tension and resentment existed, but weren't spoken of, so conflict was perceived as something frightening and threatening. As children, if my siblings and I began to quarrel, we were banished to separate rooms. When we knew there was conflict between our parents, we rarely witnessed them working through a sensitive problem successfully. They didn't fight nor even openly confront each other; problems were simply avoided and not talked about. Since I didn't observe problem-solving in Mike's family, I can only describe what I saw in his parents and heard directly from him. His mother was very forthright in speaking her mind, while his father was somewhat meek, unless he was drinking. When a conflict arose, it could quickly escalate into violence, involving both pain and humiliation. We both feared conflict, but for different reasons.

Conflict occurs in all close relationships. People are by definition different from each other, so it is inevitable that any two people will sometimes come into conflict—which can be defined simply as a difference in what two people want, need, or think. However, it isn't the conflict itself that creates difficulties; it's how we handle it. If conflict leads to criticism and blame, it becomes a disconfirmation—a threat to the way we believe we are. When our self-concept is threatened, we will naturally strive to protect it.[2]

Few of us understand that there are healthy and unhealthy ways of protecting ourselves from painful threats, depending on how available they are to our conscious awareness. A "coping mechanism," for example is considered healthy because it is a *conscious*, purposeful effort to respond to a personal affront or problem. It might mean calmly questioning a person about an offensive remark, ignoring a criticism, focusing on something positive, finding a remedy or solution, or seeking help from others. A defense mechanism, on the other hand, is an *unconscious*, automatic, reflex-like response to protect the individual from experiencing excessive anxiety. It functions in various ways to keep the self-concept intact, unchallenged, and unchanged, meaning the painful feelings must be kept out of our awareness. Because feelings then "go underground," the defensive mechanism is referred to as "repression." [3]

When a thought, feeling, or need has been repressed, that doesn't mean it simply fades out of existence altogether. Instead, the repressed feelings and tensions continue to operate as unconscious determiners of behavior, because the original causes of the repression tend to reoccur, but under different circumstances, throughout life. It is a sign that repression is at work when we refuse to examine our motives for a given action, or selectively forget something that has happened in the past. Defense mechanisms make it possible for us to continue believing we are the kind of person we want to believe we are, an effort to deceive ourselves, so consequently, they may result in some distortion of reality. We were born with a natural intent to be curious and open to learning. Defense mechanisms, on the other hand, are learned strategies to protect us from fearful situations. To be protected is to be closed, hard, and defensive; to be open to learning is to be soft and curious. They are mutually exclusive; we can't be both at the same time. Though we freely choose our intent, it happens so automatically, we usually are unconscious of making the choice.[4]

> *"An unacknowledged intent is like a shape you stumble over as you're walking through your own living room in the dark. It's your living room; you know it well.*

Walking through it ought to be easy. But when it's pitch dark all you can know is that there's something there hindering you—and you won't find out what it is or be able to avoid it in the future until you're willing to turn on the light and look."[5]

Recently I read through letters that Mike wrote to me while in Viet Nam expressing his anticipation of getting home and being a father to Leslie, and I believe those hopes were sincere. But the circumstances that prevailed once we became a family set the stage for both of us to follow the patterns that existed in our families of origin. Having been Leslie's only parent for a year, my relationship with her already mimicked my enmeshed relationship with my mother. Because of my head start, I already viewed myself as the more competent parent. Mike had a role model of a weak, unreliable father and a strong-willed mother. Neither of us had the knowledge or awareness to function without the influence of both those precursors. *"Protecting against emotional pain is a pattern learned in childhood, once necessary for a child's survival, but no longer productive for adults."*[6]

The reality of our situation was that we both were insecure parents, sorely in need of support and affirmation from each another. Instead of acknowledging our fears and asking for the help we needed, we both adopted defense mechanisms that protected us from our feelings of inadequacy. Had I been more secure in my own parenting role, I might have been more reassuring to Mike. Had he been more confident, he might have insisted on taking more responsibility with our children. Instead we fell into easy ways of fooling ourselves. I could blame him for not taking a more active role in our family, and he could blame me for being controlling, excuses for us both to withdraw into our own familiar preoccupations. *"If every time a person was threatened, he or she put on a heavier suit of armor, then in time that person would be immobile—safe but out of touch.*"[7]

Could it have been different? Phebe Cramer, in her well-researched book, *Protecting the Self*, addresses two important questions: (1) If we are concerned with growth and self-understanding, shouldn't we want to know how we might be deceiving ourselves? (2) If defense mechanisms are beyond our conscious awareness, how can we learn about them in ourselves?

Cramer defines three types of defense mechanisms, denial and projection being the most common, each one representing a different level of complexity and maturity. Denial, the simplest form of defense mechanism, is the refusal to see, hear, or understand a thought, feeling, or perception of some aspect of reality in order to avoid anxiety associated with its existence. Denial can begin very early. Cramer describes the use of unconscious denial in her four-year-old daughter, who was given the gift of a mirror by her aunt. One day the little girl presented the mirror, broken, to her mother, saying "I didn't break it." Her mother, seeing the look of confusion on her face, could see it wasn't an effort of conscious deception—a lie. In that moment her daughter believed what she said in order to protect herself from either self-reproach or reproach from her mother.

Projection, a more complex mechanism, involves attributing one's own undesirable thoughts, feelings, or intentions to others in order to avoid acknowledging them in oneself.[8] Projection is more common in older children and adults and was the defense mechanism that I used when I complained that Mike was not spending more time with the family. It was too painful for me to believe that he would rather spend time with his men friends than with me, so I projected my own hurt onto Leslie and Dan, and presented it to Mike in terms of the children needing him, not me. It was easier to perceive his inattention as a rejection of them. I believe now that I would have been more effective with Mike had I been completely honest and confessed my own fears of being rejected by him. This might have opened up a completely new line of communication between us.

Defenses work because we are not aware of their function. We project our own hurt, anger, or envy onto someone else to absolve ourselves of the discomfort of painful or unacceptable thoughts or feelings. To realize we are doing this we would have to acknowledge our own unacceptable feelings. Such an admission would be cause for self-reproach and anxiety. Cramer reminds us that human thinking is not always logical or reality based when it comes to protecting a vulnerable self-image, so that even the most conscientious and intelligent person may resort to self-protection through the use of defense mechanisms. We are particularly prone to return to a childhood behavior when we are under stress.[9]

Marriage and family therapists, Jordan and Margaret Paul, believe that the only effective way to bridge the distance that is created between two people due to defense mechanisms is to understand the powerful hidden motives that keep us fixed in our present behavior. They use the term "intent" to refer to the unconscious motivation that dominates and creates the most difficulties in relationships—the intent to protect ourselves against any pain, especially that which comes from disapproval and rejection.

If a relationship is to grow, two people must dismantle the defenses that get in the way of freedom and intimacy. An outside observer is often more apt to identify the nature of a defensive behavior in someone else because they don't share the same need to protect the self. This is when a sensitive therapist or a caring relationship partner can be of great help in bringing into consciousness the existence of a dysfunctional defense mechanism. Once a person recognizes and understands that he or she is being defensive against some threatening impulse or feeling, the person may achieve voluntary control over the defensive behavior. "*To be aware of the operation of the defense should thus render its disguise function ineffective.*"[10]

If pressures against change are too frightening, we may ignore or distort the reasons for change in order to avoid the fear and uncertainty that almost always are involved. In hindsight, I think Mike and I were both feeling shut out and unimportant. Since our fear of being rejected and losing one another's love diminished our own confidence, we projected that lack of confidence onto a therapist who might have helped us. We don't live in a process-oriented culture, so when we see a problem we don't like, we judge it and want to change it rather than understand it. We look for an immediate solution rather than seek to understand why the problem arose. I was learning all the pertinent theories and applying them to other people, but I wasn't able to apply them to myself.

I think we both used all three categories of protective behavior that the Pauls describe. *Compliance* is giving ourselves up to avoid a conflict by denying our own feelings or needs. *Control* is trying to change the other one by making him or her feel guilty or afraid. *Indifference* is ignoring the conflict and withdrawing into separate activities in order to imply that we couldn't be hurt or controlled by the other. Before we could find a mutually satisfying solution to our problems, we would have to understand more about ourselves and each other. We would need to shift our focus from a power struggle to an adventure in exploration and discovery. Then maybe we would be able to ask ourselves why things were the way they were and what was getting in the way of each of us getting what we wanted.[11]

Once a conflict brings our fundamental beliefs and fears to the surface, the resolution will be a combined achievement in that both partners will have changed as a result of new awareness. The resolution is often one that was not even imagined before the exploration began.

References:

[1] Buber, Martin, 1965. *The knowledge of man.* New York: Harper.
[2] Jourard, Sidney with Ted Landsman. 1980. *Healthy personality: An approach from the viewpoint of humanistic psychology.* New York: Macmillan Publishing Co.
[3] Jourard 1980.
[4] Jourard 1980.
[5] Paul, J. and Paul, M., 1985. *Do I have to give up me to be loved by you?* Minneapolis, Minnesota: CompCare Publications, p. 7.
[6] Paul & Paul 1985, p. 10.
[7] Jourard 1980, p. 212.
[8] Cramer, Phebe. 2006. *Protecting the self.* New York: The Guilford Press.
[9] Cramer 2006.
[10] Cramer 2006, p. 30.
[11] Paul & Paul 1985.

9

DEATH AND DIVORCE

Suddenly everything about our existence is unfamiliar, as if we've arrived on an alien planet. Mike and I are drawn together in mutual shock, anguish, and need of support from one another. Talk of our troubled relationship is a far distant matter. The tumor is a highly malignant medulloblastoma located just above Leslie's brain stem, the part of the brain that controls the autonomic nervous system, motor coordination, and balance. It's the size of a lemon, the doctor says. We fly to New York for the emergency surgery that takes place on May 20, 1985, near the end of what has been Leslie's second semester at Hunter College. A further complication of her condition occurs three days after the surgery to remove the tumor, when Leslie suffers a stroke. The extent of brain damage caused by the surgery and stroke is unknown to us or her doctors. Still they proceed with radiation treatments during her semi-conscious state.

These are difficult hours, days, and weeks, during which I examine some of the beliefs I've held since I was a young child. It came naturally to me to find security in a child-like faith in a spiritual being I called God, who knew and loved me personally. Nothing in my life until now has caused me to question the biblical promise that "all things would work together for good" as long as I continued to trust and try to do God's will. I think about a devout Christian couple I knew of who had a young daughter who was brutally raped and murdered, and still they clung to their faith. But I'm asking, what then does it mean to trust in God's care and keeping if those things can happen? My mother says this is to test my faith, and this is how I've coped in the past with any trying experience. But why does Leslie have to suffer in order that I might be tested? This would be cruel. I've never understood the Old Testament story of Abraham being tested by God to see if he would be willing to slay his own son. Why would a loving God ask a father to kill his son? I'm feeling hurt, angry, and betrayed by what I've been taught all my life about a supreme being, to whom I consecrated my life, and from whom I could receive guidance, protection, and providential care.

When Bonnie comes to visit, she brings a book by Harold Kushner for us to read together, *Why do Bad Things Happen to Good People?* It addresses all the questions I'm asking right now. Kushner holds to a belief in a God that is not all-powerful and therefore predicts that suffering will come to all human beings randomly, regardless of one's virtue or belief. With that assumption I wouldn't look to God as the source of protection from loss or suffering. In some way this makes more sense and is less hurtful than the notion that I'm being tested or punished by a vindictive guardian, but it raises other questions. Am I no different than anyone else in relation to this God? Does the creator of all things really have no personal interest in me? Is this God only involved in the big picture, putting in motion the creative process and evolution, then standing back to see what happens?

I'm drawing comfort from the thought that I may be no different from all the other parents who have children in this pediatric neurosurgical ward at New York University Hospital. Leslie's hospital roommate, a girl her age, has been in an automobile accident. Her head is clamped inside a vice in order to prevent any further damage to her brain, and she can't speak. Another child down the hall is in a coma from nearly drowning, the damage to his brain still unknown. The parents of these children are just as concerned about their child as I am about Leslie. Is this why I feel no inclination to pray? Wouldn't it be the height of arrogance to ask for special consideration?

I'm consoled to think that I'm just another member of this multitudinous human family, subject to all the threats to life and limb that everyone else is. Perhaps I can hold on to a perception of a God who has compassion for the world at large, and perhaps has even provided some means of restitution, like that of what Christians profess. But the next best step for me is first to decide how I'm going to deal with this and then rely on the support of other people in my life who also love Leslie, and that of the doctors and nurses who are doing their best to make her well. But I also won't expect any miracles.

Some years before, I read Viktor Frankl's book, *Man's Search for Meaning*, and in the hospital library I discover another book by him, which I quickly devour. His core lesson for me is that the difference between one who is destroyed by adversity and another who is strengthened by it is simply a *choice*. I'm finding this awareness to be of greater comfort and strength than any previous confidence I've had in a personal religious faith. It's an idea that I can draw on that gives meaning at every moment my brain is functioning. I have a choice as to how to think, feel, and act.

It so happens that the mother of the girl who is Leslie's roommate is bitter and resentful about her daughter's tragic accident and the resulting damage to her brain. Though she tries to conceal her anger about her daughter's fate, it comes out in a harsh, rancorous manner and tone of voice in her communication with her daughter. I can understand how the mother feels, but I worry about how her attitude might be affecting the girl. This is helping me realize that what I want more than anything in the world is to be good for Leslie. Frankl's book has made me aware of a choice I can make. So I make a conscious decision to be optimistic, compassionate, brave, and open to discovering something positive to do or say each day, not just with Leslie, but with the doctors and nurses who are trying to help her. This task I've assigned to myself is enough to give me the meaning I need, and with that meaning, I'm finding strength.

By early July Leslie is showing signs of awakening, so is moved to a rehabilitation unit adjacent to the hospital. A regimen of chemotherapy begins along with physical and speech therapy to aid in her recovery. Because her balance and coordination are profoundly compromised by the surgery and stroke, she is unable to walk, speak clearly, focus her eyes, or swallow. In spite of these massive disabilities, we are deeply thankful that her cerebral cortex has not been damaged. Her thought processes and the personality characteristics that make Leslie who she is are still intact. It's a joy to be able to communicate with her again and to observe that she is still lucid and contemplative in her thinking, even though she struggles with her speech.

I've been in New York with Leslie now for nearly four months. Mike is requesting flight schedules into New York so he can be with us during days off. A trusted college student of mine stayed with Dan until school was out and then Mike brought him to New York so our family could be together. In August we are able to take Leslie in her wheelchair on the plane to Phoenix to another rehabilitation hospital nearer our home where intensive therapy can continue. By early September we bring her home to Prescott and our family resumes some measure of normalcy.

Having resigned from my teaching position at the college, I continue to see a few clients in my office at home. We purchase a computer and a "talking books" recorder for Leslie and by using an eye patch over one eye, she's able to type and complete a correspondence course in American Literature. Mike is a co-caregiver in regard to Leslie's needs when home on his days off. He has arranged for a driveway to be bulldozed up to the second story of our split-level house so we can load Leslie in her wheelchair into a van equipped with a hydraulic lift. Every night when Mike is away working, he calls. The crises associated with Leslie's illness are frequent, and I depend on him for support in regard to them. Side effects from chemotherapy—nausea, loss of appetite, and severely low blood counts—are serious obstacles and sometimes life-threatening. More than once Mike has arrived in Los Angeles to begin a trip and then has to turn around and come right back home. If at all possible, he is here when I need him.

Dan seems to take the adjustments in stride, but cancer isn't easy for a sibling of the patient. He enjoys good friends at school, doesn't complain, and he provides companionship for Leslie when she sorely misses her friends. I worry constantly about Leslie. It disrupts my sleep, so I worry about how I will survive on so little rest. Nurses at the hospital have trained me to operate the IV catheter through which she receives nourishment directly into her bloodstream until she is able to swallow. Once she is finally able to eat some, her appetite is poor, especially after chemotherapy, so the intravenous feeding is to begin his junior year in high school, a difficult adjustment for him. He and Mike both face a loss of friends and familiar activities, so we retain a condominium in Prescott where they can stay when they return there for visits. Having adjusted to that loss already, Leslie and I look forward to the change.

Though Leslie enjoys a few months of relief from her symptoms, by November there are signs that the new chemotherapy regimen isn't sufficient to kill the new growth of cancer cells; her condition begins to deteriorate rapidly. Her personality, wit, and ability to deal with the present situation remain the same, but she is gradually losing her short-term memory. She can't remember our move to Salt Lake City and she frequently confuses our current house with our house in Prescott. To follow a mental process that requires more than several minutes of concentrated thought is difficult unless we assist her in following a sequence. It is devastating for us to witness what Leslie has feared most—the loss of her cognitive powers, but mercifully it lessens her anxiety about her illness. My mother comes to be with us during the Christmas holidays, but the sadness for her and our family is almost unbearable. Two weeks after Mom returns to Tulsa, Leslie dies.

Neither Mike, Dan, nor I have known such grief—unspeakable grief. It's as if each of us has pulled away and crawled into our own little dark hole to search for comfort. Mike begins to spend more time in Prescott with his pilot friends. Dan goes along with him at times to visit his friends. I have nothing to return to in Prescott. I begin writing about Leslie as a way to hold onto her, fearful that I might forget something if I wait too long. I feverishly seek activities to fill the huge void her death has left.

In Salt Lake City, a "peace network" is organizing around the presidential bid of Jesse Jackson. Leslie heard him speak in New York and was inspired by his message of equality and justice for the minority poor. I'm compelled to do something in memory of her, something she might have done. I go alone to the first organizational meeting and am moved by the group of people who are crammed inside a tiny old house near downtown—people of every color, socio-economic class, and people with disabilities are there—united in a common cause. I think maybe I can be a part of a movement to break down the barriers that sustain injustice in our country. I tell Mike about my new prospects with the peace organization.

He's not pleased. We have met a couple through his reserve helicopter squadron, and are enjoying their company. He doesn't want me to tell them about what I'm doing. "It could affect my top secret status," he says. My anger flares.

"I don't care. I'm going to do this no matter what." Then more calmly, "I'm more excited about this than I've been about anything since Leslie's death. I don't want it to come between us and I don't want you to feel threatened by it." Then we drop the subject.

I'm contacted by a neuropsychologist who is organizing a support group for families with children with brain tumors. Knowing I've been a family therapist, he wants to know if I'm willing to lead the group. I meet with him and one family to explore the possibility, thinking it might be another way I can use my experience to help others. For several months I work with the doctor co-authoring a booklet we will use for families in the support group.

I also write a prologue and several chapters to be the beginning of a book about Leslie, which I take to a writers' workshop in Park City. When it's my turn to present my manuscript, I feel put down by the instructor's comment: "I think it's too soon for you to write about your daughter." She too has lost a child. I pay an extra fee to have one of the guest professional writers critique my manuscript and his advice will prove to be helpful, twenty years later.

After one trip with his dad to Prescott, Dan tells me the parents of his best friend have offered to let him live with them for his senior year so he can graduate from Prescott High School. I don't want him to go, though I know he isn't happy in the Salt Lake City high school. He's the only student of color there and has made only one good friend, another boy whose family has just moved to the city, but neither of them has become involved in social activities. I don't want to be alone when Mike is gone, so I plead with Dan to stay. There's a good community college in Salt Lake City where he can find job training opportunities after he graduates, but the more I try to persuade him, the more determined he is to leave. One day he throws a can opener down on the kitchen floor in anger. "I'm moving to Prescott in the fall, no matter what you say." I don't want to fight with him anymore.

Dan gets a temporary summer job in the city and continues to make plans to move to Prescott. Mike has never unpacked all the personal memorabilia he had on his office wall in our home in Prescott, so I know that is where his heart is too. Mike is going to drive one of our cars down there one weekend, so I decide to go with him. My job at the community college has been passed on to someone else and I don't relish the idea of jump-starting my counseling practice again, but I think I should at least consider going back to Prescott. As we approach Prescott from the north, I'm flooded with memories of the last year there with Leslie and I fight back tears. I try to imagine living in the condo, but when we get up Saturday morning, Mike leaves for the airport and doesn't come back all day. My friend Sally has moved to another job in Flagstaff and there isn't anyone else here in Prescott I want to call. On Sunday morning Mike leaves again for the airport, so I pack my bag, call a taxi to the airport, get on the feeder airline to Phoenix, and fly back to Salt Lake City. A note on the kitchen counter in the Prescott condo explains to Mike that Prescott isn't going to work for me.

I'm starting to conceptualize the changes that are taking place since Leslie died. My observations strangely fit into what I understand about family systems theory—that families function as a unit, each member contributing something important in maintaining equilibrium. Leslie's passion and force must have been a powerful balancing factor, because since she died, I'm feeling a strong motivation to establish more emotional independence from both Mike and Dan. It's as if her death has infused me with new confidence and strength that will somehow restore balance to a disrupted system. I want to assert my beliefs and attitudes more than I ever have before. What started out to be campaigning for Jesse Jackson in memory of *her* has turned out to be a very clear expression of my own convictions and political leanings, beliefs that will put me in conflict with Mike. How is it that Leslie's death has had this effect? I've been thinking a lot about my promise to her months ago, that if she dies, I will find work I enjoy. She was aware that teaching and counseling were drains on my energy. She also knew I became bored with work that offered little change or diversity. A return to work that feels restrictive or oppressive will be a betrayal to both Leslie and me. I want to explore some work possibilities here in Salt Lake City, opportunities that I don't have in Prescott.

One day I notice an ad in the classified section of the newspaper for a job with Novell, a computer software company headquartered in Salt Lake City. I've not heard of it, but I ask around and learn that this is the company that developed the first networking software that enables personal computers to be connected to one another. Not only that, it can support a complex system of computers in different locations all over the world. I also find out that the University of Utah is a user of their product. The ad says they are looking for someone with a master's degree in education who has technical writing experience to do course development in their education department. This sounds exciting! In this job I wouldn't be expected to deal with people's personal problems, so I would have time to withdraw into a little cocoon to heal emotionally. Things change much faster in the private sector than in public education, so I also wouldn't get bored. I know I can write, but I expect to come up short in technical skills. I pick up the phone and call the University of Utah operator who puts me in contact with the data processing department. I speak to a computer technician who is happy to accept my offer to pay him fifty dollars if he will tutor me in a crash course on Novell's software next Saturday. This gives me the confidence to respond to the newspaper ad and schedule an interview. I don't learn much in my one day of tutoring, but I do mention to my interviewer that I made an effort to learn about their product. She concurs, however, that my lack of technical skills will be a drawback, so I leave the interview feeling discouraged.

A week goes by and I hear nothing, so I apply at the university women's center for a counseling job and I agree to an interview with them, but I'm not nearly as excited about another job in the counseling profession. To boost my spirits, I fly to Oklahoma City to spend a three-day weekend with Ellen in a new apartment she has recently rented. Monday morning, having returned to Salt Lake City the night before, I'm awakened by a 7:30 a.m. phone call. It's the woman who interviewed me from Novell! Will I come in again to meet the education program director? In that interview I'm offered the job. I buy two prints, one of Central Park and one of

Washington Square, Leslie's two favorite places in New York, have them framed, and hang them in my new cubicle. After I get to know the woman who interviewed me, she tells me that the main reason I got the job was that I wanted it badly enough to hire a tutor to learn about their product.

Dan moves into the home of his friend in time to start school at Prescott High School in the fall. I communicate with the boy's mother frequently to be sure she continues to feel comfortable with the arrangement. Mike is genuinely happy about my job, and his days off spent in Prescott become more and more frequent. I'm concerned about our relationship. I can't recall ever feeling so out of touch, so unable to make a connection, but I don't quite know what is happening. I believe I'm on a positive track, that I'm in the right place, that it's the right time, and that I'll see my way through this, no matter how it turns out. I'm learning to follow my own instincts rather than what someone else expects of me, and that's what Leslie did so much better than I.

In October Mike and I agree to a trial separation to begin in January. On a weekend that Dan comes to Salt Lake City for a visit, together we tell him of our plans. He's devastated and totally unprepared for this news. We explain it is an experiment—that we are both unsure about the future of our marriage and we need this time before we make any permanent decision. Mike will make the condo in Prescott his primary residence, while keeping a layover commuter apartment in Salt Lake City. We will sell the house and I will find an apartment nearer my work. I will keep all Dan's personal belongings with me and I promise he will have a room of his own wherever I am. The three of us spend Christmas together, but I have no written record or memory of what we did to celebrate; I'm sure it was painful.

I find a beautiful three-bedroom apartment that makes up the lower level of a split-level home in a nice residential area near downtown Salt Lake City. Dan returns to Prescott when the holidays are over, and Mike helps me move in and even meets the older couple who live upstairs. The day we close the sale on the house and leave there for the last time, Mike breaks down and cries. "It's so sad," he says. I know it is, but I can't cry. I'm in automatic mode, going through the motions, not allowing myself to feel much of anything.

We agree to have dinner together once a month to stay in touch with how we are feeling and to be a support to Dan. Mike and I attend Dan's graduation together in Prescott in May. We ask him what he would like for a graduation present and he says: "A trip together somewhere out of the country." We decide on the Virgin Islands and Mike schedules his work so we can spend a week there in June, but at the last minute he decides to go to an air show instead. Dan and I go to the Virgin Islands without him, but it isn't much fun. On our last afternoon there, when Dan leaves to go to the swimming pool, I take a lawn chair out to a grassy spot overlooking the ocean to write in my journal. I sit there for a while watching some brilliant red hibiscus flowers sway in the breeze quietly beside me. I begin to feel a new strength that maybe now I have enough information that will give me the courage to leave my marriage.

I know that marriages don't end because of the faults of one. I've read that when a marriage is strong at the onset of a child's illness, the child's death can strengthen a marital bond, but I also read that the death of a child has destroyed many marriages. The bonds were weak between us before Leslie got sick, so I have to face the reality that Mike and I may neither have the will nor the capacity to recover what we have lost between us. During the ninth month of our separation, I fall ill with bronchitis and stay home from work for a couple of days. Feeling vulnerable and lonely, I dial Mike's number at his apartment in town on the chance he might be there. He answers the phone.

"It's me. I'm not feeling well, and I'm afraid we might be making a mistake," I say.

"Well, we can talk about it."

"No. I just want to know if you would be willing to get back together and try again. I don't think you need time to think about that. I need to know now."

There's a long silence. Then he says, "No, I don't think I can do that."

"Okay. That's all I need to know. Thanks for your honesty," and I hang up. Instead of feeling let down, I'm relieved. His straightforward admission lets me know that he's sharing in the responsibility of ending our marriage. This was something we were deciding together and it would be best for both of us.

I hire a lawyer and file for divorce. I know there's a three-month waiting period, so the divorce will become final at the end of our year of separation. I'm nervous the day I go to talk to the government official who will decide if I am justified in ending my marriage. I'm prepared to tell him this long story to assure him it isn't something I'm taking lightly. I sit down in front of his desk where he has the papers spread out before him. He doesn't look up.

"Where was your last shared residence?" he asks. I give him our last Salt Lake City address.

"Where are you currently living?" I give him my apartment address.

"Where is your husband living?" I give him Mike's address in Prescott, Arizona, and explain that he has a commuter apartment in Salt Lake City.

"That's all I need to know … if you'll just sign here."

"What do you mean—that's all you need to know?" Surely this isn't all there is to it.

"Your husband left the state. In doing so, he legally abdicates his responsibility in the marriage."

"Oh." It really is that simple.

I have examined my motives for getting a divorce and it's important to me to be clear that I'm not ending one relationship in order to replace it with another. I also don't want to think of my marriage and parenting as a failure. If the success of any life experience is measured by how much we learn, then all of it can be meaningful and valuable. People change, our needs change, and if a relationship is no longer meeting our needs, hopefully we have the courage to move on. Leslie met more challenges in her twenty-one years than most people have in eighty, and Dan is embarking on new challenges for himself. During the three years of Leslie's illness, she and I had an intense personal relationship. When I could see that she was going to be as dependent on me as she was when she was an infant, I thought of it as having a second chance to make up for the mistakes I made the first time around. She, too, wanted to make it good for both of us. We focused on one another's needs, continually making an effort to be appreciative and considerate of one another. I have no regrets about my relationship with her, and if I never have another relationship as meaningful as that one, it has been enough. I know I will be okay if I never remarry.

Now that I'm single again, I'm looking forward to spending more time with my most loyal friend, Ellen, who has also suffered a tragedy in her life. After Ellen completed her PhD at UCLA in 1979, she accepted a position in Brussels to teach within a UCLA adult education program there for U.S. military personnel. Because Ellen's moving out of the country was unsettling for her parents, she made a trip home to Oklahoma City a few weeks before her departure to reassure them that she could fly home in just a day or two in the event of an emergency. I receive a shocking telephone call from her a few days after she arrives there. Her father, so dreading her leaving, had left Ellen and her mother sitting at the breakfast table one morning, gone out to the garage, and shot himself in the head, a successful suicide. This left Ellen with no recourse but to cancel her Brussels plans and stay in Oklahoma to care for her despondent mother. Shortly after her father's death, she got another position teaching philosophy, religion, and English at Rose State College in Oklahoma City.

The first Christmas after my divorce, Ellen, Dan, and I meet at a nice hotel in Scottsdale, Arizona to celebrate the holidays. Dan is living with Mike in Prescott, waiting tables at a restaurant downtown, and attending Yavapai Community College where I used to teach. Ellen and I help Dan find a used pickup truck for transportation to and from work and school, and I co-sign on the loan. Possibly because he isn't motivated enough, or he lacks the support he needs, or he is still too unsettled from all the changes that have disrupted his life, Dan eventually drops out of school and decides to enlist in the Marine Corps. Mike is happy with this decision, and though I distrust the influence of the Marine Corps, I hope that it might provide some needed structure for Dan.

My job with Novell is exciting, challenging, and fun. After one year of developing courses, I'm put in charge of the company's "train-the-trainer" program. Product sales are expanding into international markets where it's no longer feasible for the company to provide training for all their resellers and technicians. My job is to develop a program whereby the company will maintain a small staff of two dozen instructors who will travel the world to provide training to associate instructors in each state or country. Those associate instructors will, in turn, train others to sell and maintain the product. It's a major transition attesting to the company's success, and I'm earning more money than I've ever dreamed possible. I have four new gold fillings in my teeth to show for it.

My grief and need for alone time have limited my social life. I enjoy where I live and I occasionally go on walks with a woman who lives in my neighborhood. She was one of Leslie's nurses who made frequent house calls at the end of Leslie's life. On the weekends I usually need to do research for whatever course I'm working on. I have a key to the office building and I often spend a Saturday or Sunday in the company library looking for articles that describe the product at its inception, when it was simpler to understand. Then I'm better able to comprehend all the new revisions that are taking place. I'm learning how competitive the field of technology is—how quickly things change—and I love the stimulation, often contrasting it to the boredom I sometimes felt teaching the same course over and over again.

The only other people I know in the Salt Lake area are my fellow employees, most of them a generation younger. I'm inclined to stay to myself and not call attention to my age, but the company has a tradition of recognizing birthdays. The education department has grown, and I'm now a program manager. I hope the day will slip by without notice of my birthday, but the afternoon of December 8, I'm given a surprise birthday party. Someone asks, "So how old are you, Kate?"

"I'll give you a hint. I was born the day after Pearl Harbor was bombed." Not one person in the room knows the year of that historical event.

By now I'm traveling all over the country to deliver training. Often I combine a trip with a visit to Bonnie's home in Maryland, a stopover in Tulsa to see John and Mom, a visit with one of Leslie's good friends in California, and once I meet my cousin from Indiana in Chicago. At the beginning of my third year, I spend two unforgettable weeks in both Hong Kong and Italy setting up training programs. I never thought I would be traveling alone in a foreign country. The company is doing so well, a group of employees are rewarded for hard work with a pleasure trip for ourselves and a significant other to Hawaii. I call Bonnie and invite her to go with me. We've never taken a trip together like this before. She flies to Salt Lake City, and after that everything is paid for, including a brightly colored Hawaiian shorts outfit for each of us.

INSIGHTS: What Can Be Gained from Human Suffering?

The writings of psychiatrist, Viktor Frankl, his personal experience of survival in German concentration camps, later impacted the work he did with people suffering from terminal illness. His perspective helped me recognize, understand, and therefore change the way I try to respond to painful experience. Two of his books were of significant help to me in dealing with Leslie's illness, and a deeper examination of them since then has continued to influence my attitude about aging.

Viktor Frankl was born to devout Jewish parents in Vienna, Austria on March 26, 1905. In his autobiography, he describes his mother as a kindhearted and deeply pious woman, and his father as stoic, with a strong sense of duty. Though his father once struck him with a walking stick in a fit of anger, he personified justice and provided his three children with a sense of security. From a very early age, young

Viktor wanted to be a doctor, and he recalls a family friend who called him "The Thinker" because he asked her so many questions. Even as a youth he pondered questions about what might be the purpose and meaning of his life. While he saw himself as a rational, thinking person, he also acknowledged having deep feelings as well.[1]

It was a natural choice for Frankl to choose psychiatry as his profession, but he was also fascinated by philosophy. An article that Frankl wrote which was published in a scholarly journal concerned the link between psychotherapy and philosophy, and the importance of meaning and values in psychology. By this time Frankl had developed two basic ideas that were to remain with him the rest of his life.

> *"First, it is not we who should ask for the meaning of life, since it is we who are being asked. It is we ourselves who must answer the questions that life asks of us, and to these questions we can respond only by being responsible for our existence.... The other basic idea maintains that ultimate meaning is, and must remain, beyond our comprehension ... something I have called 'suprameaning'... in this we can only have faith."*[2]

In these two statements Frankl differentiates between two kinds of meaning, one that we are personally responsible for ourselves and that must be of our own creation, and another far-reaching meaning that is beyond our understanding. He often referred to psychiatry as "the healing of the soul," leaving to theology "the salvation of the soul." As a psychiatrist, he avoided any reference to his personal religious beliefs.

By the time Frankl was twenty-four and still a medical student, he had parted ways with the philosophical and psychological theories of his two most influential teachers, Sigmund Freud and Alfred Adler, and had begun to formulate his own theory. He used the term "logotherapy" as the name for his theory, taken from the Greek word "logos" which denotes "meaning." His emphasis on one's *will to find meaning* as the primary motivational force in a human being was a departure from Freud's pleasure principle—*the will to seek pleasure* on which Freudian psychoanalysis is based, or Adler's *will to seek power*, on which his individual psychology is based.[3]

The premise of Frankl's theory is that we are responsible for assigning meaning to our lives—not in a broad, general sense, but rather a specific meaning of a person's life at any given moment, which may differ from person to person, from day to day, and from hour to hour. He used the analogy of a question posed to a chess master:

> *"'Tell me, Master, what is the best (chess) move in the world?' There simply is no such thing as the best or even a good move apart from a particular situation in a game and the particular personality of one's opponent. The same holds for human existence."*[4]

It was the immediacy in Frankl's placement of responsibility on the one suffering to find meaning in their experience that resonated with me. I was not finding comfort in my religious faith, and though Frankl acknowledges that religion can be one way a person can find meaning, it wasn't working for me. Frankl was describing how dying patients and quadriplegics were coming to terms with their fate. He called my attention to the fact that no matter what happens, it is not just an option, but the responsibility of each person to choose the way in which she bears her burden.

He also reminded me that life has a way of making us see that there is a gap between what one *is* and what one can *become*. I knew that a change was needed in my thinking because the ways that were familiar to me in dealing with stress were inadequate for this situation. I needed something that would be there in each moment, something practical and tangible I could hold onto. Frankl was task oriented. He believed that we discover our meanings through action. He quoted Goethe:

> *"How can we learn to know ourselves? Never by reflection, but by action. Try to do your duty and you will soon find out what you are. But what is your duty? The demands of each day."*

Frankl proposed three possible ways to find meaning in life—even up to our last conscious moment—each one realized through one of three kinds of values—creative, experiential, and attitudinal values. First, we may find meaning by creating something of value. We mistakenly limit creativity to the arts, when it can be a deed we want to accomplish, a chosen vocation, or a worthwhile goal to achieve. Second, we may find meaning through direct experience with what we believe to be good, true, or beautiful—being receptive to the wonders of nature, art, music, or literature. These values can be fulfilled by the mere intensity with which they are appreciated, independent of any action. This would include the experience of becoming fully aware of the essence of another human being, learning to love that person, and seeing the potential of the beloved person, which may not yet be actualized. Third, we may find meaning by facing a fate one cannot change, a hopeless situation that is neither fruitful in creativity nor rich in experience. This group of values, called *attitudinal* values, is among the deepest values because they lie precisely in one's attitude toward the limiting factors in one's life. The opportunity to realize attitudinal values is present whenever a person is confronted with an unavoidable destiny. The way in which one accepts the inalterable fate, the courage one manifests in suffering, the dignity one displays, is the measure of one's human fulfillment.[5]

After Frankl graduated from medical school, he spent two years as an apprentice in the University Psychiatric Clinic and another four years working in a mental hospital. By 1937, when he was thirty-two years old, he opened his own private practice as a specialist in neurology and psychiatry. By this time he had sharpened his diagnostic skills and further developed the precepts of logotherapy, which he was making into a book he entitled *The Doctor and the Soul*. In March 1938, Hitler's troops marched into Austria, bringing his private practice to an abrupt end. Most Jewish professionals immediately applied for visas to other countries, but Frankl was caring for his aging parents, so he accepted the offer of a position as chief of neurology at Rothschild Hospital in Vienna, hoping this would provide him and his parents protection from deportation to the concentration camps.

It was at Rothschild Hospital that Frankl met and came to love Tilly Grosser, a station nurse. Tilly and her mother had also been given the benefit of protection from deportation to the camps because Tilly was a nurse. In 1941 Tilly and Viktor were one of the two last Viennese Jewish couples to obtain permission from the National Socialist authorities to wed. Not officially, but *de facto,* Jews were forbidden to have children. Jewish women, found to be pregnant, would be deported immediately to a concentration camp. The medical establishment was instructed not to interfere with abortions on Jewish women, so when Tilly became pregnant, she chose to sacrifice the fetus she was carrying.

As the situation in Vienna grew more ominous, Frankl completed his first draft of *The Doctor and the Soul,* in the event that he might be deported, and he sewed it into the lining of his coat, thinking that at least the basics of logotherapy might survive him. Still, he didn't know to what extent that the principles in his book would be tested in his own life. As Viktor and Tilly both feared, the day came when a new regulation came out canceling their protection from deportation. Nine months after their wedding, both Viktor and Tilly and their families were deported to the Theresienstadt concentration camp, Hitler's "model ghetto," known to be less reprehensible than most. It was here that Frankl experienced his first trauma of being in a concentration camp. He was among many well-educated Jews who were forced to do hard physical labor under dreadful conditions. In bitter cold weather with little means of heating the prison huts, the prisoners received a daily meal consisting of a bowl of thin soup and one small piece of bread. Nights were spent with nine other men resting on a tiered wooden plank with only two blankets to share between them, meager clothing, and ill-fitting, if any, shoes. One day, after a few hours of hard labor and indescribable torture, Tilly saw him being dragged back to his barracks with over 30 bodily wounds. She rushed to his aid, bandaged his wounds, and took care of him best as she could.[6]

It was at Theresienstadt that Frankl's father died of pneumonia and starvation at the age of eighty-one. Tilly was granted a two-year exemption from transfer to Auschwitz because she was working in the Nazi munitions factory, but Viktor, his mother, and brother were scheduled for transport to Auschwitz, the very name associated with gas chambers. While Viktor knew Tilly would want to go with him, he pleaded with her not to volunteer to do so. Still Tilly did volunteer without his knowledge and was approved for transport also.

Fifteen hundred persons traveled by train for several days and nights, eighty people in each coach, everyone struggling with luggage carrying personal possessions. Viktor and Tilly had a few minutes together before the men were separated from the women. The SS guards with loaded guns had spread out blankets into which they were to throw all their possessions. Frankl tried to take one of the guards into his confidence, desperately explaining that the roll of paper they discovered in his inner pocket was the manuscript of a scientific book. "It contains my life's work. Do you understand that?" he pleaded. An amused and mocking grin spread across the guard's face. In a matter of minutes, all those of Frankl's group were stripped of everything, including all their clothing, before being herded into a room where their heads and entire bodies were shaved in preparation for showers. With great relief, they noted that it was water that dripped from the nozzles. Their nakedness brought home the fact that nothing was left of their former lives.[7]

Prisoners lost everything they had ever owned, they knew nothing about the fate of their loved ones, and they had no idea of how long the war and their imprisonment might go on. Worst of all was sadistic treatment they received at the hands of Nazi guards, or sadly, fellow prisoners, who were given special privileges for cooperating in the torture of their comrades. Many prisoners lost all hope and any sense of their personal dignity, essentially giving up on the possibility that anything good might come to them. Frankl observed the different stages prisoners went through, the most dreaded being apathy—a lack of emotion, indifference to how one or anyone else feels. He saw that there is a fine line between the state of mind of a person—one's courage and hope, or lack of them—and the state of immunity of one's body. He observed that there were more deaths the week between Christmas and the New Year holiday. He reasoned that the explanation for this wasn't because of harder working conditions or the deterioration of food supplies, but that the majority of prisoners had lived with a naïve hope that they would be home again by Christmas. When that time grew near, and there was no encouraging news, their disappointment overcame them. Under the influence of an environment that didn't value human life and dignity, that robbed one of his will, and made him an object to be exterminated, the person suffered a loss of his core values.[8]

Many times Frankl questioned his belief in human liberty and the principles of logotherapy that he had written down with such conviction with his own hand. Are we no more than a product of environmental factors? Does our behavior here in the concentration camp prove that we cannot escape the influences of our surroundings? Do we have no choice of action? He recalled those individuals who had run into the electric wire fence on the first day of their imprisonment, committing suicide rather than face a despairing future. But he also remembered the examples of a heroic nature—people who, months later, had endured physical and mental torture, and were still walking through the huts comforting others, giving away their last piece of bread. What had made the difference? Was this the very question that could give meaning and purpose to his camp experience?

It gradually became clearer to the doctor that the sort of person the prisoner became was the result of an inner decision, and not the result of the camp environment. He became acquainted with some martyrs who suffered and died in the camps while bearing witness to the fact that this last remnant of inner freedom hadn't been lost. The way they bore their suffering was a genuine achievement, a choice they made that could not be taken away, the very freedom that makes life meaningful and purposeful. This experience could enliven and exemplify all that he had written about attitudinal values.

"... everything can be taken from a man but one thing: the last of the human freedoms—to choose one's attitude in any given set of circumstances, to choose one's own way. And there were always choices to make. Every day, every hour, offered the opportunity to make a decision, a decision which determined whether you would or would not submit to those powers which threatened to rob you of your very self, your inner freedom."

What the doctor had to learn himself (and therefore, what he could pass on to despairing others) was that it did not really matter what we expected from life, but rather what life expects from us. Instead of looking for meaning outside of ourselves, we could turn that search around and ask ourselves this question: how can I make this day, this hour, or even this moment meaningful to me?

Most despairing prisoners believed that any real opportunities in life had passed, yet in reality there was always an opportunity and a challenge, some future goal to which one could look forward, even if it was just a good meal or a warm bed to sleep in. One positive thought could become an inner triumph, or one could ignore the challenge and stagnate as did a majority of the prisoners. Whatever thought that one found to instill hope, it had to consist, not of just talk and meditation, but of positive action. That meant that meaning would be different for every person, from moment to moment, because the person, himself, had to create that meaning. In Frankl's case, their incarceration was their fate, and though all other freedoms had been taken from them, there was one freedom they still had left, and that freedom was that they could respond to their experience in whatever way they chose. The core lesson for him was that the difference between the prisoner who was destroyed by suffering and another who was strengthened by it was simply a *choice*, a choice one made each moment by moment.[10]

Frankl's life had been spared due to a number of fortuitous happenings, the most important of which was his last assignment as a doctor, to prison blocks in a Bavarian camp where people were suffering from typhus. This disease resulted from terrible sanitation and was carried to humans by fleas, lice, and ticks. A fervent desire to rewrite his confiscated manuscript helped Frankl to survive when he succumbed to the typhus fever himself. While ill he jotted down notes on little scraps of paper that would help him recall the contents of his manuscript should he live to the day of liberation. He believed that activity helped him overcome the danger of cardiovascular collapse. But as the war bore on, from verified statistics, he knew that the odds of his surviving were very slim, and he began to lose hope that his "mental child" would survive him. From then on, Frankl's hope ceased to rest in the possibility that he would survive the concentration camps and be able to rewrite his book. He reasoned that if his meaning and purpose in life was contingent on his survival and he died, then his suffering would have had no meaning. Meaning must exist whether one escapes death or not, or ultimately life would not be worth living at all. *"A man's life retains its meaning up to the last—until he draws his last breath. As long as he remains conscious, he is under obligation to realize values, even if these be only attitudinal values. As long as he has consciousness, he has responsibleness."*[11]

In 1945 Frankl was released from the Bavarian prison camp, where he had nearly died of typhus. The day he returned to Vienna, he learned that his wife, Tilly, his brother, and mother had all died in Auschwitz. Though these enormous losses caused an inevitable depression, Frankl decided to remain in Austria and return to his psychiatric work. He felt a strong connection to Vienna, especially to psychiatric patients who needed help in recovering from the effects of the war. He began by passionately reconstructing and revising the manuscript that was destroyed when he was first deported. More than ever before, he believed that the human quest for meaning was the key to mental health and human flourishing. His experience as a prisoner had forced him into a situation where the ideas contained in his manuscript were put to the most severe test. All that he had learned from his prison inmates during their shared ordeal affirmed a form of therapy that his book advocated for people suffering a terminal disease, but it would apply to anyone undergoing unavoidable hardship or misfortune. The same year he dictated in nine days the book, *Man's Search for Meaning*, about his experience in the concentration camps.

Two years later he married Eleanore Schwindt, who was also a nurse like Tilly, but was not Jewish. Elly accompanied him on lecture tours and supported him in his life's work. He chaired the neurology department at the Vienna Policlinic Hospital for twenty-five years and is credited with establishing logotherapy as a means of helping patients resolve their emotional conflicts. He died at the age of ninety-two.[12]

The Doctor and the Soul was the book I found in the hospital library when Leslie was so sick. My observations of the mother of Leslie's roommate raised the question: How am I going to deal with this unexpected and unavoidable misfortune? What value could I draw on to help me answer this question that life was presenting? It was up to me to decide how to respond. I came away from that experience with the awareness that there is always something to learn, and therefore meaning, in every situation if I choose to look at life in this way.

I don't always live up to its lesson, and make a wrong choice without thinking it through and giving myself enough time to clarify the value I'm acting on. This usually happens when I'm swept by fear. As an adult Dan has let me know that he suffered much more than I realized during the time of Leslie's illness and death. Since Leslie's needs were so critical, it probably didn't feel safe for him to add any more demands to the mix. I realize now that my level of anxiety about Leslie prevented me from being as sensitive as I might have been to the needs of both Mike and Dan. My short-sightedness at that time has been a deeply felt regret. I was aware of literature that addresses the effects on siblings when a child dies. Often the remaining child or children feel pressure to make up for the loss. This may have been a factor with Dan, but I also think he suffered from being left with caregivers while I was in New York so we wouldn't have to take him out of school. It doesn't help to dwell on past mistakes, but it does make me want to be more sensitive to the needs of others in the small circle of my closest relationships, especially during the most stressful of times.

Though I do see myself as capable of making the kind of positive choices that Frankl writes of, I do wonder sometimes, with attachment theory as a basis for thought, that some people may have been so deprived of nurturance during the critical years, and perhaps more sensitive to deprivation in general, that they aren't able to make these attitudinal choices I'm discussing here. There are those who believe, as the philosopher Sartre did, that we are all "ultimately free," that happiness can be decided, so that it becomes a moral choice. If we go so far, then sadness is unnecessary and depression is a sign of laziness. But might there be some people, for whatever reason, who may not have the courage to make the choices that will set them free? They may be cut off from the rest of humanity just as some people are in poor, war-torn, developing countries. Some may rise above poverty, but most of them won't.

In my relationships with others, it is always my greatest dilemma to decide whether or not to perceive someone as able to make what seems to me an obvious choice for the better. Is it just a matter of getting more support and encouragement? Or is one so frightened and in need of protecting oneself that making a needed change is beyond one's capacity? I don't think that I could ever say someone was beyond hope, but I also don't want to assume that anyone is to blame for their human struggles. Is there a balance between the two?

References:

[1] Frankl, V. 1997. *Viktor Frankl recollections: An autobiography.* New York: Plenium Press.
[2] Frankl, V. 2006. *Man's search for meaning.* Boston, Massachusetts: Beacon Press, p.109.
[3] Frankl 2006.
[4] Frankl. 1973. *The doctor and the soul.* Translated from the German by Richard and Clara Winston. New York: Vintage Books, A Division of Random House, p. 61.
[5] Frankl 1997.
[6] Frankl 1997.
[7] Frankl 1997.
[8] Frankl 2006.
[9] Frankl 2006, p.66.
[10] Frankl 2006.
[11] Frankl 1973, pp. 44-45.
[12] Frankl 1997.

10

NEW LOVE

Dan comes to spend the summer of 1990 with me before he is to leave for Marine Corps boot camp in September. I look forward to having quality time with him, showing him my work place, and having him see that I'm getting along fine by myself. By now Novell has moved their operation to Provo and I've purchased a condo in Midvale, a suburb just south of Salt Lake City, in order to shorten my commute. My patio opens onto a terrace with a nice swimming pool, which I hope Dan will enjoy with me. I know he's working out to get in shape. Though I've felt that I had a good relationship with Dan, I'm pushing back some feelings of anxiety about his visit. I fear a widening emotional distance between us.

One of my co-workers is hosting a barbeque one night and I want Dan to go with me so I can show off my handsome son. Dan can be charming when he wants to, but he is resisting doing something he knows I want him to do. He agrees to go with me, but wears his sloppiest clothes and makes little effort to be sociable. He's having trouble with one of his knees, so I make an appointment for him to see an orthopedic doctor, who recommends arthroscopic surgery and a knee support while he recovers from the procedure. I take him to a sporting goods store to buy the support and an attractive young girl waits on us and provides helpful information in selecting the best product. I have no inkling that I have said anything during this transaction that might have offended Dan, but when we get out to the car, he lashes out at me in anger. I have embarrassed him in front of this girl. I'm dumbfounded, but apologize while recognizing that something more is going on with Dan than I'm aware of. Is it separation anxiety, worry about boot camp, or some deep-seated resentment toward me? I don't know, but maybe creating some space between us would be a good idea.

It's a warm Sunday morning when I wake up and notice what a beautiful day it is. I wish I had a friend to do something fun with—another single woman perhaps, like me. Though I'm not a church-goer, I've heard about a nearby Unitarian Church that is known for its liberal activism and inclusiveness. Perhaps I might find a kindred soul there. So I go and I'm pleasantly surprised to find a gathering of people, all seated in a circle in a large room, discussing paganism. This is different, I think, and I listen and observe, paying little notice of a man who has quietly arrived late and is sitting outside the circle. When the discussion is over, as I'm walking toward the exit door, suddenly this tall, distinguished man is standing right in front of me! He seems to have come out of nowhere.

"Hi! My name's Tom," he says as he reaches out to shake my hand. "I haven't seen you here before. Are you new to South Valley?"

"Yes, I am—I've never been here before. In fact I've never even been to a Unitarian Church! I thought the discussion was very interesting."

"Welcome, then! How long have you been in Salt Lake City?"

"Almost three years now, but I've been working mostly, so I haven't met many people."

"Well, if you're not a Mormon, and you're new to Salt Lake City, this is a good place to start."

I laughed and admitted that was part of my strategy. That having gone well, Tom suggests we go outside and find a place to sit down in the shade on the grass and get better acquainted. During this first two-hour plus conversation, we learn that both of us have been married before, not only for the same length of time, but for the same exact twenty-five years! We both have also left the religious affiliation that we inherited in our families of origin. He grew up in a large Mormon family in Tucson, and I explain about the Laymen's Home Missionary Movement, my former religious affiliation, which he knows nothing about, and that doesn't surprise me. Both movements began in the late nineteenth century, both had a charismatic leader, and both claimed to have the truth about the origins and destiny of mankind.

Tom smiled and said, "So I grew up in the 'only true church' and you grew up in the 'truth.' We have a lot in common." We both laugh.

"Yes, but I'll admit yours has prospered a great deal more than mine. I'm sure it took a lot more courage for you to leave your group than it did for me to leave mine." Then I learn that it has, indeed, been a difficult process for Tom, the issue that ultimately ended his marriage and continues to strain his relationship with his two adult daughters. Then we talk about our work and how we feel about what we're doing. Tom is the principal of a junior high in Murray, another suburb of Salt Lake City.

"Junior high kids can be a handful," I say, "but it's a fun age to be around—before they reach the drama of adolescence. I remember my son getting in trouble for dropping water balloons from the school's second floor balcony when he was in junior high."

"That sounds typical," Tom says, looking at his watch. "Do you date at all?"

Surprised by his directness, I say, "No, not right now. Dan, my son, is visiting me now, getting ready to go into the Marine Corps in September. He's had to deal with so many changes over the past two years, I'm not sure how he would deal with my dating right now. It's just not a good time."

"I understand," he says and he reaches into his shirt pocket and hands me his business card with both his work and home phone number. "After your son leaves, if you're interested, I'd like to see you again."

When I get home, I place Tom's business card in my bedside drawer where I know I will be able to find it. I think about him a lot; everything I learned in that one conversation suggests he's a person of strong character, courage, and integrity. The date Dan is to report for duty in San Diego is postponed until October. The delay is frustrating for both of us; we're getting on each other's nerves.

One day I take the business card out of the drawer, stare at it a few moments to gather courage, and then I pick up the phone and call Tom. He seems a little surprised, but is glad to hear from me. We decide to meet at a park that is halfway between our two homes to go for a walk. I get there first and am waiting in my car in the parking lot. I'm nervous. What kind of car will he be driving? I hope not a sports car. I want it to be a car that suggests economy, practicality, and no pretense. I'm relieved when he drives up in an older model Chevrolet station wagon. This little park is called Flat Iron Mesa because it's on a high plateau between two canyons in the foothills of the Wasatch Mountains that provides a 360 degree view if you walk all the way around its perimeter. We talk about our relationships, our work, and I tell him more about Leslie. I learn about his philosophy regarding his students: he believes it's more effective to help kids learn to discipline themselves rather than coercing certain behavior. He tells me about seeing a mission statement sign in a car dealership that reminds employees that they are there for the customers. He decides to put up a sign with the *school* mission statement in the teachers' lounge at his school reminding the teachers that they are there for the students. To his surprise, some of the teachers object, so he changes it to the *principal's* mission statement.

He invites me over to his house to watch a football game with him and his brother Clark. What will his house be like? It's neat, clean, comfortable, and also not pretentious. When he learns I have a plumbing problem, he comes over and fixes it. I make dinner for him to return the favor and, while I'm in the kitchen preparing our meal, he falls asleep on my couch. Stroggy (short for Stroganoff), my beloved cat (that was Leslie's pet), is also asleep on his stomach. A wave of affection washes over me.

Tom has to chaperone a school dance and invites me to go with him. I notice how comfortable he is with the students, how much they like him, and the shared playfulness between them. When the party is over, he takes me on a tour of his school, which has increased in size many times over the years. I become disoriented in the maze of hallways and tell him so. "Good," he says. "Maybe I'll have a chance if I can keep you that way."

One night he takes me out to dinner and a concert at the tabernacle in Temple Square. He falls asleep listening to the music, but makes up for it by singing to me on the way home. He has a beautiful bass singing voice.

The blissful anticipation I feel prior to seeing Tom each time leads me to drop out of a computer drafting class I am taking to learn the software. I've never done such a thing! Instead of learning the most popular CAD program as I had hoped, the instructor is promoting his own software invention that isn't nearly as good. He pleads with me not to drop out and even tells me he'll pass me without my taking the final. But I have something better to do. I write to my mother and tell her that everyone should wait until they're forty-eight to start dating.

> *"I didn't think I would start falling for someone so soon, but the more I get to know Tom, the more I see what a jewel he is, and I think I would be crazy not to explore this further. He's a rare combination in that he grew up with wholesome Mormon values, yet he is a free and questioning thinker. At fifty-three, he seems to be less conflicted and more stable, clear, and accepting of himself than men in their forties, who are still fighting the age thing. Maybe by the time they reach fifty, they've come to better terms with it. The nicest part of it is that he seems to be very fond of me! We never run out of things to talk about."*

Tom tells me that after his divorce, he attended a workshop called "Understanding Yourself and Others." In fact, he learned so much from it, he took it a second time. It helped him to better understand the breakup of his marriage and address his feelings of failure. Maslow's theory of self-actualization and Erikson's psychosocial stages of development, frameworks I taught in my human development classes, are familiar to him. We both want to grow and learn from our past mistakes.

I knew Tom was dating several women at the time we met, and I think he might still be seeing one of them now. We are sitting together during a service at the Unitarian Church when I write him a note. "What would it take for you to stop seeing other women?"

"Just ask me," he writes back. After church we go outside and sit in his car to talk about taking this one step closer to an exclusive relationship. "If we decide to make this commitment," Tom says, "I promise you that our relationship will be my highest priority." Little does he know how good that sounds to me.

Formidable glue is beginning to form between us, strengthened by a value and belief that our relationship will only flourish through honest and open communication. My mother once told me that, as a small child, I freely expressed my thoughts and feelings. As I grew older, I learned that I risked being hurt or rejected if I openly disagreed with someone or exposed a tender hurt. I can see that Tom needs to talk about his thoughts and feelings as much as I do.

The angst of adolescence, the guilt about sex, and the fear that I might not be liked are all gone now; this is total pleasure. One day I'm in the car driving to West Valley City to look for a used refrigerator. I hear Lori Morgan singing *"He Talks to Me"* on the radio. I'm so moved by the song, I stop on my way home to buy the cassette tape so I can play it for Tom and tell him that this is how I feel.

One early fall weekend, we decide to go camping in Tom's pickup camper. A light snow falls in the Uinta Mountains. We are standing on a bridge overlooking a trickling stream, when Tom mentions that, after his divorce, he considered joining the Peace Corps.

"I'll marry you if you join the Peace Corps!" I say on impulse, revealing how much I hunger for adventure. He laughs, but I'm embarrassed and I quickly change the subject. But his remark makes a strong impression. Would he really be willing to trade the security of his job at his age for such a risky escapade?

The prospect of an overseas adventure begins to come up in our conversations again. I tell him about an analogy I read in a book somewhere that described the benefits of immersing oneself into a different culture. "A fish is not aware of the water in which it lives and breathes until it is removed from that environment—then it becomes keenly aware." Maybe living in a third world country for a time might provide the change and adventure we both are drawn to, and it might also help us see values we take for granted in a new light.

Ellen comes to spend the Thanksgiving holidays with me and I invite Tom to have Thanksgiving dinner with us. She knows I'm thinking seriously about him. She likes Tom and after he leaves, she says, "I think you should marry him." Later she teases me: "However, since you have already been married once, it's only fair that I have a turn before you marry again." My marriage to Mike didn't jeopardize my friendship with Ellen, but I had plenty of opportunities to have time with her alone by planning at least part of her visits to Prescott to coincide with Mike's airline trips. My regular visits to Tulsa to see my parents are also providing opportunities to see Ellen in Oklahoma City. But I suspect that if I am to marry Tom, it might be different, especially if we continue to explore the idea of leaving the country for a time. I reassure Ellen of my commitment to our friendship, even if it does involve a change.

By December Tom and I are talking about getting engaged, but I'm concerned about the effect this will have on Dan. "Would you like me to talk to Dan?" Tom asks. He knows Dan has a break in his training and is coming to Salt Lake City to spend a few days over Christmas. I welcome his support, hoping Dan will respond positively to a man-to-man talk. I prepare a Christmas dinner for the three of us and later in the afternoon, Tom asks Dan if they can talk privately. Dan agrees and I go upstairs. Tom tells him about our feelings for one another, but that I won't agree to an engagement right away if I know he isn't comfortable with it. Tom explains that Dan's feelings are important to both of us, and Dan responds, "I want whatever will make her happy."

In January Mike and I meet in San Diego for the impressive ceremony that concludes with Dan becoming a real Marine. The physical and mental challenge of boot camp has tested his limits and my impression is that the rigorous training has toughened him in ways that I question. I have doubts about what it may do to his emotional health, but he is making his choice. Ironically, he is assigned to the Marine Corps Air Station at Yuma, Arizona for his first duty station, close enough to Mike that he can go to Prescott for visits.

It's a cold and wintery day, when I experience something in my relationship with Tom that reveals an unfamiliar fear. I'm blind to it at first, only experiencing a feeling of panic when Tom verbally expresses a strong feeling of affection for me. It's something about his intensity I suppose, that frightens me. I don't mention it at the time, but after we part, and the more I think about it, the more panic-stricken I become. I attribute my anxiety to a fear that Tom might not take care of himself emotionally in our relationship, that he would become too dependent on me, and that I would become responsible for his well-being. I am so terrified, I phone him and tell him that I've decided that we should break up. He's incredulous. "But why?" "What has happened? I thought everything was fine between us."

"I know, I know, but I'm afraid we're not going to be good for each other," I insist. "I can't explain it, but I'm sure it's what we should do."

"I'm just now leaving for my men's group tonight, so I can't talk now, but we'll talk later," and we hang up.

In less than thirty minutes, I hear a knock at my door. I open it and Tom is standing there in his overcoat with a suit coat and tie underneath. I'm relieved and happy to see him, a reaction that surprises me. But he looks distressed.

"I couldn't concentrate on the discussion, so I just told them I had to leave," he says.

"Well, I'm happy to see you, and I'm glad you came." I invite him in to sit down. I sit on the couch and he pulls up a chair directly in front of me.

"So tell me what's going on?"

"Well, I know this must sound so crazy, but I've just been feeling that maybe you're going to need me too much. That makes me afraid that you're not going to take care of yourself emotionally—and that really scares me."

Tom was calmer, now that we were talking. "What exactly happened to make you feel this way?"

"I'm not sure, but I know it was when we were upstairs and I was sitting on the bed. You said something that was affectionate … I don't remember exactly what it was … something about how much you loved me."

"So you think that because I really care about you, I'm not going to be able to take care of myself?"

"Yes," I said. "I'm afraid you're going to become too dependent on me."

"So what is it that you would prefer I do—not care about you?"

I smile slightly at the contradiction. "Maybe that would help."

"If I know for sure that this is really what you want, I can walk out of here right now. But is this really what you want?"

"No, I'm not sure now. I was so glad to see you when I opened the door. It surprised me that I was so glad to see you."

"So what does that mean? It sounds like you're wanting me to prove something—how can I prove to you that I won't need you too much? If I leave here and never come back, will that fix things for you?"

"This does sound crazy doesn't it? I'm feeling less afraid the more we talk. Let me try to explain. I developed this framework when I was doing marriage counseling. Usually when people have difficulties in a relationship, it's because the two people aren't secure within themselves. If their personal identity is weak, it will be too threatening to get close to another person because they're afraid of losing themselves. In that case, they do one of three things—try to dominate their partner, submit to their partner, or they'll simply withdraw—any one of those things to avoid intimacy. This seems to be at the root of almost any problem in a marriage. If we haven't done the self-work, we won't be prepared for the together-work."

"I think what you're saying makes sense, but I don't think that's why my first marriage failed.

"Why did it then?"

"I don't think either one of us was willing or able to devote ourselves completely to the success of our marriage. I think both people have to be fully committed to helping their partner get their needs met. If the relationship isn't working for one or the other, ultimately it won't be sustainable," Tom explains.

"But that sounds like you have to give up your own autonomy in order to make a relationship work. I think that's what I was afraid of."

"Do you really believe that if each individual is wholly developed before the marriage, shared intimacy is just neatly going to fall into place? You don't say anything about what has to happen in the relationship in the long term. Sure, it helps to have a positive self-concept to begin with, but we still have to learn how to communicate with each other so we'll know how to take care of each other. That's where I feel like I failed. Maybe you're afraid that *you* won't be able to take care of your*self* in our relationship, and you're projecting those fears onto me," Tom suggests, reminding me of his level of sophistication about psychological processes.

"Hmm ... I learned in therapy that my mother depended on me because she was probably not getting what she needed from my father. In a way, that meant I was expected to fulfill an adult role, which created a lot of anxiety for me. So maybe you're right. Maybe I'm afraid that any real intimate relationship will be too much for me. Mike may have felt safe to me because he didn't expect very much. Maybe neither of us made a real emotional commitment. While I thought all along that it was me who wanted and needed more intimacy, I'm seeing that it probably was both of us who were afraid. Now that I have someone who's willing to make a real commitment to me, it scares me because I haven't known what that means before."

"Well, I don't want you to think that I see this as a one-sided thing. It never is. I'm sure I have my own fears about intimacy," Tom says. "I'm close to being paranoid about the possibility of failing again. Maybe you've picked up on that and it's triggering your own fears. Each of us has to take our part of the responsibility. It's probably something we should continue to explore."

Tom's ability to deal with my fears calmly and a willingness to deal with it together is reassuring, and the evening ends with my believing that the traumatic episode I've experienced is due to temporary cold feet. We both feel an immense relief. We move ahead with plans to be married in April. I list my condo with a real estate agent a few days before leaving on a week-long business trip. I figure it will probably take all the spring months to find a buyer. Much to my surprise, the agent calls me while I'm still in Boston to say she has already received an offer for my asking price.

"Looks like I'm going to have to move in with you sooner than I'd thought!" I tell Tom that night on the phone.

This also means that the time has come to address an issue with my mother. Bonnie has told me over the phone that Mom was surprised to hear from Bonnie that Tom and I are sleeping together. In a letter to Mom about the sale of my condo, I also write:

> *"I don't expect you to accept or condone, but I do hope for your understanding. My attraction for Tom has been very multifaceted, the most dominant aspect, I suppose, being the degree of emotional comfort and security he brings to me. Our sexual relationship has evolved slowly, at much the same rate that our intellectual and emotional relationship has grown. Both of us have anxieties about the prospect of a second marriage. We both are fearful of being hurt again. My anxieties go far deeper than I would have ever acknowledged before meeting Tom. Our sexual sharing has provided a reassurance and comfort for both of us. I think there are some things you can't learn about another person without being as vulnerable. We're not hurting anyone else and neither of us feels guilty about it."*

Mom writes back expressing her own traditional views about sex being preserved for marriage, but she ends with a statement of acceptance: *"My love for you and our relationship with one another goes beyond these kinds of things."*

We are married on Leslie's birthday, April 5, in Tom's home by two Unitarian ministers, a husband and wife. We write our own marriage vows and our three children, Arlene, Ronda, and Dan are our only guests. I prepare a nice dinner for all of us and Dan folds the napkins in a fancy way he learned at an upscale restaurant where he worked in Prescott. He seems proud and strong and I hope that the Marine Corps is good for him.

INSIGHTS: Why We Simultaneously Desire and Avoid Intimacy

I return to the topic of adult attachment styles, a topic opened in Chapter 5, in order to explore more deeply the reasons behind the avoidance of intimacy. The anxiety episode I describe in this chapter was the first major conflict Tom and I confronted in our relationship. We made a correct, though limited, diagnosis at the time—that we both faced fears of failure in a second marriage—but we understood little about the origin of those fears, their depth, or their persistence. We also didn't understand the role attachment insecurity or defense mechanisms had played in our first marriages. The one difference in our favor was that we did recognize my sudden withdrawal as a potential problem and we were both committed to tackling, head-on, anything that jeopardized our trust in one another. With the little awareness that we had at the time, we were able to take a first positive step toward dealing with our conflict—we talked about our fears.

My irrational response to Tom's expression of affection was something I had not experienced before that I could recall. When I had negative feelings toward Mike, they were usually in connection with disappointment or anger. Generally, I saw myself as the one who sought more connection, while seeing him as the one who was resisting closeness. In this case with Tom, it was the first time I'd ever experienced myself as the one wanting to withhold. My fears of being swallowed up by his affection were real and they involved a strong desire to avoid any degree of closeness that might result in a loss of my freedom or autonomy. I had not consciously experienced this kind of fear with Mike.

Tom, too, could see how he might have had a part in triggering my fears. He recalled his insecurities at the time of his first marriage. He had returned from a mission with the Mormon Church, which encouraged returned missionaries and single young women to get married as soon as possible. He had also spent two years in the Navy as a hospital corpsman. He remembered having serious doubts about whether or not he was financially prepared for marriage, and if taking that step would be wise before he had finished his college education. He was uneasy about his future wife's urgency to marry, but decided that perhaps her determination could help them both make it work. Once the knot was tied, he tried to put aside his doubts. This second time around, he was more certain that he was making the right choice for himself, so he felt it imperative that we succeed. He believed himself capable of making our relationship work, but his fear of failing once again could have been interpreted by me as desperation.

Hazen and Shaver's 1987 study originally described the three levels of attachment styles in adults. The Secure style was characterized by ease of trusting and getting close to others. The Anxious style indicated a desire to merge with a partner, coupled with a fear of not being loved sufficiently. The Avoidant style, the one that most closely described my early reaction to Tom's expression of affection, was as follows:

"I am somewhat uncomfortable being close to others; I find it difficult to trust them completely, difficult to allow myself to depend on them. I am nervous when anyone gets too close, and often, love partners want me to be more intimate than I feel comfortable being.[1]

Three years after the Shaver and Hazen study was published, Kim Bartholomew, a researcher at Stanford University, wanted to further examine the motivations of adults who score predominantly "avoidant" in close relationships. While infants have an innate tendency to bond with their primary caregivers, she observed that adults who were categorized as avoidant could vary substantially in their resistance to becoming attached to others. Unlike children, adults differ in how consciously aware they are of unfulfilled attachment needs. Though fear of intimacy and fear of commitment were common themes in the literature, little attention had been given to *why* these adults avoided close relationships. She proposed that there could be four different attachment styles rather than three if the Avoidant style was divided into two categories based on two different motivations.

A four-cell model was proposed that included Hazen and Shaver's Secure and Anxious styles plus two distinct Avoidant styles: *"individuals who desire close attachments but avoid them out of fear, and individuals who claim to neither fear nor desire attachment."*[2] The degree of anxiety they experience in their relationships with others seemed to differentiate between the two types of avoidance, so she developed a relationship questionnaire that included items based on both dimensions of avoidance and anxiety. Bartholomew explains that no one will uniformly match the description of a single attachment style because our images of the self are derived from many experiences over a person's lifetime. Some may show differing degrees of similarity to two or more styles. But by identifying these attitudes that have emerged in the research, we can generally determine that we approximate one style more closely than another.[3]

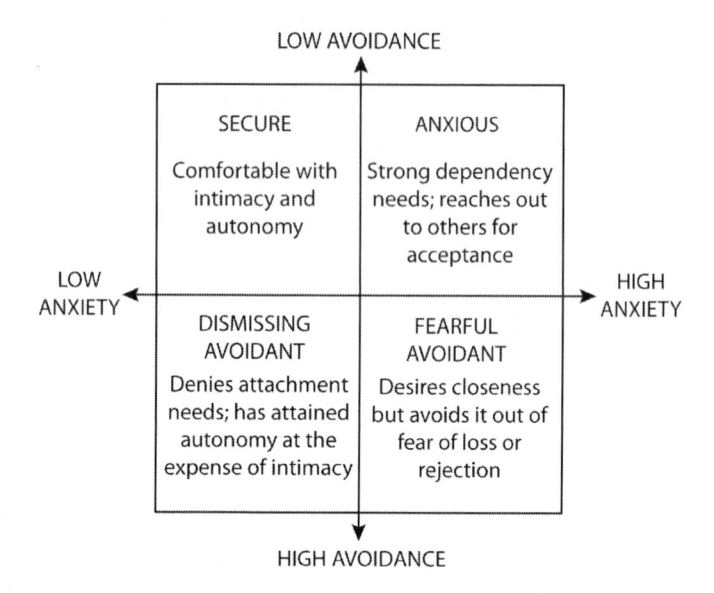

```
                    LOW AVOIDANCE
                         ▲
         ┌───────────────┼───────────────┐
         │    SECURE     │    ANXIOUS    │
         │               │               │
         │ Comfortable   │ Strong        │
         │ with intimacy │ dependency    │
         │ and autonomy  │ needs; reaches│
         │               │ out to others │
         │               │ for acceptance│
  LOW    ├───────────────┼───────────────┤   HIGH
ANXIETY ◄┤               │               ├► ANXIETY
         │  DISMISSING   │    FEARFUL    │
         │   AVOIDANT    │   AVOIDANT    │
         │               │               │
         │ Denies        │ Desires       │
         │ attachment    │ closeness but │
         │ needs; has    │ avoids it out │
         │ attained      │ of fear of    │
         │ autonomy at   │ loss or       │
         │ the expense   │ rejection     │
         │ of intimacy   │               │
         └───────────────┼───────────────┘
                         ▼
                   HIGH AVOIDANCE
```

My interpretations of attachment theory as I have described it have led me to believe that I have spent most of my life working through the different aspects of an insecure anxious attachment with both my mother and father. But when comparing the Anxious and Fearful Avoidant attachment styles, I believe I have manifested characteristics of both, depending on the person I am relating to and the situation.

As an adult I recognized in myself a tendency to be drawn to people who were lonely or depressed, probably due to my relationship with my mother. What I didn't understand at the time was that my mother's disclosure of feelings she wasn't comfortable sharing with my father exaggerated my own sense of importance. She needed me to hear and affirm her feelings and, the more I became adept at doing that, the more secure she felt, and consequently, the more I could also feel secure.

But of course I couldn't do this all the time—not even most of the time. So being close to someone became associated with a feeling of inadequacy. I think the expectation that I will not be quite enough for another person became a part of my personal blueprint for relationships that Bowlby and others describe. This has played out in several ways.

I suspect my attraction to Mike had something to do with the fact that he didn't display a need for my emotional affirmation. Possibly at that stage, Mike was "dismissing avoidant" and I was "fearful avoidant," so he felt safe to me. Mike didn't display any dependency behavior that might have triggered my feelings of inadequacy. The downside to that was that he was prone to make decisions that involved me without discussing them with me beforehand. What did emerge during my marriage to him was a desire to have a partner who was more like my father, someone on whom my children could depend, so it was tempting to see myself as having the greater capacity for relationships and to be the more competent parent. Most of the time, we were on parallel tracks, making a real emotional connection infrequently. By avoiding intimacy, we both developed a strong sense of autonomy.

When I met Tom, I was instantly attracted to his quiet, calming confidence, his willingness to talk about and listen to feelings, and a scrupulous desire to do the right thing. He represented a combination of positive traits in my parents. He felt safe to me too, but for a different reason. Possibly for the first time, he made it comfortable for me to get in touch with my most insecure feelings. I had never before seen myself as an anxious person. In spite of my disappointment in my marriage to Mike, I had in fact enjoyed my independence and the freedom it afforded. My tendency to form my strongest friendships had been with single women, because I had so little in common with married ones. With whatever magic it took,

Tom was also able to acknowledge his own insecure feelings with me so that we both were able to take the first baby steps toward building a secure relationship with one another.

References:

[1] Hazan, C. & Shaver, P. 1987. Romantic love conceptualized as an attachment process. *Journal of personality and social psychology*, Vol. 52, p. 515.
[2] Bartholomew, K. 1990. Avoidance of intimacy: An attachment perspective. *Journal of social and personal relationships*, Vol. 7, 149.
[3] Bartholomew 1990.

11

AN AFRICAN ADVENTURE

In a mountain lodge about sixty miles from Salt Lake City, where Tom and I have gone for a short wedding trip, our first telephone interview with the Peace Corps recruiter takes place. Though teaching school is in the distant past for both of us, use of that background is the quickest way for us, as a couple, to get an overseas assignment together. Our applications have been accepted and we are being reviewed for an assignment. Are we sure we're ready for a two year separation from our families and friends? Are we prepared for a change in our diet, living conditions, and all the deprivations we will encounter in a third-world country? Can we handle having to work with inadequate resources? The reality of this fantasy adventure is beginning to sink in.

We're to report for orientation in Atlanta, Georgia, September 22, 1991. Tom resigns from his job at the end of the spring semester in order to get his house ready to turn over to a rental management company. I decide to continue working until mid-August. The day finally comes when we load two carefully packed and weighed suitcases, a small computer and printer, a heavy solar-powered battery pack to power them, and Stroggy, my cat, into our car for the first leg of our trip to Tulsa to say goodbye to my mother and John. Leslie's beloved pet has high sentimental value in the family, so Mom has agreed to take care of her while we are gone. My sister, Bonnie, in Maryland, has agreed to be our financial and business liaison while we're out of the country.

A reception is held in the hotel in Atlanta the night we arrive. Here we meet the others in our group, the first Peace Corps volunteers to be assigned to Zimbabwe to fill a teacher shortage in this newly independent African country. Twenty-three young people fresh out of college, a thirty-year-old woman, two men in their early forties, and Tom and me (old enough to be parents to most of them) comprise our group. A three-day program prepares us for culture shock and introduces us to the country that will be our home for the next twenty-seven months. Pertinent to what we will be doing in Zimbabwe is that the country has only been liberated from British colonization since 1980 after a long period of guerilla activity. The country's name was then officially changed from Rhodesia to Zimbabwe. Prior to their independence, the country was run by wealthy white British landowners who maintained tight control over the majority African population. Under the new leadership of a war hero, Robert Mugabe, land that was usurped by the British is gradually being turned back over to the Africans, creating great instability and an almost mass exodus of the lighter-skinned population. We are being prepared to enter a culture that still reflects an apartheid regime.

As we deplane in the capital, Harare, I can see huge shade trees covered with lavender blossoms that I learn are jacaranda trees. The sight of them, along with brilliant fuchsia bougainvillea shrubs blooming everywhere, and the musty smell in the warm humid air is intoxicating, a sight and smell that I will always associate with Africa. We receive an impressive welcome at the airport from U.S. Embassy officials and Zimbabwe government dignitaries. Our arrival is on TV that night and a picture of our group is in the newspaper the next day.

We're bused to the Zimbabwe Electricity Supply Authority (ZESA) National Training Centre, a facility normally used to train employees to work for the government-owned electric company. Complete with a dormitory and dining hall, the training centre is our home for eleven weeks of training in Zimbabwean culture and language to prepare us for our teaching jobs. At a reception one evening at the home of the U.S. Ambassador to Zimbabwe, we meet a large group of Americans who are either a part of the ambassador's staff at the embassy or are working in Zimbabwe with the U.S. Agency for International Development (USAID). While this organization's mission is to end extreme poverty all over the world, it is no secret that its workers, like Peace Corps volunteers, are in these third-world countries, not just to help people, but to advance the interests of the U.S. government. Not all of them share our values for being here. Some think dark-skinned people will never be able to run a democratic government successfully, while others are fully committed to assisting the African people in developing their potential.

Once our training is over, we are assigned to teach in two high schools in the Midlands Province, a high plateau with moderate temperatures. Both of our schools are in Mbizo, a township located nine kilometers (six miles) from a larger town, Kwekwe, which is centrally located on the highway that connects the two major cities, Harare and Bulawayo. During apartheid only lighter-skinned people lived in the cities or towns. The darker-skinned people were restricted to living in townships, which were always nearby to provide a workforce for the larger town. Generally the townships are densely populated and most of the housing is limited to survival-level existence.

When we arrive in Zimbabwe, eleven years after independence, there are some Africans who can afford to live in the towns or cities, but the great majority still live in the townships. Mbizo's population is forty thousand. Its shopping area, consisting of a small grocery store, a post office, and a bar, is located on the road from Kwekwe as you enter the township. A large dirt parking lot at the shopping area is full of small kiosks run by women selling fresh vegetables, fruit, and eggs. The township's only telephone booth is also located here.

A unique feature of both Kwekwe and Mbizo is the existence of a huge U.S. owned Union Carbide chrome smelting plant located on the road that connects the town to the township. Three smokestacks continually discharge pollutants into the atmosphere, but no one complains because it's the major source of employment for people in Mbizo. Nineteen residential sections, all with dirt roads, comprise the township. Only one section, the one closest to the shopping area, has running water and electricity. All the rest consist of concrete block structures of different sizes with asbestos roofs, and the family cooks outside. In these sections it is not unusual for four or five families to be sharing one outdoor toilet.

The two high schools where we will teach were built since the country achieved independence, and both are located on the main road going through the township. Tom's school is considered the most advanced, and my school is the most overcrowded. Secondary schools in Zimbabwe consist of Forms 1-4, which correspond to Grades 8-11 in the United States. Tom is assigned to teach Form 3 boys in Vocational

Skills and I will be teaching Form 1 and 2 boys and girls in English. Class periods are thirty-five minutes long and eight subject periods constitute a school day. I'm terrified to learn that there will be as many as fifty students in each of my seven classes (one period provided for planning). We struggle with the question of how we can best make a contribution. We don't want to be just another light-skinned person who knows what's best for them. How can we nurture the freedom to value themselves *for themselves* and not for someone else? We remind ourselves that our main reason for coming here is to examine our own values in light of another culture. We have more to learn from them than they will ever learn from us. We speculate that whatever meaning comes from this, it will probably emerge out of the individual relationships we form, not government programs or service projects. This turns out to be true. Following, I describe just a few of these special people.

Mr. Chipanda

The Zimbabwean authorities assume that we will prefer to live in Kwekwe, but we insist on living in the community where our students reside. Otherwise we will be likened to other light-skinned people who live in Kwekwe, most of whom are racist and have never set foot in Mbizo. Due to the acute housing shortage in Mbizo, we are being housed temporarily in Kwekwe. One afternoon there's a knock at our door. We both go to answer it. A handsome young African man, probably in his thirties, is standing there.

"Hello! Are you Mr. and Mrs. Price?"

"Yes," we both say as we shake his hand and invite him to come in and sit down.

"I'm Chipanda—Champion Chipanda. I teach math and agriculture at Mbizo High School. I understand that you're both going to be teaching in Mbizo."

"Yes, that's right," Tom says.

"And I hear you're looking for a place to live."

"Might you know of something?" Tom asks.

"Well, for the past two years I've been building a house for my family in Section Five." Tom and I are aware this is the only section in Mbizo that has water and electricity—and some of the other teachers at our schools live there. "Progress has been slow," he continues, "because I have to pay for materials as I can afford them. I would consider renting the house to you if I could get enough rent that would help me finish it. The electricity hasn't been connected and there are no kitchen cabinets, but there's a kitchen sink, and the bathroom is finished."

"Where do you and your family live now?" I ask.

"We live in Section Four, but our place is small and we've just had our first baby."

"Aren't you anxious to move into the new house yourself? Tom asks. We're going to be here for two years. That's a long time to wait to get the benefit of all the work you've done."

Mr. Chipanda smiles. "Yes, and what you say is true—but you don't know what it's like to build a house in this country. Your renting my house for two years could help us in several ways. ZESA is run by the government and the government is very corrupt. You're expected to pay bribes to get anything done. I'm not willing or able to do that. I've been waiting to get the electricity connected for months and they keep putting me off. I could be waiting forever, for all I know."

"We're familiar with ZESA. We stayed in their facility in Harare during our training, but we didn't know it was corrupt," Tom said. "I'm not sure we can help you with that. I don't think the Peace Corps will be willing to pay a bribe either."

"No, no, no," Mr. Chipanda is quick to say. "I'm not suggesting that. If the people in the ZESA office know that two teachers from the United States are waiting to get in my house, I think it will make a difference. They live in Mbizo and you may be teaching their kids, and they'll also be confident that the electric bills will be paid. The two years you'll be living there will help us get ahead financially. I've talked it over with my wife, Maina."

"When would we be able to move in?" I ask.

"It will all depend on ZESA. I'd like to think we could get the electricity connected before school starts. They won't approve the house for occupation until that happens."

"There's another thing we need to tell you," Tom says. "We're volunteers so the U.S. Peace Corps will be paying our rent. Any kind of a rental contract will have to be worked out with them. Is that okay with you? If they will agree to this, we'd be honored to live in your house."

Mr. Chipanda is a cooperative and dependable landlord during the two years of our stay in Mbizo. Our home is a comfort and mainstay during two very challenging years. He and his brother Abraham take care of our yard and garden, and are proud of the banana trees and many beautiful flowering shrubs they plant and cultivate here.

Agnes

Well into our first term of teaching, a woman comes to our door asking if we might need help with housework. She explains that her husband was killed in an automobile accident, leaving her to care for her fourteen-year-old daughter by herself. She lost everything she had to her husband's family, that being the traditional custom when a man dies. Tom and I resisted taking on hired help when we first got here, even when a line of people needing work formed at our gate the day we moved in. It felt too reminiscent of the apartheid era. But we're tiring of doing our laundry by hand in our bathtub, and it takes too much time away from lesson planning. We hire Agnes on the spot to help us one day a week. After laboring hard for several hours on her first day, I suggest she take a tea break, a custom Africans adopted from the British. I pour two cups of tea at the table, but I'm surprised when Agnes takes her cup to the far corner of the living room and sits down on the floor.

"Oh no, Agnes! You needn't sit on the floor—come here to the table and we'll visit a little while. She complies. I ask her about her daughter and the rest of her family and I soon learn that she longs to marry again, but fears that the burden of her daughter will keep suitors away.

"I'm afraid they won't want to pay any lobolo (bride price) to my family for me. I'm not worth as much with a daughter," Agnes explains.

"When a man pays lobolo for a woman, does that mean he owns her?" I ask.

"Yes, it does, and it means he loves her and will take care of her."

"But you say a dependent child decreases your bride price. What else makes a difference in how much a man must pay?"

"Being pretty is very important and since I'm almost forty now, that isn't good—they like younger women. How much education she has also makes a difference. The more years she's gone to school, the more her lobolo will be. This is why I make sure my daughter goes to school, but it's very hard for me to pay her school fees."

I decide to explain gender equality to Agnes. "In the United States, we don't have anything like lobolo because we believe that if a man has to pay for a wife, that puts her in a lower position. If she's his property, like a horse or a cow he might own, that implies that she isn't equal to him. A woman in the United States chooses to get an education so that she can get a good job herself and won't have to depend on a man to take care of her. Mr. Price and I consider ourselves equal in our status and value as an individual. I would never want him to pay for me because that would mean I'm not equal to him." I see Agnes struggling to understand.

"Do you mean Mr. Price got you for *free*?" She's dismayed. I'm dumbstruck. My logic has fallen on deaf ears because of a different cultural perspective. To Agnes, I'm cheap merchandise. What a lesson this is! I will have to tread carefully if I'm to influence my female students to continue their education—for reasons other than increasing their lobolo.

Miriam, Sithembile, and Sarah

I begin discussion gender equality in my classes, and three of the brightest Form 2 girls have chosen topics on gender discrimintation for the school speech contest. They're meeting with me after school one day to discuss their speeches. Miriam's topic is "Should Girls be Educated?" so I ask her to explain her reasons for thinking that education is important for girls.

"Our parents want to get as much lobolo for us as they can when we marry," she answers. "They wouldn't pay to send us to school if there was no reward."

"Does going to school make you more valuable as a person?" I ask.

"Oh yes," Miriam answers. "If a man is willing to pay a good lobolo for me, it will mean that he cares for me very much!"

"What if no man wants to marry you, or what if your husband dies or is disabled? Might there be other reasons you would want to get a good education?"

Sithembile says, "I would like to be a teacher someday. I want to get an education so that I can go to teachers' college, but I still want to get married—and I want to have children."

"In our culture, it's more important for boys to get an education than it is for girls," Miriam says.

"But doesn't that lead to women being dependent on men to take care of them?"

"Yes!" says Sithembile, "and that's why there are sugar daddies." Her speech topic is "Sugar Daddies, Good or Bad?"

"Sithembile, explain to me what a sugar daddy is?"

"It's an older man who pays money or gives gifts to young girls in exchange for sex."

"Is that good or bad?"

"It's a bad thing, because many girls end up getting pregnant and then their sugar daddy disappears. Some of these girls aren't even out of high school, or they haven't gone to school at all."

"So what happens to these girls?"

"Either their parents or another relative has to take care of them because if a girl has a child, a man doesn't want her. Even her family is ashamed of her," says Miriam.

"So why does a young girl get involved with a sugar daddy?"

Sarah speaks up. "I think it's because their parents don't care about them, or their fathers have left to go into the cities to get jobs and their mothers don't have enough money to care for them. They're fooled into thinking the sugar daddy will take care of them." Sarah's speech topic is "Should Lobolo Be Paid?"

"I'm not sure I understand how paying lobolo is any different that having a sugar daddy.

"If a man pays lobolo for you, it means he has more respect for you," Miriam says.

"Not necessarily," says Sarah. "He's still buying you—like a broiler chicken." All the girls laugh.

"You laugh about that, but what does it mean when someone owns you?"

"It means you will have to do what he wants, not what you want," says Sarah.

"But that isn't all it means," I say earnestly. As long as women consent to be bought and sold like property, they will never be free to develop their fullest potential. Help me understand. You seem to understand that it's wrong for one race to see themselves as superior to another. I don't understand why this doesn't apply to gender. Why is it so hard to see that it's wrong for men to see themselves as being superior to women?

"I guess it's because it's just always been like that," says Sithembile.

"So who's going to have to change it? I'm not suggesting that you go to war with men, but it certainly wouldn't hurt to start pointing out to boys that it would be to their advantage to have a wife who is their equal. Not only can she contribute something to family financial support if she is educated, but also by sharing this responsibility, fathers will have more time for their children." By the time our meeting ends, I hope that I've made some progress with the girls. But on my way home that day, Sarah calls to me to wait up for her. I'm pleased she wants to walk with me and I ask her how she feels about our discussion.

"I thought it was good. I'm going to tell my boyfriend about it."

"Oh? Tell me about your boyfriend. Is he interested in gender equality?"

"I don't know about that, but I know he'll like the idea of not having to pay lobolo. He's from a very poor family. His father abandoned them and he hasn't seen him in years. His mother has to get along on whatever her brother is able to share with her, but her brother has a family of his own.

My boyfriend loves me very much and I love him too, but it's been hard enough for his mother to pay his school fees; I know he could never afford to pay my family lobolo."

I begin to understand why Sarah has responded so positively to my talks in class—more so than any of the other girls. She isn't as motivated by the ideal of equality as she is by seeing lobolo as an obstacle to getting something she wants. Another reality check for me.

Jeffrey

In Zimbabwe students are "streamed" into classes based on scores achieved on standardized tests the previous year. Most students in the A sections of each Form are fluent in English, but there are some in the G through K sections who still can't speak a word of English and can barely write their names. In order to keep it fair for teachers, every teacher is assigned sections of both highs and lows. Since I'm a volunteer and a guest in their country, I'm assigned both the 1-A and 2-A sections, but to make it fair, I'm also given the 1-K and 2-G sections, the highest and lowest sections in both Forms. Though Jeffrey is in my 1-A class, he is less mature than most of his classmates, and for some reason, latches onto me early in the term. Bright and possessing a sweet disposition, he comes from a nice family; his father is headmaster at a rural school.

Jeffrey aspires to be a great basketball player. At the All-Sports Day event, where I am in charge of measuring the discus throws, Jeffrey assists me by retrieving all the thrown discs. Most of the time, it's painless to nurture him. He walks with me to and from school and frequently drops by our house to visit, so we are well aware that his mother is expecting a new baby soon. He's beside himself with excitement the day his new baby sister arrives and he insists that Tom and I come to his home to see her the following afternoon.

Later in the term, my section A students write to pen pals who are high school English students in the United States. Jeffrey's pen pal is a girl to whom he writes:

"On January 5th this year, my mother gave birth to a baby girl she named Lucy or Moreblessing. It was just wonderful. We really hope she will grow to be a beautiful and wonderful girl. I love her very much. She can see and she makes meaningless sounds which I enjoy most. I always rush home whenever we finish our lessons at school because I do not want to spend even a minute away from the pretty one who I think is just like you."

Mark

We meet dozens of school graduates without jobs who are discouraged. The economy is depressing and having been submissive for so long, young people haven't been taught to think creatively or to generate their own opportunities. Mark is an unemployed young man in his early twenties, who visits us frequently at our home. Since he's often under foot, Tom takes him on as an experimental project. They begin exploring the idea of a second-hand shop or the possibility of him volunteering his labor in order to learn a job skill. I discover a Word Perfect tutorial on my computer and I'm teaching Mark to use it.

The Zimbabwe annual school schedule consists of three three-month semesters with one month off between semesters. During our breaks, we spend one week in Harare for workshops, two weeks working on secondary projects, leaving one week for recreation and exploring more of the country. For our first excursion, we decide to visit the Great Zimbabwe Ruins, an ancient ruined city in the southeastern hills of Zimbabwe, from which the country got its name. Mark is excited when he hears of our plans.

"That's very near my family home! Would you mind if I traveled with you? It's been since December that I've seen my family."

We agree to this, knowing that Mark's family lives in one of the rural areas that's been drastically affected by drought. As the oldest child in his family, he's looked upon as the only hope for his parents and three younger siblings who subsist on farming.

"Would you be willing to stop over on your way to meet my family?" Mark asks.

Knowing we will be afoot with luggage once we leave the bus, Tom asks, "How far is your family's home from the bus stop?"

"Oh, just a short distance," he says.

We've been in Zimbabwe long enough to know that Mark is probably hoping that we can help his family in some way, so we purchase a ten kilogram sack of their staple food, "sadza" (maize meal), to take with us along with a sack of our garden vegetables. Our trip on a slow, rickety bus takes all day and it's dark by the time we reach Mark's bus stop, a place along the road which appears to be in the middle of nowhere – no sign of civilization in sight. Much to our dismay, our sack of sadza is nowhere to be found. Apparently someone stole it when the bus was crowded with standing-room-only passengers. We set out in the darkness carrying our luggage and the sack of vegetables, following Mark on the dirt path that leads to his home. When we've been walking over an hour, I ask Mark how much longer we have to go.

"Just a little further," he says. But the "short distance" Mark had described turns out to be twelve kilometers—over eight miles! Finally we arrive at a cluster of mud and grass huts which house Mark's family and other relatives. Not expecting us, they're already asleep, but Mark gets them up to meet us.

They offer us food, but knowing of the severe food shortage, we refuse and give them the vegetables, apologizing for the loss of the sadza. We pitch our tent near their huts and eat the only other food we have in our backpacks—two avocados and two oranges—and we spend an unsettling night. I awaken early in the morning with fever and chills, disguising my flu symptoms after we dress and greet the family.

Looking around us at what might be beautiful country, everything we see is either dead or dying; there isn't a blade of green grass anywhere. The family's herd of fifteen cows is down to three and it's doubtful these three will make it until the rainy season. Only a half-dozen goats appear to be surviving the drought. The family group consists of Mark's parents, a younger brother, two sisters, one husband, and two small children. The children are dressed in hand-sewn scraps of fabric pieced together. The only furniture is one wooden chair and thin mats are spread out on the floor where the whole family sleeps.

We learn that there are vast numbers of people living on this land with each family allotted only a few acres on which they scratch out a living. Mark tells us that his family receives a minimal ration of maize meal from the government which is keeping them alive. Since I'm not feeling well, we postpone our trip on to the Great Zimbabwe Ruins for another time. We leave Mark with enough money to get back to Mbizo and we tell his family goodbye. Mark's father points us in the direction of a road where we might hitch a ride out to the highway and he instructs his oldest daughter to carry our bags! Tom won't hear of that and carries the two pieces of luggage and I carry our personal belongings in my backpack. At Mark's suggestion, we stop at the community borehole (a hand-pumped well) in the valley below that supplies water to approximately one thousand people in that area. Women and children are at the borehole filling buckets with water to carry on their heads back to their homes. The experience of meeting Mark's family in this poverty-stricken area is one of our most sobering times in Zimbabwe. Still, the little children laugh when they see us washing our faces and filling our water bottles.

Johanes

Johanes is chosen by his classmates to be their class monitor. Though only in Form 1, he is seventeen, older than anyone in the class, so he commands respect. Johanes walks with a noticeable limp, which I learn is the result of an injury he incurred in an automobile accident when he was in the sixth grade. He fell behind in school because the nearest high school in the rural area of his home is nine kilometers away, a distance too difficult for him to walk. He recently moved to Mbizo to live with his uncle so that he can go to school. He is bright and dependable and I can rely on him to help maintain order in the class, follow up on class assignments, and collect notebooks when they are due.

Very early one Sunday morning, we hear someone knocking at our back door. I quickly dress and find Johanes on our doorstep looking distressed. Tom is just getting up too, and we invite him in where we can all sit down. "Is something wrong? I ask.

"My uncle says that I have to go back to the rural area where my parents live. My mother is here to take me home."

"Why is your uncle sending you away?" I ask.

"He says that my father has not been sending him the money for my food, so unless I find somewhere else to stay, I'm going to have to drop out of school." His unspoken plea is for us to take him in.

"We'd like to help you, Johanes," Tom says, "but as Peace Corps volunteers, we aren't in a position to take on the responsibility of one of our students." I'm torn because I trust Johanes and believe he's caught in the middle of a family feud, but it only takes one shared look between us for Tom and me to know that we dare not get further involved. Johanes leaves to return home with his mother, facing an uncertain future.

The next morning we get up early to go to Kwekwe for our week's supply of groceries. We return home to find Johanes and his father waiting for us on our front porch. Johanes and his mother traveled all Sunday afternoon 160 kilometers to his rural home. His father, apparently not so willing to give up, returns to Mbizo with his son, traveling most of the night to reach our house.

Mr. Zimuto, a frail, thin man, greets us and shakes both our hands. Johanes appears exhausted and ridden with anxiety, but says nothing. His father wastes no time getting to the point.

"I'm here to plead with you to take my son for the rest of this school term. If he can finish Form One, then I hope to get him in a boarding school next year. I will pay you. Johanes will work hard to help you. My son is a good student. Yes?" He nods his head and looks at me earnestly.

"Yes, Johanes is a good student," I say.

"Please. Please. He works hard. We know of no one else who might take him."

"Have you made every effort to work out things with your brother?" Tom asks.

Mr. Zimuto slowly shakes his head, looking down at his feet. "There's no hope there. Farai and I have had trouble for years. He agreed to take Johanes, but there's been a misunderstanding. I'm afraid it's impossible."

Tom and I look at each other and Tom turns to Mr. Zimuto. "Wait here while we talk inside."

We go inside and close the door. "What's your thinking?" Tom asks.

"I don't know. He does seem pretty desperate."

"When is the term up?"

"December 3rd is the last day of school."

"October is almost half over—that's less than two months. I'm willing to take him in if you are," Tom says. "Let's just make sure that he knows it's only for the remainder of this term."

"Right. That's fine with me too."

So Johanes moves into our spare bedroom with his meager belongings and an earnest desire to have our acceptance and approval. He helps with the meal preparation, dish washing, trips to the market, and he does his own laundry. When not doing his homework, he enjoys having an abundance of things to read. We tell Johanes he can make sadza anytime he wants, but he prefers to eat American. The night I make meatloaf, he says it's the best meal he's ever had.

One week I help him prepare a speech for the school speech contest. Hoping he will find an inspiring topic, I suggest he look through a book of collected quotations that Tom and I read at breakfast every morning. He likes a quote by Helen Keller: *"I am only one; but still I am one. I cannot do everything, but still I can do something. I will not refuse to do the something I can do."* When I tell him the story of Helen Keller, he decides to include a summary of her life in his speech, which is to speak the mind and feelings of a disabled person.

One mid-November day, I can't find our calculator and I remember that Johanes borrowed it a few days before. He's gone somewhere so I go into his room to look for it. When it's not in plain sight, I search in less obvious places, finally finding it in a backpack under his bed along with my sunglasses, two new chapsticks, some nail clippers, and five books. I'm shocked and ready to send him home, but Tom has a cooler head and thinks we should talk to him before doing anything so drastic. "He's just a kid," Tom says, "and he might learn something from this that will affect the rest of his life." We knew the level of poverty in Zimbabwe would make stealing more tempting, so we agree to talk to him that evening.

"Johanes, today I was looking for our calculator and I found it along with some other things that belong to us in your backpack." His eyes widen and he looks genuinely surprised, but he doesn't say anything.

"If it was your intention to keep these things for yourself without asking us, then that is stealing," Tom says, "and we can't have someone living in our house that we can't trust." He still doesn't say a word and we can see that he's afraid.

"Honesty is very important to us and we can listen if you can help us understand," I say. We wait, but he's frozen. "I even thought about sending you home when I found these things—that's how concerned I am." Then he begins to cry.

"If there's something that you need, you can always ask us for anything," Tom says, "and we'll be honest with you if it's something we can give, but we can't tolerate your taking something without your talking to us about it. We can even accept that you've made a mistake and forgive you this time, but we need to know that it will never happen again." Johanes continues to cry, but still he does not admit to taking the things, nor does he apologize. Apparently he's too frightened to say anything. He obviously has strong feelings about it, so we hope that our warning will prevent it from happening again.

Since our confrontation, Johanes is more conscientious than ever about helping around the house. He never fails to come to the kitchen at preparation time offering to do anything, and he always washes the dishes. I regret that I jumped to an extreme and grateful that Tom helped me to look at things more rationally. We invite Johanes to work a jigsaw puzzle with us one night and, not having ever seen one before, he is captivated by it.

It's the last day of school and there's to be a staff party at Tom's school that night. Johanes is to leave for his home in the rural area the next morning and is at home all afternoon by himself. Tom's school party is postponed until the next night, so we get home early while Johanes is away telling his friends goodbye. Something tells us to check his bag. We find pens, pencils, stationary, stamps, jewelry, radio earphones, and books. But worst of all is a pile of jumbled parts that once constituted Tom's spare watch, a camera, and binoculars.

When Johanes comes home, we confront him with our discovery and disappointment.

"How did you think we would feel had we not discovered our loss until after you left?" I ask.

"I thought you would forgive and forget as you did the last time."

"Johanes," Tom said, "we were serious when we told you that we couldn't tolerate having someone in our house that we couldn't trust. It would make us too uneasy to have you here with us all night. Our intention isn't to be cruel, but you will have to leave here tonight. We care about you and we're concerned about your future. It's a serious offense to steal and destroy someone else's property. You will continue to wreck your relationships with others until you learn to resist that temptation."

"I'm sorry," he says. "I'm really sorry."

"I accept your apology, and that does give me hope for your future," Tom says.

"I can no longer help you find a boarding school position for next year, Johanes," I say, "for fear this could happen with someone else." Tears fill his eyes. I can't understand why he has risked jeopardizing our trust.

"Please, I don't want to leave tonight. Please let me stay until morning."

As hard as it is, we both tell him that isn't an option, so he gathers his things and leaves. We don't know where he stays that night, but we know his aunt and uncle still live in Mbizo. We want to believe that the consequences of his behavior might have an effect, but we fear this pattern may be too ingrained. Even later we miss other things he didn't acknowledge taking. Trying to balance our awareness of the level of poverty to which Johanes was accustomed and our expectation of honest and considerate behavior is absorbing a good part of our contemplative energy.

Hleko

By the end of our first year in Zimbabwe, Tom and I have cut our last ties to the Christian religion, partly by viewing it from African eyes. Considering their war of independence, we are surprised at the degree to which the Zimbabwean government still promulgates Christianity in the schools. To us, it is just another way to imply that the "white man's" religion is superior to their own. Every Christian denomination has missionaries in Zimbabwe competing for saved souls. From our observations, even when Africans join a Christian church, they don't give up their traditional beliefs. One day a girl in another classroom has what I conclude to be an epileptic seizure. Word spreads quickly that the girl is under the influence of a deceased ancestral spirit taking vengeance upon the girl's family. The deputy headmistress, a Catholic woman, is summoned to exorcise the evil spirit from the girl's body. She prays with fervent urgency until the girl returns to normal. We come to see their beliefs are no more bizarre than some Christian teachings, but their traditional convictions at least afford them greater dignity.

Hleko is a tall, slender and handsome Form 4 boy whose quiet mysticism and love for writing poetry has captured my interest. He is sitting in a chair beside my desk waiting for my critique of a story he is writing for a contest sponsored by a U.S. magazine to promote African fiction writing. His topic is "Is There a Place for the Traditional Healer in our Modern World?" He has written a story with strength and honesty that describes his people's encounters and reliance upon the tribal witch doctor. As he reads aloud, he frequently turns to look at me for a reaction, his eyes betraying his fear of my scrutiny. Will she scoff at my strange beliefs?

"Your story is beautifully written, Hleko, and there's really nothing that needs correction, but I do have one suggestion."

"Yes?"

"I think it might be very powerful if you could give us a clear visual image of the young boy when he sees the spirit of fire and do this in the form of a poem that you could use as an introduction to your story." Relief crosses Hleko's face and his smile mirrors the gratitude I'm feeling for his trust.

"Oh! I would love to do that! I will work on it tonight. I try to write a poem every day, and this will be my poem for today. Thank you, Mrs. Price!"

Hleko stands up to go, but I ask him to sit back down because I have something to show him that I haven't shown to anyone else since I've been in Zimbabwe. I open one of my desk drawers and take out a booklet that I compiled soon after

Leslie died that includes a picture of her and all the poetry she wrote from the time she was six years old until she died.

"My daughter loved to write poetry, like you do. She died five years ago. I thought you might enjoy reading this."

"I'm sorry to hear about your daughter, Mrs. Price, and I will love reading her poetry. I'll be very careful with your book."

In just a few days, Hleko stops by the library to turn in the final copy of his story for the contest. In addition, he gives me a poem he has written about Leslie. In it are these two lines: *"They say you are white, but to me you are pink. They say I am black, but to me I am brown."*

Teresa

Only a few teachers at our schools reach out in an effort to get to know us on a personal level. Teresa, another English teacher, invites me to her house for lunch one Saturday. I learn that she is married to a successful business man who works in Harare, but that he only comes home occasionally. They have two young children who live with her. She expresses an interest in learning more about American marriage, and I gather that she isn't very happy in her own. I tell her that, like Zimbabwe, attitudes are changing about gender roles, and the trend is toward viewing marriage as a union between equals, but there are still some religions in the United States that advocate male dominance. I ask her if some of the things we learned in our culture classes are true. In some households, do men sleep on beds while women and children sleep on the floor? Do some men beat their wives and children? Teresa acknowledges that in some families, these things are true. But then she questions me about fidelity in marriage.

"Is it considered a virtue in the United States?" she asks.

"Generally speaking, I would say it's considered a virtue, but that doesn't mean infidelity rarely happens."

"In Zimbabwe, men are expected to have sexual relationships outside their marriage, but if a woman does, he will divorce her, and even take away her children. It isn't fair."

Teresa doesn't pass judgment on her husband, other than complaining that he doesn't come home very often. The subject doesn't come up again, but since we both enjoy writing, we agree to meet on a regular basis to give each other feedback on short stories we're working on. Then one day I happen to see Teresa from a distance in a park in Kwekwe. She is sitting on a bench with a man. Since one rarely sees married couples together in Zimbabwe, I assume the man isn't her husband. Not long after that, Teresa stops coming to school. When I ask about her, one of the other teachers tells me that she was divorced by her husband for being unfaithful. Her two children were taken from her and she has been banished to South Africa. I often wonder what has happened to her.

Mr. Makwindi

We assumed that once an African population achieves independence and the educated ones gain a sense of power to form a middle class, these people, many of whom are school teachers, will want to raise the quality of life among those who are less fortunate. While there are many who reflect this sentiment, some choose to lord that power over the weakest among them—the children. We underestimated one of the worst results of colonization and the racial oppression that was the rule of law for so long. Some of the teachers at our school are there, not to help children, but because of the status it gives them. They are stern, autocratic, and punitive. We see an entire class on their knees and elbows in the dirt for over an hour because some students haven't turned in their homework. Some children are beaten in front of their classmates for minor infractions, like wearing the wrong color of socks with their uniform.

Mr. Makwindi is *not* one of these teachers. He is conscientious and genuinely wants to help his students succeed. He teaches the Form 4-A English class, the top English class in the school. One day he asks me if I will help him teach his class how to do a research paper. By then I have created a small library in the school consisting of used books Tom and I have solicited from the United States, including one set of encyclopedias and many magazines. Together Mr. Makwindi and I do a quick inventory in order to come up with a list of possible topics the students can choose from to spark their motivation. We teach the class together and I agree to be available to any of the students wanting consultation. It is so gratifying to cooperate with one of the best teachers and to feel his support, since most of the teachers show little interest in what I'm doing. The following term Mr. Makwindi and I work together again organizing a school speech contest. We coach them on expression, delivery, and gesturing, and it's amazing how much they improve with just a little practice. The contest winners will go on to compete in a district contest.

Coincidentally, Mr. Makwindi's wife teaches math at Tom's school. When we learn that we are to bring a "Zimbabwean counterpart"—a teacher with whom we work, to our next in-service training in Harare, Tom and I invite Mr. and Mrs. Makwindi to be our counterparts. The workshop is to be on integrating environmental education into English language lessons. Any time there is a mixed group like this, cultural clashes are common, and this workshop is no exception. During a cooperative group project, Mr. Makwindi and I lock horns on one aspect of our task. Our differences center around the emphasis *they* put on the facts that should be taught, and *our* emphasis on a creative problem solving process. We're able to find peaceful ways to disagree and we're still friends when the session is over. The week turns out to be a fun time getting to know each other as couples. The training is held at one of the nicest hotels in Harare and all our meals are provided, so it's a rare treat for the four of us.

Itai

In our second year of teaching in Zimbabwe, I organize a Writers Club that will have the responsibility of writing a school newspaper to be published twice a month. In 1990, the year before we came here, Robert Mugabe instituted multi-party elections, a significant step toward creating a democratic system, the reason that the Peace Corps was invited to send the first group of volunteers to this country. I want my students to be aware of how important newspapers are in a democratic system. We won't be able to print multiple copies, but I will print three copies on my solar powered printer from my computer. Tom is constructing three bulletin boards we'll attach to the outside of the school buildings in three different locations, so the students and faculty will have easy access to reading it.

From our class discussions about the violence and uprisings that led up to the official abolition of apartheid in South Africa, I learn that some students have strong feelings associated with the demise of apartheid in 1991. In particular, the release of Nelson Mandela after his appalling twenty-seven year incarceration evokes a fervent desire to learn more about democracy. This is especially true of the writings of one of my students Itai. Having been an avid reader since he learned English in his early grades, Itai seeks out sources of books to which few of his classmates are exposed. I believe that he and others like him deserve a wider voice, and a thoughtful newspaper can be a way they learn to exercise their right to free speech in a country grappling with democracy. The Writers Club, in a democratic election, elects Itai as its Editor-in-Chief and Mukululi, another high-achieving student, as his assistant.

One of the first issues the writing group wants to tackle in their newspaper is the problem of teachers not showing up for their classes. The students are appreciative of teachers who take their job seriously. Education is highly valued and seen as the only route out of poverty. They know their parents make great sacrifices to pay school fees and buy uniforms and many in their communities can't afford to send their children to school at all. Since students are "streamed" into sections based on standardized test scores, teachers with a low morale anyway tend to dislike the low-ability classes, so those are the children most frequently neglected.

Itai is fearless, ready to take on the powers that be, so in the first edition of the newspaper, he writes a strong editorial protesting teacher irresponsibility. I'm on good terms with our headmaster who has been supportive of my extracurricular projects, so I don't anticipate this to be a problem. But in the next issue, Mr. Musimhi, a conscientious English teacher and soccer coach, who devotes hours of volunteer time working with the team (which won the championship this year), writes a letter to the editor in support of Itai's editorial. The next thing I hear is that Mr. Musimhi is being transferred to the rural area, and Mr. Makwindi is certain that it is because of the letter he wrote to the newspaper. Mr. Makwindi told me that some of the most guilty teachers complained to the headmaster. I'm sickened to hear this, because it has been an act of courage for Mr. Misimhi to support the students and he has done it in a tactful way, even acknowledging that he, himself, could be more conscientious. After spending a sleepless night and getting counsel from Tom, I confront the headmaster in his office the next morning. I tell him that it appears to me that he is displaying his authority in defense of those teachers who are most in need of correction. "Do you really believe they are right?" I ask him.

He's flustered and I see that he's in conflict, and he asks an honest question. "What would you do?"

"Well, first of all I would let the students know that you care about their concern. As to the offending teachers, I would say, 'If the shoe fits, wear it.'" But this frightens him.

"I don't think you understand what kind of a regime I've grown up in," he says. "Only whites were headmasters under apartheid. I don't want the teachers to feel oppressed as we did."

This is a point of view I hadn't considered. "I can understand why you feel the way you do, and I know that it takes time for any system to change. But that doesn't make it right for the teachers to neglect their duties."

I leave his office feeling that I can no longer trust him. The result, however, is that Mr. Musimhi is not transferred, but is sent to the Science department, I suppose as punishment, and I am assigned two additional low-ability classes. (The headmaster doesn't know that I enjoy these classes because I have greater freedom to diverge from the prescribed curriculum.) This only strengthens my desire to uphold what is just for the students.

I wonder how long it will take for the newspaper staff to raise the issue of beating, and it doesn't take long. An emergency assembly is called to publicly beat a boy who questions a teacher's authority. Though the students don't approve of what the boy did, none of them like it that he is punished and humiliated publicly. Itai writes another editorial likening the incident to the master-slave era, an accurate comparison.

Beating is actually illegal, but no one adheres to this. Many teachers believe they would relinquish total control if they did not beat kids. In the next staff meeting, the headmaster issues a warning that I'm not to print anything in the school paper that has anything to do with school policy. After the meeting, I remind him that he has emphasized "free speech" and that he has persistently refused my offer to let him read the newspaper copy before I post it. Has he changed this policy to censorship? He doesn't answer my question.

Itai often comes to our house to discuss changes that are taking place in his country and he's fervent in wanting to advocate democracy in the schools. Tom and I are both aware that he's more willing to confront the headmaster in principle than I've been. After the headmaster issues this latest warning, Tom cautions Itai to exercise discretion in the degree to which he challenges the system, lest he jeopardize the existence of the newspaper and his own status as a student. He gives him good advice on how he might be most effective in making changes at the school—one little step at a time. I'm reasonably confident that the headmaster will not thwart the efforts of these exemplary students. For the remainder of the year, the newspaper becomes a popular item containing articles on academics, sports, clubs, book reviews, and letters to the editor. Students and faculty together delight in seeing their names in print.

The U.S. Embassy Wives group donates a used typewriter which I'm leaving in the care of Itai and Mukululi so they can continue the newspaper after we leave Zimbabwe. By using a typing tutorial on my computer, five girls and seven boys on the newspaper staff learn how to type. I tell them that they are to do their last edition completely on their own, and trust each other to do the final edit of their articles. I'll not see it until it's posted at school.

Tom and I are in the final stages of getting rid of our household furnishings and mailing boxes of personal items home. I arrive at school on Monday morning for a teachers' staff meeting. I haven't yet seen the last edition of the newspaper that has been posted. Mr. Makwindi informs me that Itai's lead editorial addresses the issue of male teachers impregnating school girls. This is a frequent rumor in the community that often turns out to be true, when a girl unexpectedly drops out of school. The headmaster himself has been so accused. He is furious and has expelled Itai from school. I know what I must do. After an opening prayer, it's the first issue on the agenda. I ask for permission to speak and I explain my motivation to allow the students to do the last edition of the paper on their own. They've worked hard all year, and I wanted them to know that I have confidence in their ability, but now I realize that was a mistake. Had I known of Itai's topic, I would have insisted on restraint. I take full responsibility for what has happened and I ask that Itai not be punished for my poor judgment. The headmaster accepts my apology and agrees to allow Itai to remain in school.

Itai knows how much I admire him, but I realize that Tom's and my encouragement has put him at great risk. As justified as his editorial was, nothing would have compensated for his being expelled from school. The teacher who will be taking my place as supervisor of the Writers' Club is intent on pleasing the headmaster. The headmaster will attempt to control the students through her and I'm not sure how this will work. The longer we are here, the more torn we are between believing in the future of Zimbabwe and fearing for its ultimate welfare. These young people are its only hope, because most of the adults are too afraid.

Our Peace Corps experience has allowed Tom and me to step out of our former lives long enough to establish a foundation for our new relationship. We have had time to learn more about our past histories, and by having an attentive listener, we've gained more insight into ourselves. We've also begun to forge a new shared philosophy that isn't so colored by our religious backgrounds. We will not forget the lengthy conversation we had one day arriving at a new definition of sin: *"Behavior that is aimed at getting one's needs met, but based on false assumptions that lead to harming oneself or others."*

When we came to Zimbabwe, we were looking for new meaning, purpose, and direction by either affirming or redefining ourselves under different environmental conditions. Without question, our patience, tolerance, and emotional stability have been tested many times, but gradually we've gained confidence in our endurance and ability to work through difficult situations. Though we came here with a kind of missionary zeal, we leave wondering if instead of helping these people find solutions, maybe we've only added to their problems. It's so easy to see suffering and think we have remedies they should apply. It's another thing to bring hope to a people who for so long have had so little to hope for. Of one thing we are certain, there are some African people we have come to love, and as I think and write about a few of them now, twenty-five years later, I wonder if they remember us as well as we remember them. I hope so.

INSIGHTS: How Unconscious Bias Perpetuates Racism

Tom and I were drawn to a Peace Corps adventure in Zimbabwe because it would give us the opportunity to examine our culturally acquired values against the backdrop of a different culture, particularly those values that involve race. We grew up in an era of transition that spanned a segregated America, a 1954 Supreme Court decision that desegregated schools, and a 1964 Civil Rights Act that abolished all public legal segregation. We can remember the time when signs were used to show people of color where they could legally walk, talk, drink, swim, rest, eat, or even be buried.

Still, with new laws forbidding legally enforced segregation, racial grouping in neighborhoods is still shaped by economic factors and large-scale migration of lighter-skinned people to more racially homogeneous suburban regions. This was true in both Tulsa and Tucson, the two cities where Tom and I grew up. Neither of us went to school with African Americans, nor did we regularly see them because they all lived on the opposite side of town. People of color in this country continue to suffer discrimination in areas of employment, housing, health care, police protection, and the quality of education. So what, if anything, has changed?

Prior to the 1980s, attitudes about race were predominantly assessed through self-reporting measures that relied on conscious attitudes and beliefs that people were willing to report—referred to as *explicit* orientations. What these measures could not show was the extent to which people were influenced by hidden mental associations that are unavailable to conscious introspection—referred to as *implicit* prejudice and stereotypes. Unless people *know* they possess an implicit bias, they cannot accurately report it. Unconscious associations have attracted attention because they have the potential of causing otherwise fair-minded people to unwittingly perpetuate inequality.[1] Years before data about implicit bias became available, Malcolm X, in his autobiography, wrote this statement about "white" people:

"I don't care how nice one is to you; the thing you must always remember is that almost never does he really see you as he sees himself, as he sees his own kind. He may stand with you through thin, but not thick; when the chips are down, you'll find that, as fixed in him as his bone structure, is his sometimes subconscious conviction that he's better than anybody black."[2]

In the classic book, *The Nature of Prejudice*, Gordon Allport points out that every corner of the earth has its own prejudices. Targets of prejudice may differ greatly, but the dynamics are much the same everywhere. At the root of most hostility and distrust are fears of the imagination. The United States is no stranger to the practice of inventing racial theories of hatred and condescension to justify the extreme cruelty of American slavery.[3] Just our common terminology we use to describe the two races illustrates the sharp lines we have devised to separate ourselves from one another. It has been the recent writings of Ta Nehesi Coates that sensitized me to the usage of the terminology of "black" and "white," which I am working to avoid in my own speech and writing.

"There will surely always be people with straight hair and blue eyes, as there have been for all history. But some of these straight-haired people with blue eyes have been "black," and this points to the great difference between their world and ours. We did not choose our fences. They were imposed on us by Virginia planters obsessed with enslaving as many Americans as possible. They are the ones who came up with a one-drop rule that separated the "white" from the "black," even if it meant that their own blue-eyed sons would live under the lash."[4]

A stereotype is an exaggerated, therefore erroneous, belief applied to one group. Research has established that our attitudes are activated outside of our conscious attention as we grow up in a culture, our home influence having the priority. A child needing approval from parents has good reason to adopt their parents' beliefs (stereotypes) and therefore their attitudes. It isn't until adolescence that individuals begin to see that there are attitudes that vary from the culturally approved attitudes they grew up with. Up to this time, a child's prejudices have been mostly secondhand, so that a process of questioning his or her prejudices, like religious or political views, becomes a normal part of growing up.[5]

Tom and I were fortunate that public opinion about racial equality was changing for the better during our adolescent and young adult years, so that in all our adult roles, we saw ourselves as being non-prejudiced people. But since our Zimbabwean experience, we can see that we carried our own implicit bias with us to that faraway country. What we knew at the time was based on our own conscious recollections from our childhood.

Tom recalls frequently hearing his father and some other male relatives refer to African Americans as "niggers" in association with some negative characteristic, usually having to do with incompetence. He remembers being frightened at the sight of a darker-skinned man lying beside a railroad track when he was about seven. However, his keenest awareness of racial discrimination didn't come until he served as a Mormon missionary in Brazil when he was twenty. This was a time in Mormon history when anyone of the "black" race, even partially, was denied entrance into the church's priesthood, so missionaries were discouraged from teaching them. Since Brazil was a country of predominantly mixed race people, this made missionary work there difficult. So, in the event anyone questionable (which included almost everyone) showed interest in joining the church, missionaries were required to present the Mormon "blood" lesson that gives Biblical credence to dark-skinned people being undeserving of church status. In 1978 the Mormon Church reversed its racial ban with no other justification than the obvious one to conform to changes in public opinion. While he believed the change was long overdue, the injustice he had perpetuated as a missionary for the church weighed heavily on his conscience.

My earliest exposure to African Americans was at the country club where my father worked in the summers. A jovial young man with a friendly smile revealing his gleaming white teeth sold the hamburgers and ice cream cones I coveted at the swimming pool snack bar. I had a very positive impression of him, and I saw that Dad respected him and the other darker-skinned employees with whom he worked, but I also noticed that Dad enjoyed greater respect from club members.

My first opportunity to meet African American teenagers was in 1956, just two years after Tulsa schools were integrated. For the first time my school on the south side of town, Thomas Edison High School, was to play football against the African American school on the north side of town, Booker T. Washington High School. On game day it was customary for representatives from both pep clubs and football teams to take part in exchange assemblies at each school. As a representative of the Edison pep club, I became acquainted with a girl named Cookie, who was my counterpart at Washington High School. Eager to do my part in furthering integration in our city, I invited Cookie over to my house for lunch on the following Saturday. My mother facilitated my invitation by providing lunch and Cookie's transportation from the opposite side of town. Mom was an active participant in a mixed race group of women that was formed in Tulsa to advance dialogue and understanding between the races. Though our efforts were well-intended, and Cookie and I shared a congenial conversation, I remember feeling a gulf between us, and knowing that the chances of our ever meeting again were probably nil.

In the 1970s, as public support grew for school integration, busing of students of color from the north side of Tulsa into the more affluent schools in the east, west, and south regions of the city was introduced to improve equality of education across racial lines. I remember this being a conflictual time for Dad in his career. He had been an athlete and African American young men were being recognized for athletic prowess. He wasn't convinced, however, that forcing integration was a good solution. Though I never heard either of my parents say anything derogatory about any particular race, I suspect that it would have been difficult for our father if John, Bonnie, or I had dated or married an African American person. For a time in my brother John's career, he was the assistant principal at an African American junior high school. More exposed to the north side community, he dated several African American women. My sister and I knew this, but John didn't want either of our parents to know.

So these were the conscious mindsets that Tom and I had in regard to race relations when we went to Zimbabwe. Soon after we got there, I read books by James Baldwin, Richard Wright, Ralph Ellison, Tony Morrison, and Malcolm X, all of which increased my sensitivity to what African Americans in my own country had suffered and what little impact racial discrimination had had on my own life. I hoped I would never drift back into that complacency. I thought more about Dan being Native American and wondered how much he had suffered from insensitivity and prejudice. It was painful to realize how much I had been influenced by "white" arrogance and how it is so taken for granted that "our ways" are better.

One day in class, a well-read Form 3 student asked me what a "white lie" was. "A lie that is harmless," I quickly replied, "and it's typically used to make someone feel good. Have you ever told someone that they looked nice when you really didn't mean it?"

"Yes," he nodded.

"That's a white lie. It isn't true, but rather than hurt someone's feelings, you say something that isn't true." *Then I caught myself.* I recognized the implication that if the lie is "white" it's okay. I wanted to eat my words. My own hidden prejudice had emerged without my being aware of it. What could I say? I had to say something, so I made a fervent apology and used it as an example of how prejudice creeps into our language without our even recognizing it. The depth of the evil wasn't lost to these sensitive young people.

"Are there black lies too?" another student asked. That was my first painful discovery of my own implicit bias.

It has only been since I've become aware of implicit bias as a domain for extensive research that I've looked back at less obvious ways I fell victim to other unconscious stereotypes while I was in Zimbabwe. In 1989 Patricia Divine published an article on the research study she did for her doctoral dissertation. In it she provides evidence of how quickly we can act on an unconscious stereotype even when we have consciously declared racial equality to be one of our core beliefs. Two groups of college students, previously identified as either low prejudice or high prejudice were asked to write down as many words they could think of to describe the stereotype of a member of the "black" race. They were specifically told that the study was not interested in their personal beliefs, but only their knowledge of a cultural stereotype. Their lists of traits included some positive (athletic), some negative (lazy), or some neutral (rhythmic) connotations. The most striking aspect of the data was that the three most common themes listed by both groups were that blacks are poor, aggressive, hostile, and criminal-like.[6]

When I read about this study, I was reminded of my initial reaction when we discovered that Johanes was stealing from us. I was alarmed, even to the point of wanting to send him immediately back to his rural home. I believe this was a reaction to my implicit bias. Tom was less reactive and convinced me we should talk with him about the importance of our being able to trust him, so that hopefully he could learn from the experience. In every other way, Johanes had been helpful, considerate, and conscientious, and he became even more so after our talk. We also made clear that if he ever stole from us again, we would have to send him home. But it did happen again, just before he was to go home at the end of the term. In tears, he begged us not to make him leave that night, but we believed that if we were to have any influence at all, we should keep our word. Still, we didn't feel good about the outcome, but at the time we could see no other alternative. After all, theft was a crime in both Zimbabwe and the United States. Since then I have wondered had we explored more deeply into the roots of Johanes's thievery, we might have been able to help him more.

Sometime later, frustrated by the lack of equipment at his school, Tom bought some new blades for the power saw in the school woodworking department, only to discover them missing a few days later. He confronted the teacher who was the only other person who had access, but the teacher denied responsibility.

"I really have no proof," Tom said to me, fuming when he came home from school.

Again I reacted with alarm at our being victims of theft. "That is so unfair! Surely there is something you can do." I believe the initial trigger was again implicit bias, but to make matters worse, this time my reaction also activated my attachment insecurities regarding Tom.

"What do you suggest?" he asked.

"At the very least, you could bring the small parts to the machines home with you every night. I'm afraid you're not taking care of yourself. You're letting these unscrupulous men take advantage of you."

Tom bristled at this. I was projecting my own fear of vulnerability onto him, which only added to his frustration. This was the first and only major conflict Tom and I had in Zimbabwe. I was erroneously concluding that since an unscrupulous man had taken advantage of Tom, then I could no longer depend on Tom as a person, an irrational conclusion coming from my insecure anxious attachment style. I withdrew, and he withdrew from me. We didn't touch in the night. I obsessed about the possibility that I'd made a mistake in marrying him. I even thought about going home (a similar reaction that I had experienced in Salt Lake City prior to our marriage). Fortunately, the next morning, not being able to bear the silence between us, we were able to talk. We both were learning that stealing, sadly, was embedded in the culture due to long-standing prevailing poverty. I came to understand that Tom was doing his best to work with other teachers in his school, and he deserved my trust in his judgment. We began to see that we were uncovering a dynamic that went far deeper than the issue at hand.

And the fear goes both ways. While our training in Zimbabwe taught us to expect distrust from African people, particularly the older adults who were oppressed by European people for such a long, long time, we were naïve in thinking that we could overcome that distrust with sincere good will. Once settled into our home in Mbizo, we began inviting one or two of the teachers at our schools and their spouses over to our house for dinner, hoping to develop some friendly couple relationships. Their response, peculiar to us, was to graciously accept our invitation with assurances that they would be there at an appointed time—and then not show up. This happened time after time before we got the message that they simply were not ready to trust us. We gave up the fantasy that we might be able to begin a discussion group with other adults to focus on the problems of racial discrimination. It was only with Mr. Chipanda and Mr. Makwindi and their wives did we begin to break through some of those cultural barriers

Stereotypes of any kind, because they are generated outside of our conscious attention, are activated in our mind quickly (automatically) and are most influential when our motivation, awareness, or our ability to reflect are compromised. In contrast, deliberate mental processes are relatively slow, controlled, and intentional. They are more influential on behavior when our motivation is strong, our awareness is keen, and we have the time to introspect before acting.[7]

This logic has led to the development of research measures designed to tap into unconscious motivations. Many studies in the last forty years are inspired by social problems that are characterized by unwanted behavior, not just discrimination due to race, gender, age, religion, and sexual orientation, but also addiction, obesity, and depression, where conscious and unconscious responses are often at odds, and where behaviors are resistant to change. The goal of these studies has been to better understand the mental processes that most influence implicit bias so that interventions could be developed that would be effective in changing behavior.[8]

These studies remind me that what is true of nations, races, genders, and religions, is also true of individuals in relationships. *"Unless mores somehow enter the fiber of individual lives they are not effective agents, for it is only individuals who can feel antagonism and practice discrimination."* The adjustments Tom and I had to make while living in a different culture were analogous to the adjustments that we were making within our relationship and we continue to make now. My supervisor during my marital therapy practicum used to say that most conflicts in marriage emerge from the single question: Are we going to be a "Smith" or a "Jones?" Each individual is not just born into a family, he or she is born into a micro culture containing its own behaviors and beliefs. Included in that is what we fear and distrust. One doesn't usually think of leaving one's country, and all that is familiar, to immerse oneself in a strange new culture as training ground for a second marriage, but for us it was a valuable beginning.

References:

[1] Rudman, I. A., Ashmore, R. D., & Gary, M. L. 2001. "Unlearning" automatic biases: The malleability of implicit prejudice and stereotypes. *Journal of personality and social psychology,* Vol. 81, pp.856-868.

[2] Malcolm X, 1965. *The autobiography of Malcolm X as told to Alex Haley,* The Ballantine Publishing Group, p. 28.

[3] Allport, G. W., 1979 (first published in 1954). *The nature of prejudice.* Perseus Books Publishing, L.L.C.Publishing, L.L.C., p. 285.

[4] Coates, Ta-Nehisi, 2015. *Between the world and me.* New York, Spiegel & Grau, p. 42.

[5] Erikson, Erik. 1980. *Identity and the life cycle.* New York: W. W. Norton & Company, Inc.

[6] Divine, P. G. 1989. Stereotypes and prejudice: Their automatic and controlled components. *Journal of personality and social psychology*, Vol. 56, No. 1.
[7] Forscher, P. S., Mitamura, C., Dix, E. L., Cox, W. T. L., & Divine, P. 2017. Breaking the prejudice habit: Mechanisms, timecourse, and longevity. *Journal of Experimental Social Psychology*, Vol. 72.
[8] Forscher, P. S., Lai, C. K., Axt, J. R., Ebersole, C.R. Herman, M., Devine, P. G., Nosek, B. A. A meta-analysis of procedures to change implicit measures. *Journal of Personality and Social Psychology*, 2019; DOI: 10.1037/pspa0000160
[9] Allport 1979, p. xviii.

12

ENTREPRENEURS

While in Zimbabwe, we talk about where we might live and what we might do to earn a living when we return to the States. We agree that we are too old and independent to be content working for someone else, so we want to start or resume a business of our own that will allow for creativity and autonomy as well. Surely we have a combined set of skills we can put to good use.

It's Christmas Eve, 1993, when we finally land in Tulsa, where a welcoming reunion of my family is in progress. After spending a week with my mother, siblings, and cousins, we drive our car we had left in Tulsa to Arizona to see two of Tom's brothers and his youngest daughter's family. While in Tucson, we hear on the car radio about an entrepreneurs' conference going on there. Maybe we'll find an appealing idea of an interesting business we would like to do this next stage of our lives.

Most of the booths at the conference are promoting franchises or multi-tier marketing schemes, neither of which is of interest to us, but there is one lone, independent exhibitor that catches our eye. He and a partner have developed software that is used in conjunction with a computer graphics program and an architectural plotter to print inexpensive weatherproof outdoor banners. While working at Novell, I learned some basic computer graphics skills and discovered that I could get so engrossed in that activity that I would forget to stop for lunch. Fifteen thousand dollars will buy all the equipment and supplies we would need to start a business and this would include a personal training period with one of the inventors themselves in our own facility. Should we want to expand our business to include currently popular vinyl banners and signs using adhesive vinyl for lettering and graphics, we would already have the necessary equipment to do that also. Their less expensive method, which he demonstrates, will give us a competitive advantage in getting started, he says. We will keep this in mind if we don't find an existing business for sale that we like.

From there we drive to Utah to spend a few days with Tom's oldest daughter and retrieve our pickup and camper that we left at her house while we were gone. Our plan is to check out two small cities we researched in Zimbabwe that meet our desired criteria—Fort Collins, Colorado and Las Cruces, New Mexico. We find several businesses for sale in Fort Collins and nearby Greely, but nothing seems a good fit, so we head for Las Cruces. There's something about New Mexico that appeals to us. Politically and historically it has been a liberal state and we like the idea of living where there are two mingling cultures. They say half the people in Las Cruces speak primarily Spanish, and the city government makes an effort to accommodate both cultures. Street names even reflect the amiable relationship, alternating between Hispanic and Anglo names. New Mexico State University is there and we both enjoy following college athletics and the cultural events that a university provides. When we don't find any interesting existing business for sale, we decide that the Las Cruces population of 70,000 people might be just the right size to grow a computer graphics business like the one we learned about in Tucson. We discover that Las Cruces already has two sign shops. One specializes in electric neon signs, and upon visiting the other, we think we can compete. None of the popular sign franchises have yet reached Las Cruces which is also a plus.

By March of 1994, we are living in a concrete block, two bedroom house on Main Street that is already zoned for business. A couple has been living here while operating a beauty salon in the carport they enclosed, and it already has space for parking. As promised, the inventor we met in Tucson has spent three days here teaching us how to operate the computer, the software, and the plotter, using a supply of eight colors of waterproof ink, eight large pens, large rolls of thirty-six inch outdoor fiberglass "paper" called Tyvek (which is normally used for building insulation), and four colors of paper the same size for indoor banners. Tom and I decide to give ourselves two months to get comfortable with the printing process, to prepare our work space, and do some landscaping outside. We'll also use one of our finished products for a large banner to put on the side of our building that faces the street with our new name: Signergy Productions. On our opening day, we sell our first banner to an equestrian farm that teaches disabled children how to ride a horse. Their banner cost thirty-five dollars, a good start.

Marketing our new product is a challenge because we have opened too late to be in the phone book, so we make up a sales packet containing all the services we can provide a customer. Tom hits the streets to contact every business in town that uses banners. Nearly every day he brings in a few orders and we figure we can survive if we can earn five hundred dollars per week. Then one day he returns from an outing with a big smile on his face. "You're never going to believe this!" he says. "I just happened to go into that big conference center downtown to see what was going on there. The City of Las Cruces is launching a campaign event to oust El Paso Electric, which has been providing electricity for Las Cruces for years. The city wants to provide that utility themselves. When I told them about our banners, they asked me how much one would cost to go *all the way around the inside perimeter of their main gathering room!*"

"Wow!" I said. "That's a long banner! What do they want on it?"

"The only graphic will be one long, long, wavy electric cord with a plug on one end, with the words "PULL THE PLUG" on all four sides of the room. So I measured the distance and told them a one-color printing job on our bright fluorescent yellow paper would be $650.00."

"That's fantastic! This is huge! This will be the best sale we've made!"

Another significant development comes a few months later. A man comes into our store and tells us that he's promoting a "Going out of Business" sale for one of the big furniture stores in town, and that he does this all over the country. He likes to completely cover the windows with banners containing his message in big letters.

"Can the banners be mounted on the inside?" Tom asks.

"Yes."

"Then we could use our fluorescent paper which would make them much less expensive."

I've already brought out the rolls of hot pink, yellow, and lime green paper to show him. "We print on these colors with black ink or on white paper with one of eight colors. Would that work?" I ask him.

"That would be perfect," he says.

Happy with his banners, this man becomes a regular customer. He calls in with measurements of windows in furniture stores all over the country and we ship the banners to him. Little by little, we find good customers who learn they can trust us. Tom used to sell Fuller Brush products door-to-door to earn money when he was in college, so he learned a lot of positive sales techniques. One of them is to trust one's customer, so for local jobs, we don't ask for a deposit, and rarely does a customer let us down. I'm getting pretty good at duplicating logos now and I enjoy coming up with new ideas while working with customers.

"I always know if I can get them to sit down with you at the computer, we've made a sale, because they feel a part of it," Tom says to encourage me.

By the end of our first year in business, we move out of our living room into the two bedrooms so we can use the living room space for retail sales. We start selling a variety of signs, flags, flagpoles, windsocks, and kites. We've also found a retired sign-maker who is cutting vinyl letters for us if we need them, so we're using some vinyl banner material now in addition to the Tyvek and paper. By the end of the second year, we've found a Hispanic family in El Paso who operate a wholesale screen-printing business, so we can contract with them to have large volumes of campaign signs or printed T-shirts made. We're also using a company in Illinois that screen-prints our custom-designed flags. We buy a house just a few blocks away our third year, so we're able to use the entire building on Main Street for our business. We remove a wall to expand retail space into what was the front bedroom, and we use the back bedroom for needed storage. Now, when we close the business in the evening, we have a separate place to go home, and this is a real luxury.

In 1998, our fourth year in business, we are able to completely remodel and enlarge our business building, substantially increasing both our work and retail space. The result is one of the most attractive small businesses in a southwestern style in Las Cruces. It comes at a time when other upgrades are happening along this part of Main Street, making our investment all the more valuable.

On the morning of September 11, 2001, two airplanes crash into the North and South towers of the World Trade Center complex in Lower Manhattan, New York City. Approximately thirty minutes later, another airplane flies into the Pentagon and a fourth flight, thirty minutes after that, crashes near Shanksville, Pennsylvania, its target believed to be either the Capitol or the White House. When we arrive at our business that morning, a customer is waiting outside for us to open. "I thought this would be a good day to buy an American flag," he says. The next morning, there is a line of people stretching from our door, clear across our parking lot and down the street, who are waiting to get inside to buy an American flag. The local television station crew comes to cover the spectacle. When our own accountant comes in to buy a flag, she sees that we're so busy, she stays the rest of the day to run the cash register so Tom and I can wait on customers.

We have a larger stock of American flags than anyone else in Las Cruces. We carry them in all sizes, from four by six inches all the way up to twelve by eighteen feet. We also carry every size and kind of flagpole, including wall-mounted types and those that are much larger and installed with concrete in the ground. In 1994, with unknowing foresight, we established a domain on the internet to sell our retail products. For a short while, we are the only company in the nation who carries flags of all the NFL teams online. So when local supplies of American flags run out about the country, our online business soars. When all of our U.S. wholesale suppliers run out of flags, Tom finds a Brazilian company that is happy to seize this opportunity to make up the difference. So while this unprecedented terrorist attack is causing serious harm to the United States economy and having a significant effect on global markets, our business is booming, and the demand for American flags stays high for another year. By the end of 2002, our clientele has doubled, and so has our gross income. We are named a Star Business by the New Mexico Small Business Development Center Network.

The next year we experiment with hiring employees we can train to help us. None of them turn out to be dependable in the long-term except the thirty-year-old Hispanic woman, Yolanda, who cleans for us. Smart and personable, we decide to train *her*. Yolanda quickly learns our invoicing system, our inventory, and many of the sign-making skills. Her quiet and gracious manner is popular with our customers, so we can't ask for a more versatile and valuable employee. The other work we need to have done we turn over to wholesale contractors. This works, but like any growing business, it also increases the stress because we are depending on others to do work we have previously done ourselves. We no longer have complete control over meeting deadlines for a project.

So how is this growing business affecting our personal growth and our relationship? We both have gained confidence in what we can accomplish together by working through inevitable challenges that arise in any business. Several of our best customers have commented on our ability to work together successfully as a couple. We have earned the respect of the business community in Las Cruces and formed some valued customer relationships, including those with some major institutions—New Mexico State University, White Sands Missile Range, Las Cruces School District, and local public radio and television stations. But the pressures of our business leave little leisure time for us together or alone time for ourselves. Working so closely together day after day raises the dilemma of how do we balance our needs for both intimacy and autonomy?

One problem is that the design work for me is more fun and rewarding because I receive more acknowledgements from public exposure. Tom bears almost all the responsibility for making financial decisions and he does much of the mundane and behind-the-scenes work. He's good at all these things and I can fully trust him, leaving me free to indulge myself in the delights of creativity. Though Tom is proud of my contribution to the success of our business, he doesn't always feel that his work is seen as being equally vital. This subject comes up one Sunday afternoon when we are relaxing at home.

"But I *do* know that everything you do is important," I protest. "The business wouldn't be here if it wasn't for you. Maybe it's bothering you when you see that I'm having more fun."

"That's not the problem and I resent your saying that. You make it sound like I'm jealous, and I'm not. I'm glad you enjoy what you're doing. I just think there's an imbalance somewhere that affects how I see myself and how you see me."

"I don't know what I can do about that," I say. "Why did you get into this if it's not something you enjoy? I'm willing to make some changes if you'll just tell me what to do."

"You keep making this my problem. It's the same old message I get from you that I'm not taking care of myself and you are. I don't believe this is true, and it's unfair."

Vaguely in the back of my brain, I recognize this as a familiar theme, but I don't want to see it. It angers me. "I'm getting too upset and I know I'm not being productive. I'm going on a walk. I don't like where this is going."

"That's fine! If you don't want to deal with this, I think it's a mistake, but maybe you're right. Maybe we need to give each other more space. Take it! Take all you want. I'm going out to the garden." He leaves.

I walk out the door, feeling like I want to slam it, but I don't. We live in a quiet neighborhood and I start walking. I'm feeling smug. I believe I'm right—that it isn't my fault that he feels he's not getting enough recognition for what he does. He's just going to have to figure this out on his own, and I just need to calm myself down. I take a dozen or so deep breaths. I keep walking—thirty minutes or more. Then the fear creeps in. What if I'm not right? I've done this before and I know my exiting the situation isn't the answer. Then a panic takes over. Maybe he's weary of my not trusting him. Maybe I'm really not good for him and he's finding that out. I could really lose him because of this. I think of all Tom's positive attributes—his dependability, his always being there for me, his being the most conscientious person I know. My steps quicken and I can't get back home soon enough to tell him I'm sorry. I don't find him in the house, so I go out the backdoor and find him in the garden. "I'm so sorry!" I wail. "I'm completely beside myself when we're at odds like this." In despair, I begin to cry. "I'm really sorry. I want to feel close to you again. I want to learn how to show you more appreciation—the appreciation you deserve. I don't want to be the star of our business. I'd rather not have it if it feels that way to you." Then he sees that I really care about him and that seems to make all the difference. The hostility between us dissolves.

These heated disputes don't happen very often, because most of the time Tom and I are attentive, supportive, and appreciative of one another, but when this uncomfortable dynamic makes itself known, it is usually at a time of stress, and we both feel the other is being unfair. Why do these arguments feel so threatening? Why are our efforts to restore consensus so urgent? And why is our talk so intense with defensiveness and blame? It is particularly painful and disturbing when the anxiety spills over into our sexual relationship. Then we both question our choice to marry. Has it all been a mistake? Are we truly good for one another or not?

An impasse will last one or two days at the least, three or four days at the most, and each one ends with the same conclusion. Worn out from finding fault and defending ourselves, one or the other will let down a defense, acknowledge a fear, and then make some gesture of affection and the mood will change. The tension dissolves. By then we often don't remember why we began to argue. Whatever it was, it doesn't matter anymore. We still love each other more than we've ever loved anyone else; there is no other person with whom we can share more core values; our union is unique, special, and worth all the time and effort we take trying to solve our problems. As painful as it can be, we both agree that the good times far outweigh the bad. When the beloved peace is reestablished, we try to understand what is at the root of our problem, and how can we prevent the painful times from occurring again?

Tom believes our episodes are destructive and that they weaken our perception of what our relationship can be, while I cling to the hope that we are learning something each time that strengthens our mutual trust in little increments. But we both agree that surely there are less traumatic ways to accomplish the same thing, and surely we're smart enough to find them. We read *The Intimate Enemy: How to Fight Fair in Love and Marriage,* by Bach and Wyden, reminding us that our ability to express our love feelings will correspond to our leveling with each other about our anger, but learning to do it in constructive ways. We make a list of communication dos and don'ts, signing our names at the bottom, confident that our responsible follow-through will help. Still, time after time, we find ourselves in the same situation again. What is it that we don't understand?

INSIGHTS: Acknowledging Our Defenses

Tom and I had enough experience to know that every relationship has conflict, and if it's managed wisely, it can help us learn more about ourselves and each other. It can help us grow. We also knew, however, that we hadn't handled conflict very well in our first marriages, so we were concerned about the intensity of our arguments, especially when they would raise the ultimate question as to whether or not our marriage was a mistake. It was confusing to experience something that could be so good most of the time and so disparaging at other times. What we didn't understand was that we were forming a stronger attachment with one another than either of us had ever had. From the beginning of our relationship, we knew we shared more values than we had shared with our first mates, and we were both highly motivated to make our marriage work. Consequently, we had more to lose when our relationship was threatened. A painful argument, while shaking our self-confidence, eroded our trust in each other. We didn't yet understand that we both entered our relationship as two anxious insecure people, prone to anxious behavior, and also capable of avoidance at times we were feeling most insecure.

Jeremy Holmes wrote and published a book in 2010 called *Exploring in Security*, which describes a process through which two people can "earn security." Written primarily for psychotherapists using attachment theory as a framework, Holmes contends that although attachment styles are rooted in early parent-child interactions, they should not be seen as fixed. Through the attentions of a caring school teacher, for example, or as an adult in the form of a good marriage, a nurturing friendship, or successful psychotherapy, a person's level of attachment security can be increased.[1] What would have been particularly helpful to us is Holmes' description of the skills that help two people feel secure in one another's presence.

Of most importance is what he calls "mentalizing," (a term first used by Bateman and Fonagy, 2004).[2] Mentalizing is a capacity to be aware of and to make interpretations about what we are thinking and feeling. It also involves attributing meaning to our interactions with another in a non-judgmental way in an effort to understand.

"I sense that I've upset you in some way. Can you help me understand how I've done that?"

Or, "I feel angry and impatient with you right now, but maybe it's because I don't understand why this is so important to you."

Or, "I can tell I'm distancing myself from you, and I don't like that feeling. I don't want to alienate you."

Or, "This feels like we're getting polarized, and I don't want that. Is there some common goal that we can work toward?"

In the developing child, the constant exchange of thoughts, feelings, and words with a caregiver is what helps to build a secure attachment, and it is these same processes that can help two adults "earn" a secure attachment, reducing the impact of previous childhood deprivation or harm. When we feel we are being listened to, non-judged, and understood, we feel safe, secure, and better able to get to the truth of what we are experiencing. Mentalizing helps to break down the defense mechanisms that project false notions about ourselves. Destructive behaviors intended to hide our vulnerability or angry behavior that cloaks our fears are acts that reinforce trauma of the past and become barriers to nurturing communication.[3]

In another work by Holmes and Lindley (1997), the authors describe their goals of psychotherapy, the primary one being to help a person reach a state of "emotional autonomy." To be emotionally autonomous does not mean isolation or avoidance of dependency, nor does it mean one must suppress feelings, including the need for dependence. Instead, it implies that we are taking control of our lives by learning to be cognizant of our feelings, rather than being ruled by them. In a relationship where two people are earnest in becoming more emotionally autonomous, they may soon discover that a negative response to the other person is often based on a faulty perception. To move from a position of insecure to secure attachment with another will involve a great deal of emotional processing of past painful events in order to get to the truth of our interaction.[4] While Tom and I knew a lot about one another's former lives, we had not yet explored the depth of disappointment we had both experienced in earlier relationships.

We certainly hadn't been able to accomplish this in our first marriages. Perhaps none of the four of us had the maturity to see things in an objective way. We didn't yet understand how we had been driven by forces over which we had little control. By now we had some hindsight about early choices we had made when dies were cast for good or ill. Due to our unique histories, we each entered our relationship with an unconscious paradigm of what healthy relating meant. I was convinced that one needs to develop a strong sense of personal identity before one can successfully merge with another person. Without that preparation, intimacy with another would be too threatening. My perspective was one of putting *autonomy first*. Tom, on the other hand, came into the relationship believing that commitment was the necessary ingredient in a healthy relationship. Partners must make the facilitation of one another's deepest emotional needs their highest priority. His perspective was one of putting *intimacy first*. . Consequently, when a conflict arose, my tendency was to pull away and withdraw into myself. Tom's was to move closer, isolate the problem, and figure out what precisely was separating us.

We wouldn't be the first couple to experience autonomy and intimacy as a contradiction in a relationship. Since our business necessitated our working closely together every day, we had little time for individual activities. I would go swimming early three mornings and week when Tom would ride his bike, and on weekends we spent some time apart, but some understanding of a "dialectic" perspective would have helped us see our struggles in a less competitive way.

In the late 1980s, Leslie Baxter began to study the dialectic component in friendships, romantic relationships, and married couples. The philosopher Soren Kierkegaard used a dialectic form of thought when he wrote, "*It belongs to the imperfection of everything human that man can only attain his desire by passing through its opposite.*" This perspective goes a long way back to the best of ancient thinkers. The Tao-Te-Ching exemplifies dialectic thinking:

> "*Should you want to contain something, you must deliberately let it expand,*
> *Should you want to weaken something, you must deliberately let it grow strong.*
> *Should you want to eliminate something, you must deliberately allow it to flourish.*

Should you want to take something away, you must deliberately grant it."

To a dialectic thinker, developmental growth and change take place amid the tension and struggle between paired opposites or contradictions. Two entities that may appear contradictory to one another may actually be two parts of a whole that depend on one another. We couldn't talk about darkness if there was no such thing as light. We begin to understand love when we permit ourselves to understand our hate. Rather than seeing something as either-or, we find that opposites can be found within each other.[5]

Baxter's earliest work established that there are three fundamental dialectic pairs of contradictions that are experienced in most relationships: autonomy vs. intimacy, openness vs. closedness, and predictability vs. novelty. It is commonly one of these contradictions that causes a minor difference between two people to become polarized. The dialective perspective recognizes the need for both, and relationship well-being is best sustained when the need for each opposite is fulfilled. It also acknowledges that too much of one without the other is detrimental to a relationship. Individual identities can get lost when there is too much togetherness, for example, but paradoxically too much autonomy can also weaken an individual's identity, since connections with others are necessary for identity formation to take place. More than that, dialectical conflicts are considered inherent to all healthy relationship functioning. Rather than viewing contradiction as harmful, it is viewed as essential to change and growth.[6] This understanding is an incentive to see what may bother us most about the other is the very thing that might be of most benefit to ourselves. In this way, the relationship helps us each to become a more fully developed person than we would have become by ourselves.

Attachment theory has helped me understand how our insecurities came into being, but the dialectic perspective is reassuring in that I can see how our struggles emerge from forces that are present in all relationships. Though our mutual insecure attachments have probably increased the amount of tension we've had to deal with, they may also have given us a stronger desire to make our relationship work. Together, both perspectives combined have comprised a strong impetus to change and grow.

References:

[1] Holmes, J. 2010. *Exploring in security: Towards an attachment-informed psychoanalytic psychotherapy,* London: Routledge.
[2] Bateman, A. & Fonagy, P. 2004. *Psychotherapy for borderline personality disorder: Mentalization based treatment.* Oxford, UK: Oxford University Press.
[3] Holmes 2010.
[4] Holmes, J., & Lindley, R. 1997. T*he values of psychotherapy* (2nd ed.). London: Karnac.
[5] Rowan, J. 2015. *Ordinary ecstasy: The dialectics of humanistic psychology.* New York: Routledge.
[6] Baxter, L. A. 1990. Dialectical contradictions in relationship development. *Journal of social and personal relationships,* Vol. 7.

13

FAMILY MATTERS

While we were in Zimbabwe, we avoided some of the problems that often emerge in a second marriage, particularly those involving in-laws and one another's children. Now that we are back in the U.S., it's no surprise that our interactions are increasing with our family members. I exchanged weekly letters with my mother while we were away and I was moved by an awareness that she, more than anyone, was the most interested in my day-to-day experiences. This helped to soften the strain that still exists between us regarding religion. John has brought her here to spend a month with Tom and me, so we can have a good visit. She is with us on the day we open our business. I'm very nervous and tell her about my hand shaking when I record the order for our first thirty-five dollar banner. She reassures me that I will do well.

Mom takes walks in the neighborhood for exercise and Tom takes her to the senior citizens center several days each week for social activities. One day he tells me that she has talked to him in the car about her religion. "I think she may want to convert me in hopes that I'll bring you back into the fold," he says.

"You're probably right. So how did you respond?"

"I just haven't said much of anything, but I would like to be honest with her. How would you feel about that?"

"Just the thought of you talking honestly to her about her beliefs—and ours—makes my stomach churn, but I think it's the right thing to do. I don't want her to have false hopes. I've not even told her myself that I no longer consider myself a Christian. That's going to be hard. Would you mind talking to her without my being there?"

"No, not if that is what you want."

So that evening, while I'm working on something in the business side of the house, Tom and my mother have a conversation. I can't hear what they're saying, but I feel my heart beating and I can't concentrate on anything I'm doing. It's still hard for me *not* to protect her.

That night after we go to bed, Tom tells me the details of their conversation.

"I think it went as well as could be expected. I told her that since she's been bringing up the subject of religion, I wanted to be honest with her. She probably suspected what was coming, because at first she resisted, saying that we didn't need to talk about it. But I told her I thought we should. I basically said that though I respect her beliefs and that I've thought about what she's said, I'm really not likely to be convinced of any Christian perspective right now. She was a little defensive and told me that I probably couldn't ever understand since I hadn't been brought up in the Truth. I said that might be true, but that I hoped we could respect one another's position, and she agreed."

I'm relieved, but I imagine that Mom is probably disappointed that her efforts have been thwarted. Over the next few days, we feel a withdrawal from her, which makes me sad, and when John returns to get her, she's ready to go back home. I try to accept this as an inevitable consequence of the reality that exists, but still, I worry about her. John is retired now and has sold his house and moved into our family home with Mom so he can care for her. Since Bonnie and I are still working, we are grateful to John that he is so willing to do this. Dad willed the house to the three of us, so Bonnie and I settle financially with John to give him full ownership of the family home.

One day I get a phone call from John. "I've had a really bad night with Mom," he says. I can tell he's upset. "She fell when she got up to go to the bathroom and she couldn't get up off the floor. The hardest part is that she cried out to me to come and help her, but I didn't have my hearing aids on, so I couldn't hear her."

"I can imagine how you must feel, but there's no way you could have possibly known. You mustn't blame yourself."

"She had to lie there all night on the floor. I didn't find her until I got up this morning."

"Is she all right now?"

"I think so. She's just sore, but I don't think she broke any bones. The worst part is that it really scared her."

"Well, it's probably a sign that we need to get more help for her. It may be that she needs to be in a nursing home."

"I don't think I can do that," he says. "Especially now."

"Let me call Bonnie. Maybe she and I can both come home and we'll all talk about it."

"I would really appreciate that."

A week later, the four of us are sitting around the dining table in our house on Madison Place. We talk about her falling and how sorry we all are that she had to go through that traumatic night. But it's Mom who brings up the difficult topic, not us.

"I think I will feel safer if I'm in a nursing home."

As hard as it is to leave the home she has lived in for over fifty years, my mother makes an adjustment to a life I suspect she never anticipated. She cared for her own mother in our house until her mother died, and there being three of us, especially two daughters, she probably expected the same for herself. We help her get settled into a nice facility that isn't far from John's house so it's convenient for him to visit her regularly. A kind and amiable lady is her roommate. Bonnie and I create a large collage of family photographs to put on her wall, and we both agree to fly to Tulsa, alternating in three month intervals, throughout the year. John keeps a promise to visit her every evening, and makes friends with all the nursing home staff in the process. His devotion is probably a factor in guaranteeing that Mom receives the best possible care. She is a sweet and submissive patient and her only complaint is that she has to wear ear plugs at night in order to sleep.

That year I begin to compile thirty years of my mother's writings into a book that she names, *Mountains and Valleys in my Life*, and describes as "accounts of some of the happiest times in my life as well as my failures and blunders and excuses for myself." It contains fifty-three chapters! During my visits to Tulsa, we collaborate about her book, giving us many opportunities to talk about her life. One particularly enjoyable day, nearing the book's completion, we spend hours going through family picture albums selecting the photographs she wants to include. She studies carefully a photo of her with Bonnie and me when I was a teenager. She reaches over and places her hand over mine before she speaks.

> *"I recently read of a metaphor regarding aging. It described two trees growing next to one another, tall and sturdy, but not touching. Only until full maturity do they touch, when their foliage finally mingles together at the top. I hope this characterizes our relationship."*

In early November Mom contracts an infection from a bedsore and is taken to the hospital. By now she has withdrawn considerably and I can no longer have conversations with her on the phone. Though we expect this setback to be temporary, her body is unable to fight off the infection and she dies on October 30, 1998 with only John at her side. In a private moment after her funeral service, John, Bonnie, and I huddle together in a hug, weeping in acknowledgement of the hard life our mother has had.

Now that we have a comfortable guest bedroom, John is coming to see us several times a year, and he's learning to help us in the business. As we get busier and there are evenings in which we have to work, we compensate for the longer hours by taking John out to eat. He has a lady-friend now whom he seems to be quite serious about, but as usual, he's conflicted about making a commitment. I watch John reach out to Tom for friendship, comparing Tom in positive ways to our father. I think that Tom can be of help to John, who is comfortable confiding in both of us. Consequently, his visits sometime result in lengthy, what have become "therapy" sessions. Tom believes our family has belittled John by perceiving him as weak and immature, so Tom is more inclined to view him as a mature adult. We explore all the many reasons that John might fear marriage and how he might overcome his reluctance, only to end up with John admitting that he really doesn't want to get married after all.

"I don't know how productive these long discussions are," Tom says once John has left.

"I know they can be frustrating, but I think you're good for him as long as you don't expect too much. He suffered the most from Mom and Dad's conflicts. I think that's why he fears marriage—and he looks up to you."

"But he's almost sixty years old! And I didn't sign up to be his father."

"I know that I get anxious when you don't respond to John as I do."

"I see that, and I like John. He has a lot of admirable qualities, but I need to develop my relationship with him without interference from you. I think all of your family has coddled him long enough."

Not long after this, Tom's brother Clark comes to visit us and once again we encounter some tension in the way we deal with one another's family. I'm aware that Clark is just eighteen months older than Tom and that there was rivalry between the two of them growing up. After Tom's divorce, he and Clark spent time together when Clark's wife was out of town or involved in her own activities. I sensed some resentment from Clark after Tom and I started dating, because Tom was spending more of his free time with me. Clark is here helping Tom put a roof over our back patio and Tom is eager to show Clark the plans for remodeling our business. As he often does, Clark responds with obvious disinterest when he sees there is something Tom is excited about. It appears to me that he's ignoring Tom to needle him, and my anger flares.

"I can't help but wonder if you're just jealous of Tom because things are going well with us," I say. I see Clark fume.

"You don't know anything about my relationship with Tom," he mutters with contempt.

I decide this may work out better if I let them deal with this alone, so I leave to go finish up some work at the business. When I'm not home by nine, Tom calls me on the phone, angry. "Leaving here was the worst thing you could have done! Now Clark is threatening to go home in the morning."

"I didn't know what else to do, and I thought it would be better if you two worked it out yourselves. I didn't trust myself to talk with Clark because I was so angry with him. I really do think he's jealous of you."

"That's no justification for your being rude."

"If you want me to apologize, I will." And so I do, but Clark still leaves early.

Then there is Dan, who has returned home from his last duty station as a Marine in Okinawa. He drives to Las Cruces to see us with his new girlfriend, a pretty Apache girl, who has grown up on the Apache reservation in eastern Arizona. Dan has been doing well at a job in Phoenix, working at a native-owned casino. He's pleasant, though somewhat aloof with me. Tom asks for some help putting up a new sign, and Dan agrees, but gets a little testy when Tom tells him what he would like him to do. We notice the tension, but the rest of their short visit goes by without any further friction. A few months later I learn that Dan has lost the casino job, broken up with his girlfriend, and is back in Prescott staying with Mike and his new wife. He comes to see us again a second time, but this time a friend drives him here because Dan is adrift without a job. His friend then leaves to go elsewhere, so we get Dan settled in the guest room and prepare ourselves for what may be a long stay. We discuss the possibility of him helping us here in our business, but he doesn't seem interested in that, so we make some suggestions about where he might apply for a job. One day he walks a distance to apply for a waiter's job at a nice restaurant, but is turned away. Another day he goes with a friend of ours on a temporary job delivering telephone books. But the next few days he seems to be content to stay at the house watching television. Tension is building. One night we take him to a university baseball game. On our way back to the car, Dan lags behind, seemingly not wanting to walk with us. A second week goes by.

That night I say to Tom, "I think we need to talk to him seriously about his plans. I suffer watching Dan flounder, but I feel utterly ineffective in knowing how to deal with him."

"I know what you mean. I'm starting to dread coming home," Tom says.

"I don't sense that he's really motivated to stay here in Las Cruces with us, but I don't know what else to suggest that he do otherwise," I say.

"Apparently he's had run-ins with Mike too, or he wouldn't have come here."

"Would you be willing to talk to him with me tomorrow night?"

Tom agrees and we discuss the points we want to make.

The next evening we ask Dan to sit with us in the living room for a conversation. Tom and Dan are sitting on the couch and I'm sitting across from them in the rocking chair.

"Dan, we're glad you felt you could come here at a time when you needed support," I say to begin, "and you're welcome to stay here with us for as long as you need to. But we do need you to make some reasonable effort to find work." Dan shifts in his position and is noticeably agitated.

"Help us know how we can best support you," Tom adds.

Suddenly Dan jumps up from the couch to go back to his room. "I'm leaving!" he says.

Tom and I both get up to follow him. "Wait, Dan," I say. "Can't we just talk together calmly about this? We don't want you to leave, especially at this hour of the night."

"No!" he yells. "I don't want to talk to you. I'll hitchhike. Just give me enough money to get back to Prescott." He starts stuffing things from drawers into his bag.

"Dan, we need to talk about this," Tom pleads. "We need to deal with it. Please come back in the living room and sit down with us." Dan continues to impatiently stuff his bag with his belongings.

I'm in acute emotional pain trying to face the reality of what is happening. "Dan, this is crazy. I'm sure we can work out something. I don't want you to leave here tonight alone. Please." But I see his determination and I believe that to argue further will be of no use.

We have no cash with us, so Tom drives over to the business to get a fifty dollar bill, and we give it to him. Watching him walk out into the dark night, carrying his stuffed duffle bag, is one of my most despairing moments as a parent.

Not long after this, Dan calls me on the phone from Prescott. He explains that he's been contacted by his birth family in Quesnel, British Columbia. An aunt of Dan's has offered to pay his way to come home to his birthplace and meet his relatives, including eleven siblings of whom he is the oldest. Dan sounds excited and I'm happy for him. I think it couldn't have come at a better time. Maybe this is exactly what he needs—to find his roots. He thanks me for all we did for him and I get the impression that he intends to stay in Canada. "Promise me you will stay in touch. I will always love you, Dan."

"I love you, too."

Not long after Dan returns to Canada, I write an article that is published in a monthly literary magazine about Mike's and my adoption of Dan and the feelings I experience when he leaves to relocate near his birth family. In the next issue of the magazine, much to my shock, there is a vehement response to my article.

"You stole that child!" a man writes. From there he describes the Canadian government's strategy to integrate aboriginal children into the dominant culture by removing them from their birth families and placing them in "white" homes or residential schools. This is the first time I hear of the policy that led to our adoption of Dan. No one in the adoption agency informed us of this. All we were told was that this baby needed a home. Though it may have been intended to ensure that aboriginal children receive an education, I am horrified to think that from the families' point of view, Mike and I were complicit in something that was destructive to their culture and cruel, in that it separated them from their children. Frantically I delve into the history of the policy that came to be known as the "Seventies Sweep." Aboriginal bands came together to hire legal help to undo the harm that was done during that decade. Reparations have been made to those now adults who were placed in residential schools. Some Canadians believe the reparations have gone too far, have been too much, exacerbating racial tensions. Unfortunately, reparations can never compensate for damage that is done from serious ruptures in one's childhood.

It isn't until 1986, the year Dan was contacted by his aunt, that the whereabouts of these children were made known to their birth families. Sherman Alexie, a Native American writer, writes fiction based on real experiences of aboriginal people. I begin to read his books in order to gain more understanding. His first book, *Indian Killer*, tells a story of an aboriginal boy who is adopted by a Caucasian family. The mother in the story is depicted as shallow, self-serving, and condescending, motivated by a desire to appear charitable when she and her husband adopt the boy. I'm sickened at the thought that she could be me, especially when I learn that the boy in the story grows up to be a serial killer.

When I tell Dan on the phone what I'm learning, he confirms the information with his own story his mother and siblings have told him. His band, the Kluskus people, live on a reserve seventy-five miles from Quesnel on a primitive logging road. The children are moved into Quesnel for the school year, while band elders remain on the reserve. His mother is only sixteen when Dan is born in a Quesnel hospital. When his grandparents hear of the danger that their grandchild might be taken from his mother, they take the arduous nine-hour journey into town in a horse-drawn wagon. Their hope is to get there in time to rescue the baby, but they are too late. Dan's birth certificate contains a release form signed by his birth mother, so if his family's story is true, and I assume it is, then she was either coerced or deceptively manipulated into signing it.

Dan stays in contact with me intermittently, but he has yet to settle into any one job, and relationships with his birth family have been mixed in their level of satisfaction. He's close with one younger brother and his mother, but has had little contact with his father. Assimilating into his native culture, not having grown up on the reserve with his siblings, is challenging. They tell him he talks differently, and he tells me they barely talk at all. It concerns him that his younger siblings aren't serious about going to school. He also experiences a difference in the Caucasian people there. In proportion to the United States, the aboriginal population in Canada is much greater because they didn't kill as many native people in Indian wars as did the United States. Consequently, there are more reserves in close proximity to Canadian towns and cities. Proximity breeds tension, and tension breeds prejudice. Dan feels that he's a misfit in both cultures.

In his third year in Canada, Dan forms a relationship with a young native woman he met when they both were working as firefighters one summer. He and Alison move in together and have a baby girl. When the child is eight months old, Alison decides that she wants her daughter to know her only surviving grandparents. She calls us on the phone, asking if she and the baby can come and spend two weeks with us in Las Cruces. She is confident that they will be welcome because we are "family." And they are. Dan chooses not to come. He says he can't afford it, but I suspect he doesn't want to be observed in his new and unfamiliar fathering role. We learn a lot about Dan's native culture during those two weeks. Like in Africa, it is more important to women to bear children than it is to marry. If a woman becomes pregnant, the success of the conception is a sign that the relationship is meant to be. She is very fond of Dan and wishes he had come with her. John comes for a visit while they are here, so he keeps them entertained while Tom and I are working.

I miss having a close woman friend while Tom and I are working in Las Cruces. I was naïve to think that the two-year separation from Ellen while we were in Zimbabwe wouldn't create distance between us. For months she didn't respond to my letters. Not understanding this, I could only imagine that Ellen was hurt and angry because I'd stepped out of her life. I finally expressed my fear in a letter after nine months of silence, bewailing the fact that I hadn't heard from her. This provoked her to write, but not to reconcile. She insisted that she wasn't angry, that she understood and accepted that our lives had changed. Her response wasn't comforting, and since then I've mourned our estrangement. Ellen has been my closest woman friend. Now that we are back home and have moved into our separate house, I convince her to come visit us. Unfortunately I come down with the flu and we don't have much quality time together. In the discussions that she, Tom, and I have together, she learns of my departure from the Christian faith, which I'm afraid she has experienced as a rejection of her. The visit hasn't healed the breach between us, and I feel a deep loss that my friendship with Ellen has diminished.

INSIGHT: The Relationship Between Insecurity and Anxiety

As one might expect, research shows that the best predictor of happiness in any relationship is a secure attachment. Secure individuals report higher levels of relationship satisfaction, commitment, and trust, while insecure individuals report lower levels of all three. What are the traits that secure people have that make so much difference? Secure people are not as apt to get "riled up" in the face of threat. They learned as children to expect their caregivers to respond to them in comforting and reassuring ways, so they don't worry so much about losing someone's affection. They have an ability to discern another's needs and to respond appropriately, because they've seen this sensitivity in their former caregivers. They are more comfortable responding to others with physical expressions of affection, like reaching out to touch, hold hands, or to hug another. During an argument, they are less apt to defend themselves or to punish another because they are not so threated by criticism. In short, what may be hard work for their insecure counterparts, comes easy for them.[1]

Fortunately Tom and I brought some important positive secure traits into our relationship. For example, we both were singled out by our mothers as being more responsive to their needs, so we had acquired many caregiving and unselfish behaviors. But we both shared a strong need for approval and neither of us could gracefully hear criticism, especially if we thought it unfair. Anxious people carry with them a sense for danger because as children they experienced mixed responses, both positive and negative, to their emotional needs. They tend to be more sensitive to others' emotional cues, picking up more quickly on threatening details specifically. They are more apt to jump to conclusions and misinterpret or exaggerate another's emotional state, fearing the worst.

I am aware, as I write about these conflictual times with my mother, my brother, Dan, Clark, and Ellen, I associate them with high levels of worry and anxiety, particularly when I perceived any indication of disapproval. This was often the case in my interactions with Clark. Looking back, I can see that I was intimidated by Tom's large family, knowing how critical some of them were about his leaving the family's chosen church. I feared their influence, concerned that Tom might succumb and return to the fold, ultimately threatening my relationship with him. Of course Tom wanted to have a good relationship with his brother, but I saw it as a threat to me. If a child becomes frantic or cries uncontrollably when separated from his or her mother, we sympathize and view it as normal. Insecure adults also have their ways of protesting a threat, but our behaviors are not as easily tolerated. I defended myself and found reason to blame. The result was to put Tom in a position of having to choose between his brother and me. Not yet having enough confidence in either of our abilities to make repairs, he sided with me, but suppressed resentment.

When my mother, John, and Dan came to visit, we encountered a different kind of problem related to our attachment insecurities. In these situations I had unreasonable expectations of Tom, wanting him to make up for my own sense of inadequacy in my relationships with each one. I've observed that when needs have not been met in our families growing up, we tend to cling in desperation to those early relationships out of a longing and hope for reconciliation. Attachment bonds are deep with our parents, siblings, and our children, and when things didn't go well with these family members as adults, I felt a desperate need to fix whatever it was. When I wasn't able to fix it, I wanted Tom to do it for me. As unreasonable as it was, and as much as I denied it, I unconsciously blamed him to avoid my own feelings of inadequacy.

As we settled into the demands of running a business, working together almost constantly, we rarely were able to get away just to enjoy one another's company in a relaxing atmosphere. Since neither of us had experienced a consistently secure relationship in our first marriages, neither of us understood how much insight and perseverance it would take to maintain a deep, secure trust. In our good times, we both could make ourselves available to the other and achieve a level of secure emotional intimacy. At times of stress, however, we were prone to protective behavior which only exacerbated an already strained situation. If Tom reached out for closeness and I was feeling insecure, I would interpret his attempts at closeness as a threat and accuse him of neediness. On the other hand, if I reached out for closeness and he was feeling insecure, he would see my attempts at closeness as a trap in which he could be accused of being weak. It's not surprising that we could easily slip into a vicious cycle of taking turns being either anxious or avoidant. In either case, when either of us felt rejected, our protective behavior heightened the anxiety in the other. This is why, later, we would question what we were fighting about, because the arguments weren't about a minor problem; they were about a shared fear that we were losing a connection with each other.

The saving grace of our destructive dynamic was that a rupture in the connection between us would create so much anxiety, we were willing to try anything to restore harmony. Eventually that desperation would overcome our need to protect ourselves. Once one of us would drop a defense, the other would be inclined to do the same. The authenticity that is revealed when someone discloses a real fear invokes empathy in the other, the fundamental ingredient that builds attachment. Had either of us been consistently avoidant, it is highly unlikely that this outcome would have occurred. The avoidant one would want to avoid that closeness so would likely get more hostile and distant as the argument progressed.[2]

It is characteristic of anxious people to intensely *want* to work out a relationship problem.[3] The fact that anxiety seems to motivate people to examine their psyches is a theme that runs through Rollo May's definitive book, *The Meaning of Anxiety*. After I wrote the narrative portion of this chapter, I took some time out to read this book. I think I intuitively knew that if I could better gain control over my anxiety, I could be much better for myself and Tom too.

While anxiety is what triggers defensive behavior, it is also anxiety that helps us move to a better place. A more in-depth understanding of this two-fold function has helped me to understand our struggles to "earn security." May begins by explaining the difference between anxiety and fear. Fear is a reaction to a specific danger that can be consciously articulated. The source of the fear can be pinpointed and if the source can be removed, the apprehension disappears. Anxiety, instead, is an unspecific, vague feeling of uncertainty and helplessness that attacks us at a deeper level and in many cases cannot be articulated or even recognized.[4]

Anxiety that leads to an anxious attachment style begins so early in one's life that the feeling of being "anxious" may have become commonplace, just a fact of life. A child is unable to be objective in dealing with a threatening interpersonal situation, usually involving relations with his or her parents. It is too frightening to admit the source of the threat because young children are so utterly dependent on their parents. For example, the awareness that my parent is incapable of taking care of me, or does not love me, is unbearable to a young child. Consequently, repression of the source of the anxiety becomes a central feature of the child's way of coping. It continues in the form of defense mechanisms as similar threats occur throughout life.[5]

The threat one is reacting to will vary with each individual depending on the origin of the threat and the value the individual holds as being essential to his or her existence as a person. The threat must be to something in the "core" of our self-esteem, how we experience ourselves as a person, our feelings of worth. In some environments it may be the threat to physical life—the fear of death—or the threat to meaningful existence—the loss of freedom and autonomy. Or the threat may be to some other value: fear of losing the love and acceptance of another person, or the fear of failing to be a successful provider to one's family. The threat can be to any other value which one identifies as being vital to one's security. (All of these are inadequate descriptions of what is threatened.) Whatever it is, the anxiety attacks the essence of our being, so it is difficult to see it objectively or separately from ourselves. "*One cannot fight what one does not know.... one is afraid but uncertain of what one is afraid.*"[6]

Just because anxiety is diffuse and vague does not mean that it is less painful than other emotions such as anger, fear, and hostility. In fact, it can be more painful because it is experienced at a deeper level, making it more threatening. In chapter eight I make the point that defense mechanisms are only effective because they are unconscious. Their purpose is to keep an inner fear from surfacing into our conscious thought. The strategy always involves some form of repression, an effort to run away from some sort of element within ourselves. As a child the repression was necessary; as an adult, it evades a problem rather than resolve it. "*Repression increases the individual's feeling of helplessness in that it involves a curtailing of his own autonomy, an inner retrenchment and shelving of his own power.*"[7]

The philosopher Soren Kierkegaard believed that our creative problem-solving capacities and our susceptibility to anxiety are two sides of the same capacity that is unique to human beings. Self-realization only occurs by moving through and understanding anxiety-creating experiences. If we don't confront our deepest fears, we set ourselves up for living a life of neurotic worry.[8] The only way we can begin to understand our anxiety is first to be aware of it. We can learn to recognize an undifferentiated anxiety because it will generally be disproportionate to a perceived threat (e.g. panic, emotional outbursts) and it creates an inner conflict, the result of repression. We can also learn to recognize our tendency to "cue off" (or repress) the threat onto something more palliative by denying our fear, defending ourselves, blaming others, or projecting our fear onto someone else. This is when we must ask ourselves, what is it that I am afraid of? This is not easy, however; I liken it to looking directly at the sun. In Rollo May's words: "*the very perception with which we look will also be invaded by anxiety.*"[8] We must be willing to endure the anxiety that this exploration evokes. We have to be convinced that we will gain more by moving ahead than we will by repeating an effort to escape. Something will eventually ring true. Once we get a handle on what that deepest fear is, and we're able to be aware of it when it happens, we've begun a process that Kierkegaard speaks of as having "*learned the most important thing.*"[9] Once we know there is a more positive way of dealing with our anxiety, a resolution is within our reach.

During the eleven years Tom and I were in business, we dealt with some normal conflicts that two people face in a second marriage. The more these crises occurred, however, the more we became aware that the threat of those problems was disproportionate to the ruptures they would cause in our relationship. We also began to recognize similar patterns in our arguments and we learned more about our unique vulnerabilities. This was the beginning of an expansion of our awareness of a pervasive underlying anxiety in both of us that was at work, but we still didn't understand precisely what deeply held personal values were being threatened. It wouldn't be until we retired with more discretionary time that a deeper exploration of those fears began to take shape. We look back on those years of building our business as valuable time spent in learning to cooperate and gain trust in one another's commitment to our relationship. But a marriage is only as strong as the two people in it, and we still had a lot to learn.

References:

[1] Levine, A. & Heller, R. S. F. 2011. *Attached. The new science of adult attachment and how it can help you find—and keep—love.* London: Penguin Books.
[2] Levine & Heller 2011.
[3] Levine & Heller 2011.
[4] Levine & Heller 2011.
[5] May, Rollo. 1977, Reissued 2015. *The meaning of anxiety.* New York: W.W. Norton & Company.
[6] May 1977, 191.
[7] May 1977, p. 200.
[8] May 1977, p. 191.
[9] Kierkegaard, Soren, 1953 (third printing, originally published in Danish, 1844). *The concept of dread.* Trans. by Walter Lowrie. Princeton, N. J.: Princeton University Press, p. 139.

14

RETIREMENT

We have an ambitious plan for our retirement, something we concocted while in Zimbabwe. We've read about how important it is to keep our minds active as we age. For the next ten years, we want to travel to different countries to live for an extended period of time, like we did in Zimbabwe, but this time without the necessity of having a job. In each place we go, we will rent a place to live where we can mix with the locals and focus our interest on getting absorbed in a new and different culture. Learning a new culture every few years, finding our way around a new location, and making new friends in each place should keep us active and stimulated, providing we stay in good health. But before we leave Las Cruces, we purchase an acre of land in a new sub-division that has just opened up on the side of Las Cruces that has been used primarily for farming and pecan orchards. We would like to build a house there, once we are through traveling.

It's been seven years since I've seen Dan, so the first country we're going to explore is Canada—British Columbia in particular for the first two years, giving us plenty of time to reconnect with him. Not long after Alison and her baby visited us in Las Cruces, she and Dan break up. She is with another young man now and they have a little boy who is two years old besides my granddaughter who is now four. They live in Williams Lake, a small town where Alison has completed a program at the local community college and works as a teachers' aide. She has been better about staying in contact with us than Dan has, so we look forward to seeing her and her family too. Our role as grandparents is extended to both children.

The letter in the magazine, the reading I did, and Dan's story prepare me for the kind of reaction we might expect from Dan's birth family. I'm concerned about the prevalence of alcoholism on First Nation reserves. Several times I have called Dan when he was incoherent or unresponsive, leading me to wait until he calls me. I fear he is drinking. For all these reasons I'm eager to make contact. We decide to rent an apartment in Prince George, a town located in the northern central part of British Columbia, an hour's drive to Quesnel where Dan is living with family members. Something about his response to our coming cautions us not to live too close. Tom and I make arrangements to meet him at an outdoor book fair that is going on in Quesnel. I'm browsing through some books when I look up to see Dan, smiling and so handsome, and definitely older. After a vigorous hug, I exclaim to a light-skinned woman standing nearby, "This is my son, whom I haven't seen in seven years!" Rather than acknowledging my happiness, she glares at me, a response I learn to expect before I tell a Canadian that I'm the mother of a First Nations child.

"Can we take you to lunch?" Tom asks Dan as we walk to our car. He hesitates, but agrees and climbs into our back seat. "We don't know much about this town, so why don't you suggest a place," Tom says. As we drive around the commercial area of Quesnel, Dan is tense and glances apprehensively at any people we see.

"Wait! There's my brother!" he says. Tom pulls over and Dan jumps out of the car and then disappears from our sight.

"Oh good! We're going to meet his brother," I say.

But in minutes, we see Dan walking slowly back to our car, alone.

"What happened?" I ask.

"Oh, he's busy now—maybe another time," is his only explanation. We continue our search for a restaurant as Dan resumes a surreptitious manner, obviously very nervous about something, we don't know what. He finally agrees to stop at a fast-food place, but it is obvious that he doesn't want to be seen with us when we get inside, so we sit outside at a table to eat. His discomfort precludes any meaningful conversation. Back in the car, Tom suggests we stop at a park to talk, but he doesn't want to do that either; he asks us if we can take him home. I get the feeling that he's made his obligatory contact with us, and this is all we're going to get. He directs us to the rear of a garage apartment, and as he gets out of the car, I make a timid suggestion.

"We'd like to have you come to our place in Prince George," I say, thinking that maybe in another town he'll be more comfortable. So uncertain of his response, I lack the courage to get out of the car to tell him goodbye, but Tom does. Since Dan's initial smile when he first greeted us, the only other positive signal we receive is that he gives Tom a genuine hug, like he means it. Maybe there's hope. But we're both troubled by Dan's behavior, not knowing what to think. It hasn't even come close to the reunion I had hoped for.

We sparsely furnish our apartment with the necessities from the Salvation Army thrift store and another thrift store chain we learn is in every town in British Columbia. We enjoy bargain hunting, and our best buy is a disjointed vacuum cleaner that Tom is sure only needs a nut and bolt. For twenty-five cents it's ours, once we know it works. We brought our bicycles with us and we begin exploring the beauties of Prince George, where two major rivers in British Columbia converge, the Fraser River that flows north and south, and the Nechako River that flows east and west. Both are huge rivers surrounded by lush forests and an abundance of wildlife, especially moose, deer, and bears. The favorite sport is hockey, and we've never been any place where there are more outdoorsy people. The first warm weekend in the spring, everyone is out running! Known as the capital of northern B.C., Prince George is a two-day drive from Vancouver, so they must not get many American tourists. Anyone who notices our New Mexico license plate wants to know why we are here—and we're always heartily welcomed. Tom wastes no time joining a hiking group composed of some very friendly people. By mid-summer, because we are so far north, the sun stays up until 10:00 or 11:00 o'clock at night, so we have hours to ride our bikes after supper. Our apartment complex is located just a short walk from an aquatic center and running track, so we both leave in the morning to exercise.

We visit Alison and her family the first time in their home in Williams Lake for the children's shared April 25th birthday. We like Alison's new partner, who is an attentive father and he and Tom begin to forge a relationship. Alison is not comfortable cooking for us, so I prepare the meals or we bring home pizza. We learn they don't eat many vegetables, but everyone likes meat and desserts. The children and I make a birthday cake, half of it chocolate and the other half white. Being grandparents feels natural to Tom and me, and the children soak up our attention, so it's a satisfying visit for all of us.

For Dan's birthday in May, we invite him to Prince George to stay with us for a few days and we send him a bus ticket.

We go to the bus station at his expected arrival time, but he isn't there. He has our phone number. Maybe he's coming on a later bus, so we return home. By nightfall we assume he isn't coming at all, but by mid-morning the next day he calls. He's been staying with a friend in Prince George. "Is it okay if I come over there this evening?"

"To spend the night?" I ask.

"Sure."

"Will you be here in time to eat? I've planned a special birthday meal and cake for you."

"It'll be late when I get there. Can we wait until tomorrow?"

"We'll plan to celebrate your birthday tomorrow at lunchtime. We'll expect you tonight. Do you know where we live?"

"I have the address."

I hang up the phone and tell Tom the news. "I guess he's getting a ride over here. I have no idea of where he's coming from."

Dan gets here about 9:00 p.m. I show him his room upstairs and ask him if he's hungry. "I can fix you a peanut butter sandwich, if you'd like."

"Can you bring it upstairs? I don't feel like talking." I take a sandwich and a glass of milk up to his room and tell him goodnight. "I'm glad you're here," I say as I close the door.

It's nearly noon the next day before Dan comes down carrying his small duffle and a jacket. Tom and I both greet him and I have the table set for lunch.

"Did you sleep well?" Tom asks. Dan acts nervous and distracted. Any other attempt we make at conversation, he resists.

Finally, "Can I have some money for a hamburger?" he asks.

"Dan!" By now I'm angry. "I've prepared a birthday dinner for you, and you want to buy a hamburger? We bought your bus ticket so you could come to visit *us*, not someone else here in Prince George. Where are you going? Tell us what is going on? This is getting real crazy."

"You're not going to give me the fucking money for a hamburger?" he barks.

"No! The main reason we came all the way from New Mexico was to see *you*. Why are you acting this way?"

He swears again and storms about the room gathering his things. Tom and I look at each other with dismay. "Are you leaving?" we both ask.

"Yes!"

"Are you coming back?"

"Probably not," he growls as he goes out the door and that's the last we see of him. My hopes are shattered, so Tom and I talk. The only thing we can imagine that could possibly explain his behavior is that he's either drinking or he's on drugs, or maybe both. For the next few days, I sink into a depression, remembering how I had encouraged him when he was contacted by his birth family. Am I to lose another child? I can't bear to think about that possibility.

One day Tom and I are in town and I notice a sign on a door indicating that it's a social gathering place for First Nations people. While Tom goes to buy something, I summon the courage to go in. I'm looking for some kind of answer. It's dark when I step in and I can barely see some stairs that lead down into a dimly lit room where about six native men are seated around a table. They stare at me in what I imagine to be a stupor, obviously wondering what I'm doing there. In my state of mind, all I see is destitution, squalor, impoverishment, and misery. I turn and rush back up the stairs to get out into the sunlight and to find Tom. I try to explain to him what has frightened me, but it doesn't really make sense. All I know to say is that I'm afraid I've just seen what is happening to Dan.

My worst fears are heightened in mid-summer when Alison calls to tell me that she has heard that Dan and a woman jumped off the main highway bridge that goes over the Fraser River in Quesnel. Dan swam out, and the woman was rescued by a passerby who saw them jump. Was this an act of foolishness during a drunken binge or an attempt at suicide? I don't know and I don't want to know. Where have I heard that you are only as happy as your unhappiest child? But Tom tells me that it doesn't have to be that way. If I'm depending on Dan to make me happy, I'm making him responsible for me, he explains. I should know that a child shouldn't be made to feel responsible for a parent's happiness. I'm responsible for myself. This is beginning to sink in and I gradually gain some measure of control over my despondency.

One day I meet two women at the swimming pool. Ironically they both are named Leslie. They invite me to go to coffee, and then laugh at me when I say I would have to call my husband.

"You have to get permission?" they tease.

I soon realize that it's been so long since Tom and I have done things independently, I'm unaccustomed to making autonomous decisions. With twenty-four hours a day and seven days a week of discretionary time, there are so many decisions to make as to how to use it. Activities alone, activities together? Individual friends, couple friends? Time at home, time away from home? Weekly coffee dates with the two Leslies are good for me.

It's been seventeen years since I have looked at the two-inch thick notebook containing my journal writing during Leslie's illness. Though I dread the process I'm facing, my motivation to write about her is strong, almost obsessive. Since I'm the only one who observed every day how brave she was, I'm the only person who can write this book. I've been waiting until we retired to begin. The book will be dedicated to Mike and Dan because there are things I want to say that I haven't been able to say to either of them face to face. This will help me find closure for that time in my life. Tom enjoys reading history, particularly about a new place he's never been to before. We set aside a certain number of hours each day while I write and he reads.

Our lease agreement is up the end of September, so I make a list of all the used furniture we bought six months earlier and post "for sale" signs in several nearby apartment complexes. We sell everything in just a few days, and even make a small profit. We will go to Parksville on Vancouver Island, where the winter temperature is milder than on the mainland. This time we rent a furnished house from an owner who likes to spend her winters in Hawaii. Though much warmer than it would be in Prince George, it is also cloudy, rainy, and dismal almost every day. When it's not raining, we ride our bikes along shaded trails that feel like we're in a rainforest. Along the coastline, we see pods of orca whales in the distance. Tom joins another hiking group and signs up for three classes for seniors on First Nations culture, South Africa, and alternative energy sources. Three days a week, he goes to the gym and I drive to the next town where there is a pool to swim. I take a writing class where I find an instructor who encourages me in my writing project.

One day I get a phone call from Dan, friendly and casual, as though nothing strange ever happened in Prince George. He tells me he's in a new relationship with a woman named Hazel, who is a widow and member of a neighboring First Nations band. They are living in her house on the Nazko reserve and they are expecting a baby. He's also applying for a firefighting job with the Forest Service in Washington State, and do I still have a copy of his resume? I have it on my computer and I promise to send it to him. Keeping up with the chaotic nature of Dan's life is an emotional roller coaster, but I wish them both the best.

Then spring arrives and we move further north on the island to a pleasant little town called Comox. Beautiful weather, a resource for freshly harvested fruits and vegetables, golf lessons and a walking group for Tom, and kayaking lessons for us both, do wonders for our dispositions. I also find a helpful editor in Comox, Anneli, who provides the support I need in writing my book, and she will eventually become a good friend. Being in such a beautiful place draws visitors. Three of Tom's brothers, a cousin of mine, and some old friends visit us that summer. Dan and Hazel's baby is born in April, her arrival stimulating mixed feelings in Dan. In one phone call, he describes the little girl as a "lifesaver" for them, but in another call, he's overwhelmed by her care. "Would you take care of her?" he asks me, in desperation.

I don't hesitate to answer. "She is your and Hazel's responsibility. I'm sure you'll find a way to manage." Something tells me that it's better that we're a two-day drive from The Nazko reserve ... and he didn't ask that we come. The Forest Service job in Washington might have been an opportunity had he shown up for the required physical exam, but he didn't. Hazel wouldn't have been willing to move to the United States anyway, he says.

※

In a used bookstore, Tom picks up a book *"Getting the Love You Want: A Guide for Couples,"* by Harville Hendrix. "Maybe this can help us," he says. I read on the back cover that the author is a therapist, educator, and a director of The Institute for Relationship Therapy, based in Dallas and New York. There are exercises in the book that are used in couples workshops across the country, and research studies show them to be as effective as three to six months of private marital counseling .

"Hmm," I say. "It looks good." Tom buys the book. The opportunity to apply some cognitive reasoning to our puzzling relationship excites us. We didn't have much time to do this while we were working. The central theme of the book is to contrast between what the author calls the "unconscious" and the "conscious" marriage, directing the reader's attention to understanding one's childhood wounds, how they influence our choice of mates, and predict the kinds of problems we may encounter in marriage. A ten-step process involving the completion of sixteen exercises will assist a couple in translating new insights about themselves into effective skills. We decide to read one chapter at a time, and then follow up by doing each of the exercises.

Our first task is to jointly create a "relationship vision." First we each write a series of short sentences describing our personal vision of a deeply satisfying love relationship, including qualities we already have and want to keep and qualities we hope to have. After sharing the two lists of sentences, we combine those values we have in common, which becomes our relationship vision:

> *"Second only to our own personal well-being is the health of our relationship, based on our belief that our relationship will only be as strong as we are as individuals. It shall be equal and reciprocal in that whatever we ask of the other, we should be willing to give ourselves. We will recognize our differences and support one another as we explore ways to meet our individual needs, while trusting that we both are seeking personal growth. Each one is ultimately responsible*

for all aspects of his or her life. We will best realize these goals through awareness and open and honest communication without blame."

Now that we have an agreed-upon vision for our future, our next task is to take ourselves back to our past and try to imagine ourselves as a young boy or girl, identifying the people who most influenced us deeply as a child—usually our parents. Then we think about what we enjoyed most about them and what we wanted from them but never got. Each one separately makes two lists—one includes the positive traits we saw in our parents and the other lists the negative traits. The point of doing this is that Hendrix suggests that people will unconsciously pair with individuals who have some traits of their caregivers, both positive and negative, because these traits feel familiar. So we talk about it and we can begin to see that this is true for us. On the positive side, I see that Tom has the calm, steady, and protective temperament of my father and the intelligent inquiring mind of my mother. On the negative side, he can withdraw emotionally when dealing with conflict, like my father, and his intense desire to engage emotionally can feel possessive and controlling, emotions I often felt with my mother. For Tom, he sees me as warm and affectionate, like his mother, and financially responsible and efficient, like his father, the positive traits. However, I can also be rigid about my opinions, as his mother was about her beliefs, and I'm prone to uncontrolled emotional outbursts, as his father was when frustrated or provoked.

Hendrix explains that during the early romantic stage of a relationship, we look at our partners and see all the good traits of our parents, setting up an expectation of need fulfillment, the illusive euphoria of romantic love. Unconsciously we assume our mates will conform to a whole list of desired behaviors, some conscious, but most are hidden from our awareness. It is inevitable at some point that most couples will begin to discover a trait in their partner that annoys them. Tom's willingness to talk about anything and everything, a trait I cherished early on, becomes an aggravation when I'm working on my book. The confidence Tom places in my "depth of thought and maturity" is dismantled when I crumble in tears at the hint of his disapproval. What appears to be a sudden reversal is simply the reappearance of a reaction we each learned to repress in our childhood. The negative traits we resolutely denied during a romantic stage are coming sharply into focus, triggering a sickening fear that our partner is destined to wound us in the same way we were wounded as children. While this exercise can stir up each other's repressed behaviors and old childhood wounds, if we can work together, it also gives us an opportunity to repair the emotional damage of childhood.

Even if we did not grow up with serious childhood trauma, such as sexual or physical abuse or the suffering that comes from parental addictions, we all are born with a complex set of needs. No parent, no matter how devoted, is able to respond perfectly to all of these changing needs. Tom and I are aware that we didn't achieve a "conscious" relationship in our first marriages, meaning that we did not use conflict to learn about ourselves and our partners as we are trying to do now. We generally avoided conflict, lacking the ability to work with it effectively. Though we have learned that we can eventually work through our conflicts, we know they occur more often than we would like to admit, and we know they can be painful. We dread conflict because we interpret it as something wrong with us, but in actuality, it is an opportunity to make adjustments that will put us in a better place. We like this positive approach because it presents the work we do on our relationship as something that will help both of us in our individual personal growth. It compels us to face unresolved issues that have existed since our childhood. This is a powerful motivator.

Our discussions about our parents and the feelings we associate with each of them are very revealing. The exercises encourage us to look inside for traits of our parents that we think are working against us. My awareness of a free-floating anxiety in the background is becoming more in focus. I recognize it as something I've always had that makes itself known unexpectedly, emerging suddenly as if it's beyond my control. I even think sometimes that I might have some sort of strange insanity that is apt to strike when I am most unaware.

Tom often speaks of our need to be "responsible" for everything about ourselves, including our thoughts and feelings, not just our actions. This is a vague notion to me, particularly when it comes to my emotions. I have thought of responsibility as referring to behaviors, like doing regular exercise, eating healthfully, showing up on time, making sure my bills are paid, etc. It feels like my emotions just happen; they are a part of who I am; I don't fully understand what he means about my being responsible for them.

He points out how often I speak of my fears as a way of explaining my abrupt reactions, implying that I'm not responsible for them in some way. He tries to explain that a fear is only rational if there is a certain undeniable danger, so if what I perceive as a threat poses no real danger, but I treat it as a valid fear, it soon becomes a reality. He's saying that I have a choice about what I am afraid of. I'm starting to look at my emotions in a whole new way. One of the exercises is on "exiting," which refers to ways we avoid dealing with a problem. The chapter in the book warns couples that the exercises will stir up anxieties that they may not have confronted before, which will be uncomfortable, and the temptation is to put the book aside. It also discusses other ways couples avoid discussing their problems—most of them we don't do, like going to bed at different times, or making plans without consulting each other. But I am usually the one that wants to "take a walk by myself" when our arguments get heated. My idea is that we will be more productive if we can cool off, but there is nothing more frustrating to Tom. My being prone to exit is probably due to my difficulty in controlling my emotions, so I have agreed to not be so quick to exit when our talking gets uncomfortable.

We are beginning to understand how we reinforce each other's insecurities. When one or the other feels we are not being acknowledged or understood, and this insecurity is expressed in the form of blame, it is quickly passed to the other and we both become defensive. In essence, we scare ourselves and then we scare each other. Clearly, we are both equally responsible when our communication turns defensive and destructive. The dynamic requires that we both work together simultaneously to gain control over our own anxiety if there is any hope of our overcoming this vulnerability.

We see that most of our arguments arise from superficial issues, when we should be looking at the underlying anxiety from unresolved childhood needs. As a child, I felt responsible for my mother, but utterly helpless in dealing with her mental illness. Even as a dutiful daughter, I wasn't able to solve her problems, and those feelings of inadequacy carry over into my relationships with the people I most love. A typical reaction is to fall into a feeling of despair, helplessness, and a loss of confidence in myself. Tom is most vulnerable to the chaos that he experienced as a child, when he felt responsible or blamed for the confusion that was going on. Sometimes this fear is exacerbated during our altercations, when he feels he's unfairly blamed for my discomfort. We know we must recognize these deep-seated anxieties in ourselves before they become so threatening that they evoke a defensive reaction.

We decide to spend our second winter in the Okanagan Valley, an area known for its fruit orchards and milder winter temperatures. We lease another furnished house on a lake that is ten miles from the town of Vernon, close enough to Dan to consider a visit from him, Hazel, and their new daughter. This will be our last six months in British Columbia, so if I'm going to make any progress in my relationship with Dan, it will have to be now.

Our house sits beneath a rugged forested ridge that is so high, it shields the house from sun until mid-afternoon. Though Tom hikes the ridge, the weather is too cold and damp and the trails too steep for me. Much of that winter, we hibernate with books, writing, and conversation, and we even resort to some occasional television in the evenings. Alison's family, which now includes three children, come to see us at Christmas. I'm so excited about having the children for the holidays, we buy a used electric keyboard so we can play and sing Christmas carols together while they are here.

I am near the end of a first draft of my memoir about Leslie. Eager to share it with Dan before we leave B.C., I spend hours at the computer in the spare bedroom writing before I place the manuscript in a large envelope and mail it to Dan. He calls me on the phone one night, crying, having just finished reading it. My treatment of him in the book, including an acknowledgment of my neglect of him during Leslie's illness, has had an impact, and he feels some vindication regarding his hurt feelings. The old familiar connection with him that I haven't felt for years is there. I cry too. I believe the book has broken through some barriers with Dan that may change the course of our relationship. I suggest the possibility of his bringing his family to Vernon for a visit before we leave, and we establish a date. The day of their expected arrival, Dan calls to say that something has come up with Hazel, and they're unable to come.

After a slow trek across Alberta, Saskatchewan, Manitoba, Ontario, and the eastern half of Quebec, we settle in Nova Scotia for our last summer in Canada. We rent the lower half of a large two-story house in Annapolis Royal, a town that dates back to the 1600s, sitting on the south bank of the Annapolis River, which drains into the Bay of Fundy. Our house is located on the northern bank of the river in the community of Granville Ferry, which used to be connected only by a ferry that crossed the river. Now a causeway has been built across the river to accommodate an electrical generating station that is powered by the magnificent rise and fall of the tide coming from the Bay of Fundy. We can watch this phenomenon from our back porch, the water level rising twenty-five feet every time the tide comes in. We can cross over the causeway to the main part of Annapolis Royal by car or bicycle.

The community of Granville Ferry is only about three square blocks of beautiful old colonial style homes, inhabited by a very diverse group of people, most of whom came here from somewhere else to buy one of these structures to renovate. They gather together once a week at a community center for coffee, home-made baked goods, and conversation. Newcomers like us, an enticing source of curiosity, are enthusiastically welcomed. When they learn we are renting just for the summer, neighbors generously offer to loan us pieces of furniture that round out the bare essentials our landlord is providing. Almost instantly we feel like we belong here!

By creating more physical distance between Dan and me, I'm able to come to a more objective stance in regard to the failed expectation I had for renewing a close relationship with him. Perhaps it is enough for Dan at this stage of his life to find a comfortable place in the culture of his birth without interference from me. If he struggles with addictions, which I have reason to believe he does, there is probably little I can do to support him until he's ready to assume responsibility for his problem himself.

Since Bonnie and her husband and a close cousin and her husband live in the eastern part of the United States, we host a small family reunion in Annapolis Royal, to which John also comes with Mavis, a woman with whom he has finally achieved some measure of comfort in a long-term relationship. The helpful factor is that Mavis has not insisted on marriage, nor do they share the same house, but they see each other almost daily and they both enjoy traveling together. Each couple takes a turn preparing an evening meal for all of us, and each day we explore some of the most interesting sites in this historical place.

From our home base this summer, Tom and I visit New Brunswick, Prince Edward Island, Labrador, and Newfoundland. We find these Maritime Provinces like going back in time to when life wasn't as complicated and stressful. They seem far removed from the political strife that is going on in the United States, though we are aware that Canada has problems of its own. On Prince Edward Island, railroads that crisscrossed the island have been replaced with bicycle trails. Cycling through the land where the story of Anne of Green Gables originated makes the simplicity of life at that time seem possible.

INSIGHTS: Restructuring Vows and Goals

The Hendrix book provided some practical needed assurance that the repetitive nature of our arguments did not mean we hadn't been making progress. It explained that relationships tend to move in spirals and cycles of both calm and turbulence:

> *"Even when you are going through the very same struggles over and over again, there is always some degree of change.... The changes may seem imperceptible, but there is movement all the same. By continually affirming your decision to grow and change ... you will be able to make sure and steady progress on your journey to a conscious marriage."* [1]

Jeremy Holmes described the same process "earning security"—when two adults form a relationship in which one feels safe enough to face the pain and fear of feelings of inadequacy. It means that one can let go of blaming others or oneself. It means developing the capacity to accept that love and hate are two feelings that are part of a whole and will inevitably be directed towards the same person at different times. An earned security perspective is consistent with being able to say, "I may feel hateful towards you right now, but I realize that I'm in the grip of an emotion, and that in reality we can choose to be either a loving partner or a depriving one." [2]

It is also the two-fold process Rollo May describes in the method of resolving the problem of neurotic anxiety:

> *"One is an expansion of awareness: the person sees what value is threatened, and becomes aware of the conflicts between his goals and how these conflicts developed. The second is re-education: the person restructures his goals, makes a choice of values, and proceeds toward the attainment of these values responsibly and realistically."*[3]

We're not to think that these processes are ever achieved perfectly—nor would we want them to be, because we would be overlooking the benefits of using normal anxiety-creating situations in a constructive way without being overwhelmed.

> *"When the organism ... is put on its mettle, aroused even by pain and inconvenience, it functions better. Simple contentment, in other words, is not the aim of life. Such things as vitality, commitment to values, breadth of sensitivity, I propose, are more adequate goals."* [4]

In order to support our new perspectives, Tom and I found the concept of friendship to be helpful in our conversations. We became aware of a subtle assumption that often becomes embedded in marriage—that we own each other. Possessiveness justifies our taking responsibility for our partner, meaning we have the right to make corrections in her or him. We found that if we viewed one another as friends, rather than marriage partners, it helped to reinforce our letting go of blame. Together we composed, first, a symbolic dissolution of our traditional marriage—

> *"for the said purpose of removing the binding relational expectations that have been assumed in our marriage contract thus far (not to include the forfeiture of any legal or financial rights). It is understood by both of us that these binding expectations have been both culturally and religiously imposed without regard for what is in the best interest of us as individuals. In order for a new and more healthful contract to be enacted for our benefit and our relationship, the old contract is hereby dissolved."*

Then we composed a mutual friendship pledge—

> *"to promote dignity and to honor individuality through active listening with the intent to understand*

and support each other through life's journey. We will attempt to do this without claims of ownership, judgment, or censorship, and with respect for the confidentiality and trust inherent in our relationship."

Along with the pledge, we created a list of new relationship vows that we would consult regularly and especially at those times when we felt ourselves faltering in our resolve.

- I will be responsible for all my thoughts, feelings, and actions, and will strive for congruence between all three. I will not be responsible for the thoughts, feelings, and actions of my partner and others.
- Involvement of my partner will be in the form of an invitation, and I will respect his/her response.
- Any rights or freedoms that I claim for myself are extended to my partner. I will not ask anything of my partner that I wouldn't ask of myself.
- I will encourage and support my partner in his/her efforts to meet his/her needs, recognizing that we may not choose to get our needs met in the same way.
- I will work towards a mutually caring intimate bond between one another through appreciation, affection, and sensitivity to my partner's feelings.
- I will communicate honestly and openly my feelings and wants, recognizing they reflect my own personal bias.
- I will listen calmly and patiently to my partner's expression of feeling without ownership, blame, or censorship, but with a genuine intent to understand and support.
- I will creatively seek new adventure, both individually and collectively with my partner.

Our new pledge and vows provided a structure that gave us both confidence and a sense of stability that we had not had before. I saw them as the culmination of struggling for a long time with preconceived expectations of our marriage that we had unconsciously absorbed from our culture, but had never carefully examined. We believed that the fact we were able to think more creatively and come up with a group of principles that we both wanted to live by was a credit to both of us. I was excited by the prospects of all that might come from our efforts. My hope and faith was in the belief that as we learned to act on these self-chosen principles, our desire to both give and receive affection would grow, our level of trust and intimacy would increase, and our awareness of ourselves and our knowledge of one another would expand. There had been no other accomplishment that I valued more than this one.

Establishing a sound and stable intimate relationship had been Tom's goal during his first marriage, and that remained an ongoing quest. The conventional marriage format, which we tried to adhere to, had yielded mixed results—some positive, but others nearly breaking our spirits and our resolve to stay together. Out of desperation, we both turned to a more liberating truth-oriented kind of relationship, declaring our formal marriage dissolved and its associated ownership vows null and void. Our simple, but powerful pledge of friendship encouraged freedom and individualism, with the inherent responsibility that goes with them. He believed that we would find not only new meaning, but a shared purpose and a greater sense of our own identities. Willingness to be selectively vulnerable, in his way of thinking, was not weak; it required courage. This was healthy, not a result of emotional insecurity. We both believed that by keeping our new vows, we would be acting out of our strengths, not our weaknesses.

In this way we could become more than either of us would be if we were alone.

References:

[1] Hendrix, Harville. 1988. *Getting the love you want: A guide for couples.* New York: Henry Holt & Company, p. 205.
[2] Holmes, Jeremy. 2010. *Exploring security: Towards an attachment informed psychoanalytic psychotherapy.* London and New York, p. 27.
[3] May, Rollo. 1977. *The meaning of anxiety.* New York and London, p. 354.
[4] May 1977, p. 368.

15

A SOJOURN IN SALT LAKE CITY

We leave Canada on a ferry from Yarmouth, Nova Scotia to Bar Harbor, Maine in October of 2007, having spent two and a half years in that country. We admire much about Canada, their sane policies for health care, gun control, and paid leave for parents (six months for each parent, giving each child a whole year of undivided attention and care from a parent). This last provision can make a tremendous difference in the psychological health of an entire generation for as long as this provision is in place. For the most part, we believe Canada's values are more in line with our own, but we hope the United States is moving in this direction. The one breakdown we see in Canada is in the prevailing attitude toward First Nations people, exacerbated by the number of First Nations people who have been forced to leave the geographical areas where they could best sustain themselves. I don't know if Dan would have fared better had he remained in the U.S. or not, but I leave with a deep sorrow about his situation and my inability to make it any better.

We are spending the Christmas holiday in Salt Lake City where both of Tom's daughters are now residing with their mates and ten children between them. Our next destination after that will be New Zealand for six months. I have cataract surgery on both eyes and, due to a lingering "pucker" in the macula of one eye, the doctor doesn't want me to leave the country for two months. Then we learn of the real estate financial crisis in the stock market which causes a sudden drop in our travel funds. We've been staying in two different vacation rentals for six weeks at a time, and decide to find one more temporary rental for six months while we evaluate our financial situation. Unexpectedly, we find a beautifully remodeled Victorian home in Sugar House, a popular residential area very convenient to downtown and the University of Utah. Unfortunately it is not for rent, only for sale, but has been discounted due to the economic state of the country.

Also affecting our decision-making is an emerging awareness that I would like to put down some roots. The excitement of moving from one place to another every six months or so has begun to wear off for me. This cozy little house in such a desirable neighborhood is enticing. The stress of my troublesome eye adds to my need to nest. Tom has mixed emotions about staying here. His ex-wife lives close to both his daughters, and his relationship with them is still fraught with their resentment about his decision to leave the Mormon Church. While we were living in Canada, an invitation to have our oldest grandson visit us there had been declined. Dealing with their feelings as well as the pervasive influence of that religion will be a challenge if we live in Salt Lake City. Tom has three brothers and two sisters in Utah, however, and rekindling his relationships with them may be a compensating factor, not to mention, we have ten grandchildren just across town we would like to get to know better.

We buy the house, take Tom's sister Millie with us to Las Cruces to get our belongings out of storage, and bring it all back pulling a trailer. Once we settle in and Tom stakes out a garden area in the back of the house, we both begin to make plans for what we would like to accomplish in our new environment. First on our list is to continue working on our relationship. The new vows we made for ourselves are helping. We keep them in a drawer in the living room where it's handy to reach at times we need to be reminded of the principles we have agreed to. As we read through each vow, more often than not, it's the first one that is applicable to whatever is going on between us. "I will take responsibility for my thoughts, words, and actions, and I will not be responsible for the thoughts, words, and actions of my partner." I now understand what this really means. We each have our own private domain that includes the choices we make as to how we meet our own needs. We have the freedom to explore, experiment, make mistakes, and decide what is best for ourselves. We are not to take responsibility for the other. If a decision impacts both of us, then the issue requires a negotiated sharing and a commitment to reach a mutually satisfying consensus. We may need to temporarily lay aside a personal preference and listen to the other's point of view before making up our mind. The solution may be a third option we haven't thought of before that only emerges from a creative effort to explore the possibilities.

Our second priority is to spend time with our grandchildren. It has come as a surprise to Tom's daughters that we have decided to stay in Salt Lake City, and though they are polite, we sense some apprehension. Since their mother has recently moved to the area also and lives halfway between both the girls in the town of Magna, a small community adjacent to Salt Lake City, they hadn't expected to have to deal with both their parents being on the same turf. There is also an issue of trust. Tom's leaving the church and his reasons for doing so are sensitive issues his daughters have not been willing to talk about.

We start slow, inviting the twin girls over to bake cookies one afternoon, and taking two of the boys to the pool where I swim. We regularly attend the boys' basketball games, the monthly family birthday parties, any school programs the children are in, and church coming-of-age ceremonies. Near their birthdays we invite each child over to spend the night and do something special with them. A "children's nook" with a lowered ceiling is part of a suite in the upstairs of our house. The younger children enjoy sleeping there. We are doing our best to fit into "one big happy family"—seventeen of us all together, including the three grandparents. On the surface, all is well, and Tom and I ease into a regular routine.

I enjoy searching for the most appropriate books to give the children for their birthdays, trying to match their reading level and interests. One Christmas Tom and I make little cloth covered books for each child expressing what we appreciate most about each one. It's hurtful when there is so little acknowledgement of these gifts. We begin to wonder if our involvement is resented.

One night on our way home from a family birthday gathering, I'm quiet in the car and Tom asks me what I'm feeling.

"Sort of numb, I guess. Each time we leave these occasions, I'm aware that I sink into a sort of funk. It takes a while for me to shake it off—but I do—eventually."

"Where do you think it comes from?" he asks.

"I'm not sure, but it's probably because it's rare that I make a real connection with anyone. Sometimes I do—with one of the children usually, but the conversation with the adults is so limited. We can talk about the weather, the children, our garden, and basketball. You occasionally bring up something that has some bearing on what's happening in the world, but each time you do, I feel the tension build."

Tom smiles. "I think I do that out of rebellion. At least it gets their attention."

"What it amounts to, I think, is that it's not safe to talk about anything I'm really interested in."

"I know what you mean," Tom says. "Anything having to do with feelings, new ideas, personal values, or principles, has the potential of becoming controversial, and therefore related to the church. Its influence pervades every aspect of life."

"I also sense that they're afraid to ask us any questions about what we think or feel," I say. "The children are affected by this too. They pick up fears quickly from their parents."

"Let's not give up," Tom says. "We don't need to bring up anything specific about the church, but I do think we should be honest with our grandkids when it's appropriate—especially if they ask us a question. They're our grandchildren and we have a right to develop our own relationship with them."

※

I finish my book about Leslie and form my own publishing company in order to publish it myself. By enlisting the help of four brain tumor foundations, they agree to endorse my book in exchange for proceeds from its sale the first year. Tom and I decide to take advantage of a program at the University of Utah for seniors, enabling us to audit any course for twenty-five dollars. Our motivation is to take classes on subjects that we missed or weren't available at the time we were in college. I have never had a course in philosophy or anthropology, so this is where I begin. It is thrilling to me to learn that I relate most to the existentialist philosophers, who accept the certainty of death, recognize that life is tenuous, and understand that true morality lies beyond commonly accepted religious and philosophical rules and values. This means that we are responsible for choosing the values we want to live by and what we consider to be right and wrong.

My philosophy professor introduces me to Ernest Becker's book, *The Denial of Death*, which profoundly affects my thinking. From my anthropology professor, I learn how we know that living species change and that evolutionary theory provides a scientific foundation for understanding anything biological or behavioral regarding humans. I haven't realized until now how much I've missed the academic world, but I see I have a lot of catching up to do. My thirst for learning reminds me of my first year in graduate school. I think I'm ripe for an "accommodation."

The second year in Salt Lake City, I have the opportunity to teach a class at the Osher Institute, an affiliate with the university that offers curriculum designed for people over fifty-five. I develop a course called *Personal Development in the Later Years*. In the process I discover new advances in the field of human development, the expanded research on John Bowlby's attachment theory, and some newer studies that go beyond Piaget's last stage of cognitive development. Specifically Jan Sinnott's work on the value of *postformal thinking* in intimate relationships has encouraged Tom and me. She has taken Piaget's ideas and applied them to a cognitive stage that usually does not develop until later in life. This stage requires a certain amount of time, experience, and effort and is characterized by a capacity to accept uncertainty and to admit that answers are often relative. Besides enjoying the course preparation, I'm stimulated by the interaction with the mature adults in my class. I'm motivated to create another course, *Relationships across the Lifespan*, and then another the following year, *Perspectives on Aging*. I teach subjects that I want to learn more about myself. By having faculty access to the university library, my resources are unlimited.

After two years of teaching at the Osher Institute, the physical demands of that work are making me more aware of my aging body. I carry a laptop computer to use with a large screen for Power Point presentations. To avoid parking on campus, I ride the bus to the university and walk up a hill to catch the campus shuttle to the Osher Institute building, carrying my laptop and teaching materials. The effects of three deep vein blood clots have compromised the circulation in my legs, so this effort is a strain. I'm thinking about creating some meaningful work that I can do at home.

When I published the book about Leslie, I learned to use the InDesign graphics program for designing and formatting books for print. I also learned all the necessary steps it takes to be a self-publisher. My editor and now good friend in Canada, Anneli, also wants to publish a book of her own. Since I'm experimenting with some possibilities for a second book, Anneli and I decide to trade skills; in exchange for her editing talents, I will design and format her book and help her through the publishing process. With this practice, I gain confidence to do this for other authors, adding it as a service I offer through my already existing company, Forest Dale Publishing. I stop teaching at Osher and for the next three years I assist three other authors with their books and help Anneli publish four more.

It's December, 2013, and I decide to have a Christmas open house December 28 for Tom's family—his siblings and the two Magna families. I print invitations, send them out, and begin making cookies to store in the freezer. Then the morning of December 23, the telephone rings. It's Bonnie. "Merry Christmas!" I say when I pick up the phone."

"No! It's not a happy day! John just died. Mavis called me. He had a massive heart attack in the night."

I'm shocked by Bonnie's news—even though there had been a warning. A week ago John collapsed while walking in the mall with a friend. While in the ambulance on the way to the hospital he called me, but I wasn't at home. Tom answered the phone. "He was frightened. He asked to speak with you. When I told him you weren't here, he said, 'I think my time has come.' I cautioned him about making too much of it and tried to reassure him."

I immediately called John back. By then he was in the hospital. He seemed calm and the doctors didn't seem to think it was serious. He hadn't been taking his cholesterol medication because he didn't like the side effects. They were to release him that day. I was relieved—surely they wouldn't be sending him home if it was serious, so I reassured him too, cautioning him about neglecting his medication.

Bonnie tells me the details. Mavis recently had a reoccurrence of cancer and is undergoing treatment, so John had been staying overnight at her house to take care of her, but they were sleeping in separate rooms. In the night he must have gotten up to go to the bathroom and then collapsed on the floor. Mavis didn't hear anything and didn't discover his dead body beside his bed until morning. She had no idea of how long he had been there.

I'm grieving. Why couldn't his doctors have known? Why couldn't more have been done the week before? We were expecting that Mavis would die first and we worried about John being left alone. Now it's to be the other way around. It's hard for me to believe that John will no longer be a part of my life. An older sibling has been in one's life longer than anyone, even one's parents. I will miss him terribly.

Tom and I leave the next morning to drive to Tulsa, meeting Bonnie and her husband at the airport Christmas evening, finding only one restaurant open. We talk about recent events. John and Bonnie and I met in Tulsa for our annual reunion six months ago. I stayed over two more days after Bonnie left. One of those evenings, John and I talked in the den in the back of our family home. He asked me if I would help him with something he had composed that could be read at his funeral. He recently had a lawyer draw up a trust and he wanted this paper to be included. He explained that few of his friends knew about his religious beliefs and he wanted them to know this about himself. Though John no longer met with our mother's religious group in Tulsa, he still hung on to many of our mother's and grandmother's beliefs, particularly those foretelling a resurrection and a kingdom of perfection on Earth. We spent several hours on his writing that night, and the next day I typed it out and made a copy for myself, promising John I would read it at his funeral. While imagining this to be maybe six to ten years down the road, we also talked about what kind of service he would like: just a gathering of his friends and time for everyone to share stories of good times together.

On December 30th, the day before John would have been 80 years old, we do everything he and I had talked about. Over two hundred people attend his memorial service. Bonnie and I stay in Tulsa for another month disposing of John's things and nearly seventy years of accumulation of our parents' belongings—things John was too sentimental to discard himself. We find scrapbooks of our mother's that go back to the 1940s. By early February, 2014, we put the family home up for sale.

I still maintain a connection with Ellen, who is now retired from teaching, still living in Oklahoma City. We talk over the phone every few months or so, taking turns calling each other. There is still an awkward distance between us, but my longing to restore our former connection is still strong. One Sunday I call and get no answer. She's usually close to her phone. I call repeatedly every few days over the next several weeks, and still no answer. I don't have a telephone number of any of Ellen's friends, so I grow more and more anxious. All I know to do is to keep calling the same number. Finally, one morning Ellen answers. She tells me that she's had a hip replaced and a crisis of depression, both of which require a hospital stay. Now she's in an assisted living facility receiving rehabilitation therapy. "I'm in a quandary about what to do with my condo," she says. "I can't climb the stairs up to my bedroom anymore."

"Do you think you'll eventually be able to move back home?" I ask.

"I don't think so." A sadness is in her voice as Ellen explains her dilemma. The facility she's in now is over twenty miles from her condo in Oklahoma City, where her friends are located and where she would much prefer to be. A woman on whom Ellen depends for assistance used to help Ellen's mother before her death. She is now helping Ellen, using Ellen's car for errands and checking on her condo. She lives near this facility so hopes Ellen will stay put.

"This is such a coincidence! I'm already planning to meet Bonnie in Tulsa the middle of October—that's only a month away! Bonnie and I have to rent a car anyway, so after she leaves, I can drive over to Oklahoma City and stay long enough to help you find another facility that you would really like. I can fly back home from there!"

"Would you really be willing to do that?" she asks with some hope in her voice.

"I would love to do it, especially knowing how important this decision could be." We begin to make plans for my visit. I make a list of senior facilities in Ellen's desired area of Oklahoma City and start making phone calls. I learn about the distinction between "independent living" and "assisted living." One helpful administrator asks me some questions.

"Does your friend deal with any dementia?"

"No."

"Is she responsible for taking her medications?"

"Yes."

"Does she still enjoy social interaction with others?"

"Yes, definitely."

"Then I think an independent living facility will be the best solution for her." I share this information with Ellen and by the time I arrive in mid-October, we've decided on four facilities she would like to see. Having been a professional single person all her life, with no expensive habits, Ellen has no serious financial limitations, so she chooses the nicest place we see—a beautiful full-service facility on twenty acres including a lake with swans! It even provides guest rooms to visitors. "I can come to see you every fall when I come to Oklahoma to meet Bonnie," I tell her the day before I'm to leave. "I've loved our being together."

"I have too," Ellen says. "If I paid for it, do you think you could come every six months?" I'm touched by her question and begin to cry.

"I would love to, but what if we split the cost because this will be for me as much as it will be for you."

So every spring and fall, I am spending three or four days in Oklahoma City with Ellen and we talk on the phone every

Sunday afternoon. We're in touch with each other—just like it was when we were roommates.

One other relationship is bringing some warmth to Tom and me during our time in Salt Lake City. I first noticed Zhou (pronounced "Joe") on the bus going to the university—the same young Chinese student who sits across from me in my anthropology class. So I ask him one day, "You live fairly close to me—I see you getting on the bus. Have you been in Salt Lake City long?"

"No, only two weeks," he says. "I'm working on a master's degree in Anthropology." I learn then that Zhou's home is in Shanghai, that he earned his Bachelor's degree in biology in China, and his goal is to get a PhD in Anthropology. This is the first time he has lived in an English-speaking country, and he has some concerns about becoming more fluent in the English language—especially upon learning that we have an essay due in our class every week. We start sitting together on the bus and walking to our class together, giving us more time for conversation. One day we discuss our essays the professor has just returned, and Zhou asks me to explain a question regarding clarity the professor has written on his paper. This begins a meaningful exchange whereby I read Zhou's essays after they have been graded, then make suggestions regarding his grammar and sentence structure. He learns very quickly, and I also notice that he checks out a whole book from the library on each topic we are assigned in class, while I'm barely able to absorb one chapter in our textbook each week. He is a voracious reader!

I want Tom to meet Zhou so we invite him for dinner. In his backpack, he brings a skillet, some raw eggs, and vegetables in order to contribute to our meal. Tom is curious about China and Zhou is a ready resource, so it isn't long before he becomes a regular visitor to our home. He can't resist buying used books, so when either of us mention a topic we are interested in, a book arrives in the mail via Amazon on the very topic. Some of the most informative books in our bookcase have been given to us by Zhou. We have known Zhou for seven years now. In January and February of this year (2019) Tom and I enjoyed a vacation house trade with a British couple from Sri Lanka. (They stayed in our house while we stayed in theirs.) While we were there, Zhou and his parents flew from Shanghai to Sri Lanka so we could meet one another.

INSIGHTS: New Insights on Aging and Death

A stubborn myth still exists in our culture that aging amounts to nothing more than dealing with an inevitable decline of our body and mind. Along with amazing advances in medical care that have people living longer as active and independent adults, new emphasis is being placed on the many advantages associated with aging, including psychological and mental development as well as continued social engagement and intellectual stimulation.

Some of the most exciting research is coming from studies done with brain imaging enabling scientists to see activation patterns of the living brain at work. New findings reveal that while acknowledging the hard realities of aging—poorer vision, hearing, and memory—the aging brain is more flexible and adaptable than once thought and it is even better at some types of intellectual tasks than younger brains. Scientific work confirms that the mind grows stronger from use and from being challenged in the same way that muscles grow stronger from exercise. We also retain our capacity to form new memories, which involves making new connections between brain cells, and even growing new ones.[1]

I was exposed to the work of Jan Sinnott, a professor of psychology at Towson University, while preparing to teach a class at the Osher Institute. I was attracted to Sinnott's description of the positive impact that complex thought can have on close relationships, hoping that it would be reinforcing to the relationship work Tom and I had been doing. I contacted Jan and this was the beginning of a meaningful correspondence and friendship. Following are three important things I learned from her:

First, most moral dilemmas that face us in our day-to-day lives are relative rather than what is absolute in human life. Therefore postformal thinking is valuable for ill-defined, ambiguous problems for which more than one solution is possible. (This happens to be the case in most human relationship problems.) Sinnott differentiates postformal thought from Piaget's fourth stage of formal thinking, in which thinkers consider a finite number of variables to be considered, expecting to find a single right answer that will hold in all similar circumstances across time. Disagreements, in this way of thinking, are regarded as signs of trouble, irritants to be ignored where possible, and eliminated when necessary. Instead, the relativistic thinker regards the perspectives of others as a source of creative thought and diversity. This requires a willingness to listen with the intent to understand where someone else is coming from and interacting on that level.

Second, and closely related, is that some moral dilemmas involve dialectic contradictions which require the ability to uncover the goodness in two seemingly incompatible views. Problem solving becomes a process of evolution in which contradictions play a key role in intellectual growth. This means that the resolution of our conflicts will encompass both of our points of view and changes in our thinking will be natural, expected, and valuable. Problems resolved in this way provide emotional support to the participants, enabling an equal commitment to make it work, and an ongoing strengthening of the relationship.

Finally, in order to participate in postformal thinking with another person, it will be helpful if we have experienced a close intimate relationship long enough to have learned that *if I think of you as a trustworthy partner, then treat you that way, you are likely to become a more trustworthy partner.* The reverse is also true.[2] The long process that Tom and I have been in for the last twenty-eight years has been learning how to be trustworthy. We are not so prone to be swept by common, every day insecurities because we understand those fears trigger a much deeper childhood fear that we have confronted and recognized as being no longer true. By gaining that control, we are able to risk stretching to meet the other's needs. It's no longer a matter of giving up something out of compromise; it's a choice we are making because we know we each will gain. We also know to expect that maintaining a balance in our relationship will be an ongoing quest, because reciprocal trust is a living dynamic process that must be nurtured through authentic dialogue every single day.

※

As we anticipated, our proximity to Tom's ex-wife, the families of both his daughters, and the tension that exists in Salt Lake City between a predominant Mormon culture and an equally robust counter-culture (though much smaller in number) has been a challenge. Our efforts to carve out a place for ourselves as grandparents to ten beautiful children have been frustrating. We both were committed to a positive outcome, thinking that by being close by and giving attention to these children, we could overcome a belief held by the parents that Tom was the reprobate their church describes him to be since he chose to leave the fold over thirty years ago.

> *"Their senses are taken from them, their understanding and judgment in righteousness are taken away, they go into darkness, and become like a blind person who gropes by the wall.... I comprehend it by saying death, hell and the grave. This is what they will get in exchange for their apostasy from the Gospel of the Son of God."* ("Preventing Personal Apostasy," Teachings of Presidents of the Church: Brigham Young (1997).

Tom's deepest disappointment has been that he and his daughters have not been able to reach the level of understanding that we hoped for, a sad predicament for many families who are caught in binding obedience to authority that is demanded in the doctrines of their religion—not just Mormonism—there are others like them. Is it possible for the bonds of familial love to endure when beliefs of arbitrary condemnation prevail? On Tom's birthday and Fathers' Day, I watched his daughters lovingly give him pages to a scrapbook of photographs containing fond memories of their childhood. Notations on these pages refer to what a good father he *was*. These gestures gave him hope that a comfortable connection could be restored, yet his efforts to converse with them about the issue that is at the root of their distrust leave him feeling frustrated and disregarded. When they see he suffers, it only reinforces their point of view.

What is it that makes people become so enslaved by a specific worldview that they will blindly disavow their love for a family member who adopts a different perspective? This is one of the questions that Ernest Becker addressed during his career as a social anthropologist, trying to understand what makes people act the way they do. He is best known for his Pulitzer Prize-winning book, *The Denial of Death*, which he wrote during the last few years before his untimely death from cancer.

Becker focused on probably the most important characteristic shared by humans and other animals—that is, that all such creatures are driven to survive, or have an instinct for self-preservation. What makes our species unique is our highly evolved cerebral cortex, giving us our capacity for conceptualizing our experience in terms of past, present, and future, and our capacity for self-awareness. We are able to communicate with one another about possibilities, plan our courses of action, and monitor our progress toward goals. These advantages have enhanced our fitness far beyond that of other species, enabling us to survive in virtually every environmental niche on Earth. Unfortunately this inheritance doesn't come without its burdens. Becker explains:

> *"Man is the one animal who does not enjoy oblivious, instinctive living. He is self-conscious, which means that he knows about life and death. The body is the thing that will die, and hence it becomes a major problem to a creature who wants to continue experiencing."* [3]

Becker argues that the fact that we are instinctively driven to survive, coupled with our knowledge that mortality is a certainty, creates a potential for anxiety we carry with us at all times. He was interested in how humans deal with this paradox—being driven to live while knowing that we will surely die.

I used a book on ageism that contained the research on Becker's work when I was teaching a class on aging at the Osher Institute. An aspect of his theory was presented as an explanation for age discrimination. I was more interested, however, in Becker's explanation as to why the awareness of death causes people to cling tenaciously to their own cultural beliefs and experience difficulty coexisting with others who espouse contrary beliefs. Becker explains that as our intellectual capacities have evolved, Homo sapiens became increasingly aware that all living things, ourselves included, ultimately wither and die. Becker emphasized that death awareness is not simply uncomfortable, it is so overwhelmingly threatening to the human psyche that it has to be repressed. We have resolved this dilemma by developing cultural worldviews, humanly constructed beliefs that provide a view of reality that guarantees safety and security in this life and beyond, in some form of immortality.

Immortality is attained in these worldviews through various afterlives promised by almost all organized religions, be it heaven for an immortal soul, Nirvana, resurrection, or reincarnation. By meeting some standard of behavior, we qualify for some way of transcending death. These "fictions" as Becker calls them, buffer our human anxiety that stems from the awareness of death. Consequently, exposure to people who adhere to a culturally different worldview can be psychologically threatening. People may react to those who are different by denigrating their worldview in hopes of converting them to their own way of thinking, or obliterating them entirely to demonstrate that one's own cultural worldview is superior after all.[4] This explains to me why the fear of death (or more specifically, differing worldviews of immortality) is so often at the root of ongoing wars, prejudice, and discrimination.

In his introduction to *The Ernest Becker Reader*, Daniel Liechty, its editor, comments that Becker took great care to respect the religious aspect of human experience and acknowledged that all immortality beliefs function effectively to dispel the terror of death. He cautioned, however, that what we may recognize as a higher power should not be frozen in man-made descriptions of divine attributes because this power can never be fully known or understood.

> *"As soon as an individual or a community claims to know this God, to speak for this God, they have created an idol, a human-made God, which will sooner or later displace human freedom with alienating subservience."* [5]

The very definition of a successful culture, religion, or philosophy is that it offers a satisfactory and convincing way of denying death. When we are young, we follow the voice and ideas of those who have had the strongest influence and we try to pattern our ideals after them. But as life goes on and we get a perspective on this, we recognize that there are many different formulas for triumphing over life's limitations. There are so many people who are trying so hard to win converts for their point of view because it is more than just an outlook on life: it's a formula for their own immortality.[6]

Since Becker's death in 1974, an impressive body of evidence has been gathered to support Becker's theory, which has come to be known as Terror Management Theory.

> *"The theory posits that to manage the potential for terror engendered by the awareness of mortality, humans sustain faith in worldviews which provide a sense that they are significant beings in an enduring, meaningful world rather than mere material animals fated only to obliteration upon death."* [7]

From this premise three hypotheses are extracted:

(a) Reminding people of their mortality should increase bolstering of their own worldview and striving for self-worth.

(b) Bolstering their worldview should reduce anxiety in response to threat and defensive reactions to reminders of death.

(c) Threatening their worldview should arouse anxiety and bring death-related concerns closer to consciousness.

Hundreds of studies reveal that reminding people of their mortality increases positive reactions to people who validate aspects of their worldviews. Also, reminding people of their mortality increases negative reactions to people who challenge aspects of their worldview or espouse a different one.[8] This would explain the discomfort that Tom's daughters have displayed in our being in Salt Lake City. While we respected their wishes that we not discuss the church with their children for ten years of our time in Salt Lake City, this has changed as our grandchildren are growing up, some marrying, and some leaving the church themselves. Wanting to support them as adults, we have become more open about our own perspectives. This has brought us closer to some of our family members, but distanced us from others. When to speak out, and when to remain silent is a moral issue for us that demands examination in each situation.

Ernest Becker's ideas have helped me see that everyone develops some kind of view of themselves that helps them to tame, subdue, or repress entirely the terror of death, and the way we choose to do that becomes an ultimate concern and value for us. Looking at it this way, we could speak of "religion" as being a part of the human condition, meaning that we are all religious in one sense; we just vary in what we choose to be religious about. I am trying to separate those conditions that I can observe or that have been supported by research from those conditions that remain unknown to the human mind. I believe the evolution of the human species has been established by scientific evidence, so I expect that the life I have is to be no different from the life of any other animal. I think the consciousness that I have of my own existence comes from my brain, and once my body is dead, I will have no more consciousness. It would be nice to know that the essential elements of my body, once they have decomposed, could be recycled in such a way to provide some nutrient to other living things. I do get some satisfaction from hoping that by writing something of my life and the things I have learned that this may get passed on to my grandchildren and others after I die, just as I have benefited from the thoughts and ideas of others who have lived before me.

As to all the unknowns about human existence, I don't think there are any absolute truths, values, or norms that are directing our choices and behavior. Consequently, I believe that it is my responsibility alone to choose my own ultimate concern and values and how I want to live my life. If I want my life to have meaning, I have the freedom to create that meaning myself while knowing that no one has the final answers, so I may well be wrong. This also implies that I acknowledge that others have the same freedom themselves, and so we may have very different ultimate concerns and values. By recognizing that our differences are based on choices, not absolute truths, we can coexist comfortably with mutual respect. We can even talk about them together without fear.

I have learned the most about myself in relationships with others, each one providing a different mirror in which to see parts of myself. Therefore my ultimate concern is to maintain and grow a small group of relationships that are most significant to me because I can be honest about my thoughts and feelings and I can trust the other to be honest in the same way with me. The strength of this kind of relationship comes from self-disclosure, and only then can it foster growth, understanding, compassion, forgiveness, and genuine affection.

I also find strength and courage in communion with the wonders and consistencies of nature: watching a full moon move across the sky above the Caribbean Sea; experiencing the energy of a powerful surf in Sri Lanka; listening to an explosion of birdsong in the trees of Australia; beholding the majestic beauty of Mount Rainier; feeling the warmth of the sun on a chilly morning walk; and seeing for the first time the magnificent amaryllis plant bloom on my window sill.

References:

[1] Cohen, Gene. 2005. *The mature mind: The positive power of the aging brain.* New York: Basic Books.

[2] Sinnott, Jan D. 2014. *Adult development: Cognitive aspects of thriving close relationships.* New York: Oxford University Press.

[3] Becker, Ernest. 1974. "The spectrum of loneliness," *Humanitas,* Vol. 10: 237-246, reprinted in *The Ernest Becker reader,* Daniel Liechty, Ed., Seattle: University of Washington Press, 2005, p. 231.

[4] Becker, Ernest. 1973. *The denial of death,* New York: Simon & Schuster.

[5] Liechty, Daniel, Ed. 2005. "Introduction," *The Ernest Becker reader.* Seattle: University of Washington Press, p. 22.

[6] Becker 1973.

[7] Greenberg, Jeff & Jamie Arndt. 2012. Terror management theory, in *Handbook of theories of social psychology: Volume 1 and 2,* Paul A. M. Van Lange, Arie W. Kruglanski & E. Tory Higgins, (Eds), Sage Publications, p. 398.

[8] Greenberg, J. S. & J. Arndt. 2009. Chapter 19: Terror management theory. A uniquely human motivation in *Handbook of theories of social psychology: Vol. 1 and 2*, P. Van Lange, A. Kruglanski, &T. Higgins.

EPILOGUE

One January day in 2019, we received some unexpected good news. An acre of land we purchased in Las Cruces after we retired was available for a building permit. Our plan at the time we bought this land was to travel for ten years and then return to Las Cruces to build our retirement home. But while we were in Canada, the developer of the sub-division went bankrupt and subsequently died, leaving a larger portion of the lots (including ours) without amenities (street paving, electricity, and water). Since then, because of legalities, we weren't able to build on or sell the property. It was worthless, and we had given up on ever building a home there.

The unexpected news was that a group of developers had bought all the remaining lots and negotiated with the city and county to complete the amenities. They were also setting aside some of the land for grape vineyards and the growing of produce.

"Instead of a golf course to entice residents, they're calling it an "agrihood!" Tom said. "We can still build a house there!"

"But don't you think we're getting a little old?" I said.

"So we are, but we're still healthy and active. There's no reason we can't build the solar home we've always wanted and we can live there as long as we can. What have we got to lose?"

I was almost afraid to join him in his enthusiasm. Our dream had been to build a house that would be energy efficient and environmentally friendly—"a gift to the earth" we called it. "It's true though," I said, "our two-story house here and the pollution in the Salt Lake valley that keeps getting worse, isn't providing an ideal living environment for us as we age."

"That's right! I think we should take a trip to Las Cruces to explore the possibility of our moving back there—and we'll make sure we can afford it."

Trying not to let myself get too excited, I compiled a list from the internet of architects, builders, and financial institutions that we would contact when we got there. In less than a week after we returned from a vacation house trade in Sri Lanka, we were on our way to Las Cruces with a spirit of adventure that matched the excitement we had before going to Africa. Within two weeks we decided on an architect/builder who had designed a group of high efficiency homes of different sizes, all with solar systems, and we obtained pre-approval for a mortgage loan from three different banks.

Back in Salt Lake City, we hired a painter to do some touch-up work on our house, and we engaged a friend and neighbor, also a real estate broker, to list it for sale. The first weekend our house was on the market, it sold for our asking price. Things were moving more quickly than we had anticipated, but we were excited and energized. I had to remind myself to slow down and eat regularly. We made another fast trip to Las Cruces with our pickup camper and one vehicle, both of which we left temporarily in an RV park. We also had to rent a house. Since we were familiar with the neighborhoods in Las Cruces, in one day we found a home that we would enjoy while our new house was being built. An airplane out of El Paso took us back to Salt Lake City, with only one month to sell unwanted items and pack the rest of our household goods.

On the evening of April 27, 2019, we attended a musical program, in which two of our grandchildren were performing. We said goodbye to them and six more who were there to see us off. Early the next morning, we pulled out of our driveway, Tom at the wheel of a twenty-six foot U-Haul truck, and I followed in the Chevrolet Impala I inherited from John. A favorite neighbor who lived across the street came out on her porch in her robe to wave goodbye, and that's the only time I cried. We arrived in Las Cruces the afternoon of May 1. The sun was shining brightly in a vivid blue sky with white puffy clouds casting dramatic shadows on the majestic Organ Mountains. It was good to be home.

The first thing we did was to locate a fitness center for Tom and a swimming pool for me, the same pool I used to swim in when we lived here before. A new walking trail with exercise machines placed at intervals around the three-quarter mile oval was constructed at the university since we left here; we could use it for walking on alternate days. I gave up bicycling in Salt Lake City, but with so many safe places to ride here, we bought a new bike for me. This would take care of our exercise needs. By the end of the summer, we found several good camping places in the cooler mountains nearby, and we enjoyed visits from two grandsons, our friend Zhou, and my sister, all of whom took pleasure in seeing the progress of our new house.

A new environment meant finding new meaning. I set a goal to finish this book by the end of 2019, which I did. I've spent the month of January working with my editor, Anneli, making revisions. We hope to be in our new house by May, and then my goal is to find a new activity I will enjoy. When Zhou was here and he saw how close we are to New Mexico State University, he suggested that I might tutor international students in English. "If I had everything you taught me about English written down in a book, I could teach English in China!" he said. I was flattered by Zhou's remark ... and I think I like his idea.

Now I am reflecting on what more I want to say to my reader before I end this project. I described what I wanted from this effort in the preface—to come to greater acceptance of myself by tracing the changes I've made, while recognizing the people whose ideas helped me along the way. Working toward this end has strengthened my confidence and affirmed what Tom and I are most proud of—that we are learning how to be better for ourselves and each other. I wanted my reader to know that this is a lifetime process, perhaps discouraging to some, but for us it's been worth the effort. We shouldn't feel badly that we have problems in our relationships, because most of our difficulties began with decisions that our parents, and their parents, made before we were born. We've been dealt a hand and we play it the best we can.

I know I've been fortunate to have a partner by my side who has wanted to make things better as much as I have. We each have a firmer trust in ourselves because of what we have accomplished together. We are grateful to be in good health with so much to look forward to. At our age, thoughts of death frequently enter our consciousness. We know that one or the other will be left without a partner in the not too distant future. I used to think that a couple in a close intimate relationship would have more difficulty dealing with the loss of their loved one, but I have learned from my studies that the opposite is true. Research that measures the degree of depression and anxiety experienced during bereavement show that securely attached couples demonstrate greater resilience. Any major loss will be accompanied by sorrow and grief, but in a trusting relationship, individuals have learned to be comfortable with their feelings, so the same will be true when dealing with a partner's death. The strong feelings of grief are not so frightening—a normal way of keeping our loved one close as we make a major adjustment.

    I believe we can continue to draw strength from the memory of our relationship. We will recall the spirit of adventure we shared in Zimbabwe, and the sense of purpose we felt while developing our business. The creation of new vows will be remembered as an act of faith in our ability to make needed changes. They still represent good principles that we can follow as we seek to establish new healthy relationships. The most powerful memories are contained in the wisdom we have acquired by asking these important questions: Can we view conflict as an opportunity to learn more about ourselves and another? When we are distressed, can we look first to see if the conflict is within ourselves? If we've lost confidence, do we believe something about ourselves that is not true? If we are blaming another, are we projecting a fault of our own we don't want to recognize? If we're disappointed in another, can we resist shouldering what is the other's responsibility? If we are worrying about tomorrow, can we redirect that energy to doing our best today? Can we remember that we will only love another to the extent that we're able to love ourselves? Can we trust that whatever our future brings, we will find new meaning?

Kathleen and Tom
Sri Lanka, 2019